The Ritz and the Ditch

DIANA HOLDERNESS

The Ritz and the Ditch

A MEMOIR

STONE TROUGH
BOOKS

*To my father Flash Kellett
and my husband Richard*

© Diana Holderness 2018

ISBN 978-0-9929497-6-1

Published by Stone Trough Books

The Old Rectory

Settrington

York YO17 8NP

Printed by CPI Group (UK) Ltd, Croydon CR0 4YY

Contents

Appendices

Illustrations

Richard and Fiona at Flat Top
Aerial view of Flat Top
Nanny Cross with Emma and Ed
With Richard and the children above Flat Top
Our invitation to the Coronation
Emma and Ed inspect James Gunn's portrait
Sammy with her son Mark, Gran and Iso
Richard swims amid the ice on Boxing Day
With Billy Brooksbank at a Garrowby Christmas
With Charlie Halifax at Christmas

Between pages 176 and 177

The Villa Cimbrone
Ursula Bethell
Pam Baring
Senior ministers at Chequers, 1963
Janie and Cath Kidston
Launching *British Dragoon*
Going down a coal mine with Richard
Anthony Eden
Grouse shooting at Bolton Abbey
Richard in the Libyan desert in 1965
Richard writing his diary in the desert
A melon-seller in Afghanistan
Henrietta Scott
Taking Hilda Slater and Eleanor Mounsey to the Palace
The marriage of Charlie Allsopp and Fiona McGowan
Emma's marriage to Nicholas Brooksbank
King Hussein of Jordan
Looking out to sea at Aqaba
Hilaré and Bob Ryder
Building the swimming pool in France
Richard and Timothy Tufnell
Richard and Brigid Ness

Richard joining the House of Lords
With Margaret and Denis Thatcher at a regimental dinner
Julian Holland-Hibbert
Myles Hildyard in his garden
Joh Seb Peake
Richard with Desert Orchid
Richard on duty as Hon. Colonel of 4th Battalion RGJ
The wilderness we transformed in France
A sketch of our house in France by Graham Rust
Richard in Port Grimaud
Ed and Katha
With John Major
Graham Rust
The Governor's house on St Helena
The steps above Jamestown, St Helena
Patrick McCraith climbing the steps
Richard on his quad bike after the fire in France
On the quad bike at Flat Top
Hugh Trenchard and Ed
Crystal Tweedie
Edward Ford
Myles Hildyard and Michael Parish
Toby and Araminta Aldington
With Mary Sheepshanks in St Petersburg
Ed in Libya
A group of us at Leptis Magna in 2010
Frances and Michael Howorth
Mark and Mary Buttle
Ed with his family

Preface

I had always hoped that Richard would publish his memoirs because he had kept copious diaries for a great part of his life. But just after we had moved from Yorkshire he died, very suddenly. It was some time later that I considered using them to help write my own memoir.

I adored my father, Flash Kellett, who went out to Palestine with his Yeomanry regiment in January 1940. He used to write and say he would try to get me out to join him and my mother, who was out there with him, sharing a house with the Fevershams and Woods, who would later become my brothers-in-law and sisters-in-law. But by the time I might have joined them, all the wives had been made to leave by the Governor, Sir Harold MacMichael, the father of Araminta who became a great friend in 1947 when we had both just married. Her sister Priscilla had worked with me in MI6 at the end of the war.

Richard had his legs blown off in the desert and, when I knew this, I was terrified of meeting him. It is so strange that we should have married, but sometimes in life odd things do happen. He had so nearly married Kick Kennedy, having us to stay in Yorkshire alternate weekends until his mother objected and said he must make up his mind. Despite a very difficult time when we were first married, our marriage was a huge success. We both thought that we would try our hardest to do things together and get to like them. Sometimes it was a great effort, but we succeeded. We also decided that as far as was possible we would be together daily. Once we made a great mistake. We didn't do this and during that time we were both unfaithful. But we decided, as did my sister, that should this happen we would always tell our husbands and they must tell us too. I have heard that the French do so, and it seems to work. It did with us, anyway. When in 2002 we were moving into Timothy Tufnell's house in Winkfield and Parliament was sitting, Richard used to come down one night and I went up to the flat in London the next. As he died only six weeks after we moved I am more than ever glad that we did this.

Diana Holderness

November 2017

Acknowledgements

Without all the help that Benjamin Buchan has given me, this book would never have been achieved and I would have found the illustrations much harder to place; he has been a real godfather to this project. I ran out of space for all the pictures I wanted and one of those in particular was of Wendy French, who bought my printing and publishing business when I moved to London four years ago. My husband Richard kept copious diaries of much of our life together and in particular of the journeys all around the world when he was Minister of Overseas Development in Ted Heath's Government. But for those diaries, it would have been difficult to remember all the strange and vivid the details of those journeys.

CHAPTER I

Myrtie and Flash

I was born in another world. It was a society and culture whose certainties and assumptions, rules and conventions, largely vanished with a second world war and by the mid-1960s were gone for ever. Despite fluctuating circumstances, my parents' pre-war life was a glamorous one: hunting and racing, steeplechasing, parties and race meetings, adventurous and exotic foreign travel. As a child – I was still only eleven when the Second World War started – I took our life for granted, unaware how swiftly this whole world, like my childhood, would come to an end.

My father – Edward Orlando Kellett, but known to all his friends as Flash – came from a fiercely Protestant family in Ireland with a military tradition. A Victorian ancestor was Admiral Sir Henry Kellett, who in the 1840s had been sent in his ship HMS *Resolute* to search for the Arctic explorer Sir John Franklin. The *Resolute* became trapped in ice – there was an artist on board and I have some of the pictures painted while the ship was trapped, as well as the sledge flag. The ship had to be abandoned but was later found by an American whaler and then bought by the US Government, who presented the ship to Queen Victoria as a gesture of goodwill. When the ship left service the Queen had a desk made from its timbers and gave it to the American President. The desk remains in the Oval Office and in use by the President to this day.

My parents married in 1926 and I was born a year later, in Bruton Street in the house next door to the one where Princess Elizabeth had been born the year before. My father's elder brother, and my grandfather's favourite son, had been killed in the First World War, so my father could have expected an inheritance. But his mother had died on the last day of 1925 and the nursery governess, Jesse, had stayed on with my grandfather. Jesse put pressure on him to marry her, as she said people would otherwise 'talk'. When my grandfather brought her over to England for my christening in the Guards Chapel, my father complained and said he didn't want 'that old bore'.

This remark so infuriated my grandfather that he went ahead and married Jesse, and disinherited my father and left everything to Canon Patten, his parson. But the Pattens very generously transferred my grandmother's money in trust to me, and when Jesse died Mrs Patten gave me the family medals, and was going to give me my grandmother's very valuable emerald jewellery, but Jesse in her old age had sold it all to dealers. Because it was in trust, my father was still able to inherit Clonacody, the Georgian family home in Tipperary. But my mother said she didn't want to be 'stuck away' in Ireland and the house was sold.

My mother was named Myrtle after the myrtle that grew on the wall outside her mother's bedroom window at her home at Landguard Manor, Shanklin, on the Isle of Wight. Her father's family had aristocratic connections – he was the grandson of the 17th Earl of Suffolk – and her father was rich. He owned big tracts of Southampton, handed down from Arthur Atherley, MP for Southampton. He left Myrtie and her sister Isobel everything except for £700 a year to his widow. Myrtie's mother's family was from Aberdeen, where her grandfather was a Writer to the Signet. They owned Echt in Aberdeenshire, which they sold to Lord Cowdray who enlarged it into a vast Victorian mansion.

Horses and hunting were an essential part of life. My paternal grandfather and my mother's stepfather (both were retired major generals) died from heart attacks out hunting, in November 1931 and November 1932. As a child we moved between rented houses, as so many people then did – in winter for the hunting, in London for the Season, close to Ascot for the racing, where they would share a house with Andrew and Doria Scott (the daughter of Earl Haig), and on the Isle of Wight in August. At the end of August my father went off to a Territorial camp for training.

For the hunting, the houses were in Leicestershire, first in Melton Mowbray and then in Thorpe Satchville. I remember a large stable yard in Thorpe Satchville where the wooden stable buckets were painted in my father's racing colours of yellow and black. In the small world in which I lived in those days I assumed that everyone had racing colours, just as I assumed every pram had a crest on the side. I can still remember being pushed in one for a long walk at the age of five. In that part of the country there were gated roads everywhere and my job in life was getting out of the car to open the gates. When I was a few years older I used to go beagling with my father.

When I was born my father was in the Irish Guards. But in 1930 he transferred to the Nottinghamshire Yeomanry (Sherwood Rangers), part of the Territorial Army. It was still an unmechanised cavalry regiment, one of the very last, when the Second World War broke out. Both my parents regularly hunted several days a week throughout the hunting season. My mother rode side-saddle and wore a bowler hat. My Aunt Iso wore a top hat, which I thought was much smarter. But one day she had a bad fall and the top hat was forced down over her face and someone, trying to be helpful, pulled it off too quickly, damaging her eyelid and leaving her with 'an untidy eye'. After that she wore a black eyepatch whenever she went to anything smart. I believe she had been operated on by Sir Harold Gillies on the kitchen table, but she then moved to Lady Carnarvon's Nursing Home in Portland Place, where there was a uniformed butler in the hall, chintz curtains and bedheads upholstered in the same chintz, close-carpeted floors and servants to convey the meals.

Like almost all my friends, I was made to ride, and it was very exciting when we were 'blooded' out hunting. Despite Nanny's protests, we were made to leave the fox's blood on our faces until it wore off, usually by the end of the day. But sadly for my parents I was always a nervous rider. I knew they minded this.

In the 1920s horses and hunting had brought my parents together with the Prince of Wales and his brothers George (Duke of Kent) and Henry (Duke of Gloucester), and they became great friends. My mother told me that, out hunting, you could treat them like everyone else and shout, 'Get out of my bloody light, sir!' if they were in the way of a hedge you wanted to jump.

In the late 1920s George V ordered the Prince of Wales to stop hunting and sell all his superb hunters. My mother kept a catalogue from the sale, by auction, on 23 February 1929 at the Leicestershire Horse Repository of 'The Entire Stud (with the exception of one old horse), the Property of H.R.H. the Prince of Wales'. Certain horses' names on the card have been marked with a cross and inside there is a short note from the Prince of Wales on St James's Palace writing paper. The notice of sale and the brief letter from the Prince of Wales are reproduced in the first appendix at the end of this book.

I remember very well my first and only sight of Mrs Simpson. The Prince of Wales had telephoned my parents in Leicestershire to ask if he could come and dine with them before the Quorn Hunt Ball and if he could bring Mrs Simpson. He did bring her, and I was allowed to stand at the top of the stairs and see them. They were both dressed as pirates.

★　★　★

My parents had a taste for adventure. In November 1933, backed by the Rootes car company who wanted to promote the triumphs of British engineering, they accepted the challenge of driving from London to Cape Town, down the entire length of Africa, in two large, canvas-topped Hillman cars. Both cars were Hillman Minx 'standard touring cars', fitted with oversize, low-pressure tyres and extra springs, and with the back seats removed to carry stores and equipment (including large quantities of Terry's Bitter Chocolate which turned pale when melted and then hardened). Flash and Myrtie drove the lead car and two mechanics drove the second one.

There were many adventures on the way. Crossing the Mediterranean from Sicily to Tripoli in Italian-occupied Libya, they were required by the authorities to sleep in Italian military outposts. The Italians had started to build a tarmac road from Tripoli to the Egyptian frontier but only a few hundred miles had been completed. The 'rest of the 1,500 miles is often more like the bed of a mountain stream than a motor road', according to an article that Flash wrote for the *Household Brigade Magazine* later that year. Very occasionally they were able to sleep in a hotel – in Wadi Halfa in northern Sudan they 'spent the night in what is about the best hotel in Africa'. But they carried no tents and most of the time they slept in the open air on camp beds under an awning stretched between the two cars.

They were lost in a sandstorm in the Sudan but rescued by a passing camel train, and they were badly bitten by mosquitoes near the Nile. The rains arrived when they had reached Northern Rhodesia (now Zambia) and what was called the Great North Road, of which Flash observed: 'This so-called road, stretching for about a thousand miles, from a hundred miles north of Abercorn to within a few miles of the Victoria Falls, is nothing more than a grass-grown track, the elephant grass in places being five to six feet high, and through this with its many concealed and very deep "pot-holes", the cars had to push their way. The greater part of this time it was raining, and our progress was sometimes rather slow in consequence!' Amazingly they only had a couple of slow punctures and they completed the 12,000-mile journey by March 1934, in time to host a party for Prince George in Durban (having sent on their clothes in cabin trunks by boat to South Africa).

Encouraged by the success of this venture, they planned to drive in 1935 through Europe, the Middle East, Iraq, Persia, Afghanistan and finally through the Khyber Pass into India. My father sought advice about roads in Arabia from T. E. Lawrence (strangely enough, we lived for a time at 18 St Leonard's Terrace in the mid-1930s, the same house that Lawrence himself had once occupied).

Lawrence, then serving in the RAF in Yorkshire under the name T. E. Shaw, replied courteously to my father by letter in June 1934: 'I have as much idea as most people of the road surfaces down the west side of Arabia, from Palestine to north of Medina, and these will not have altered in the time that has passed since I was there. If this area interests you, I shall be very pleased to tell you anything I know.' He asked my father to bring a map with him to their meeting.

Once again my parents – and the Hillmans – were up to it and the journey of more than 9,000 miles was successful. At one point Flash was captured by bandits, but quickly released. They travelled home in style, on their friend Lord Moyne's yacht *Rosaura*. On board was a monkey, being brought back as a present for me. But the monkey died en route. I was terribly disappointed, although I'm sure my nanny was pleased. (There is a photograph of the monkey on deck with Lord Moyne, who less than ten years later would be assassinated by a Jewish terrorist in Cairo.)

I have some photographs of the two journeys, but they also took some cine films. When I was in Jordan in the 1960s the Jordanian Government said they would very much like to see this pre-war film of their country. So I got in touch with Rootes, who had kept possession of the films because they had financed both of these long-distance trips, only to discover that at the beginning of the war the company had burnt them all. Obsessed by the supposed threat of imminent German bombing raids, Rootes had considered the films too flammable. (I was reminded of London Zoo killing all its dangerous snakes at the very beginning of the war in case they escaped.) What a pity. I would have loved to have seen those films again.

★   ★   ★

My father learned to fly. He thought it would be useful in case the pilot died! His flying clothes were always kept in a chest in the hall. He once flew low over the house and threw down some chocolates for me. I also remember Sir Victor Warrender (later Lord Bruntisfield) landing in our field in his autogyro (a sort of early helicopter). He had come to play in a village cricket match with Flash. His youngest son, Robin, was a great childhood friend but I never saw him again after the war.

Some press cuttings in a family scrapbook report that Flash accepted a wager of £500 (£32,000 in today's money) in the summer of 1936 to walk from Thorpe Satchville to the Ritz in London, a distance of 110 miles, in less than forty-eight hours. A motor car would be following him. I don't know if he won the bet, but he must have been very fit indeed even to consider it.

My parents were often abroad. They went to America, where Cecil Beaton took a photograph of them with the Marlboroughs and Loelia Westminster. (Myrtie returned with a list of all the things Americans did which she knew we would copy – and she was right. I have put them into a short appendix at the end of the book.) They went big-game hunting in Kenya on several occasions with the Marlboroughs or Lord Carnarvon (known as 'Porchy'). But sometimes they actually travelled abroad because they were short of money – such was the strength of the pound in those pre-war days. The house would be let, complete with all the servants – one winter to Bob Laycock and Antony Head, who had three months' 'Hunting Leave' from the Army – and I would be sent to stay with my grandmother or my Pease cousins.

I have no doubt at all that Flash and Myrtie loved each other deeply. I have learned over the years that both were from time to time unfaithful, but they would always return to each other with huge pleasure. Nowadays many people may be shocked. But having talked to contemporaries about their parents, I think this behaviour – and its not being kept a secret from one's husband or wife – was not uncommon before the war, or in my own youth, or even that of my half-sister who was twenty years younger than me. Such an attitude is now perhaps more French than Anglo-Saxon, but is perhaps none the worse for that.

My parents shared many things and in particular an outlook which meant that they enjoyed the fine things in life when that was possible but were also quite prepared to rough it when necessary. Either extreme was preferable to the humdrum middle. My father once said to me that he'd married my mother because she liked 'the Ritz and the ditch'. I realise that's also what I have liked all my life.

CHAPTER 2

A Thirties Childhood

I adored my father. He had great style, as became even clearer in the war when he had command of his Regiment. He was a man of action, but at the same time he always dressed beautifully and took care to change the carnations in his buttonhole morning and evening. My mother had been left a lot of money, and my father spent it. The family fortunes seemed to fluctuate wildly. At times my parents couldn't pay the rent and my pocket money was stopped.

But there were times of plenty too. Mothy Tufnell, who later became one of our greatest friends, vividly remembered the first time he saw my father in the 1930s. His nanny said to him, 'Come quickly to the bottom of the drive. Captain Kellett's car is on fire!' My father was standing in a morning coat beside a smoking Rolls-Royce. Another car had stopped and its owner was saying, 'My dear Flash, let me give you a lift.' Mothy heard my father reply, 'Please don't worry. I've got another one coming along behind.'

I was an only child, but I don't remember feeling lonely. My Aunt Iso's daughters, Sammy and Susie Pease, were like sisters, and in Leicestershire my mother used to arrange for little boys to come and spend the day with me, or I with them, which I loved. (Years later when my mother suggested, 'Darling, you don't really like women, do you?', I said that perhaps that was because she had always encouraged me to make men friends.)

There were two boys called de Pret Roose whose mother (a sister of Jean Smith-Bingham, whose husband later married Iso) was very rich. They lived only a few miles away and I often went there for the night. The elder boy, Michael, was the first love of my life – I never liked his brother John (who years later almost ended up in prison). One day, after I'd been given a miniature Crown Derby tea service, I thought I would give it to Michael when he came to tea. As I was handing it to him, John jumped up and grabbed it. I went for him at once, trying to strangle him. I was pulled away and sent to bed. But I must have done some real damage because in those days few people went to hospital and he was in Melton Mowbray hospital for a week. I was left lying in the dark, no one speaking to me. My father came and told me I must apologise. But I refused to do so.

There were lots of children's parties. At tea-time the nannies were usually stationed behind our chairs with old Milk of Magnesia bottles containing Grade A milk fetched from the farm before setting out. It was always considered safest to bring your own milk. We travelled in a car with a glass partition between the chauffeur and us, rugs tucked over our knees and a box carefully packed with layers of tissue paper containing the party dress. On arrival we would be shown up to a big spare room where we got into our dresses.

At the end we all lined up to say goodbye and thank you to the hostess. Once when I'd been scared of the conjuring tricks and hated the party, I refused to say thank you. It was stalemate – until I compromised by saying, 'Nanny says I must say thank you.'

Elizabeth Fortescue's family lived in Thorpe Satchville and she was part of my early life. We went to dancing classes and spent days together, tobogganed and went to parties. Sunny Blandford was another childhood friend. He was a year older than me but we bicycled together a lot when his family lived in Leicestershire, before his father inherited Blenheim. I was staying at Blenheim one Easter when there was a fire practice for the two private fire engines parked at the end of the Nursery passage. I was so terrified of the alarm that I went and got into Sunny's bed, where I was found by Nanny and smacked hard 'for doing such a nasty thing'. I had no idea what she was talking about.

Perversely, as children we much preferred manufactured or shop food to the home-made variety. The Harrisons of the Harrison Shipping Line had a huge house in Grosvenor Square and there was excellent home-made ice-cream made by the cook. But the great excitement was the visit of the Walls Ice Cream man on a tricycle which said 'Stop Me and Buy One', and we were allowed to go downstairs and would each be bought a choc bar. It was the same at tea with the Mildmays at Dogmersfield Park (which we always called Dog-Mess-in-a-Field) in Hampshire, where we were thrilled when the baker called and we were given 'baker's bread' rather than the bread made in the house.

At one party at the Harrisons, Jeremy Cubitt and I were much the youngest, so we sat behind the curtains in a little-used smoking room. We were discovered there holding hands and were fished out. From then on he used to come over frequently and we went on bike rides together. Tragically he killed himself in his twenties – but that's a later story.

★   ★   ★

My grandparents' house in Trewsbury in Gloucestershire held a particular fascination for me. My grandmother was obsessed with the threat of fire. Every upstairs room had a neatly folded-up canvas tunnel that you threw out of the window and the first person going down it had to stick out their elbows as they went down, to stretch it out. Then the children shot down it. At the beginning of every visit we always had to practise this.

There was only one bathroom in the house, which was my grandparents', so my cousins and I always had a hip bath in front of the fire – lovely for us, but not so lovely for the housemaids carrying up the brass cans of hot water. There was a lift in the house but it rarely stopped exactly at the floor level, and as children we were always terrified having to step up or down. And there was a huge pack of terriers, about sixteen of them. We were sometimes taken out with them all in the car, which had talc windows.

I was fond of my grandmother but later, when I was well into my teens, I became aware of a horrible habit that she had. Given half a chance, she would look in my bag or in my desk, and read my letters. When I had lunch with her at the Guards Club, which I did quite often, I made sure to take my bag with me when I went to the loo. I always ate exactly the same thing whenever I went and my grandmother used to say to the parlourmaid, 'Miss Diana will have her usual – potted shrimps and brown bread and butter.'

Manners were important. If people were staying, we had to go down after tea and proceed around the room, shaking hands with anyone we hadn't met the day before. Often they'd be wearing different clothes or had a different hairstyle and it wasn't easy to tell if we'd already met them.

Good manners to servants were particularly essential. When I was about twelve my mother was having lunch at Highclere with her great friend, Porchy Carnarvon. (He was known to us as Old Porchy. His son, known as Little Porchy, became the Queen's racing manager.) I was at lunch too and there were about fifteen people in all. I was sitting next to Porchy, who was telling me how you could tell when a pear was ripe. It was only ripe for three hours, he said. I was listening to this as I helped myself to a second vegetable and I never said thank you to the footman holding the vegetable dish. My mother, from the bottom of the table, suddenly said, 'Diana, you didn't thank George. Leave the room!' I got up and left. I shall never forget leaving that table, my shoes squeaking in the silence. It was the best lesson I've ever had. I have never not thanked anyone since.

I have a number of childhood memories that seem unrelated, though perhaps they are linked by a sense of calamity, even potential catastrophe. At 1 Eaton Place there was a food lift from the kitchen in the basement up to the dining room on the ground floor. I was downstairs with the footman and thought it would be fun to see if I could get up to the ground floor in the lift. I climbed in. Not comfortable, but just possible. From the basement he pulled on the rope, but after moving a few feet it broke and I was stuck between floors. They got me out eventually, but it was terrifying. A second memory was an early revelation to me of my father's fiercely Protestant faith. I had been to tea with a little girl and she had shown me a small statue of the Virgin Mary. When I told my father he said, 'You're not going there again!' Nor did I.

Then, a little later, there was *Jane Eyre* and the purple dye. I had bought a cheap copy of this masterpiece in Woolworths for sixpence and I was reading it under the bedclothes with a torch in case nanny came in. When I got to the point where Helen Burns died of TB and Jane Eyre was so upset, so was I. My tears rolled onto the book and the purple dye of the book cover rolled onto the sheets. In the morning I tried to make the bed myself, not leaving it for the nursery maid to do. But I was discovered and severely reprimanded.

Miss Beakey arrived in 1935 as a nursery governess and was to play an enormous part in our lives, for better and for worse. In Thorpe Satchville I had had lessons with Elizabeth Fortescue and their governess Miss Sedgley in the mornings. I then had Miss Brooking living in as my nursery governess, but she was discovered to be a typhoid carrier and had left forthwith. Anna Beakey was different. She came from a farming family in southern Ireland and had been well educated. She had worked and taught in France since leaving her Irish convent at the age of seventeen and she spoke beautiful French.

That summer of 1935 my parents took Beakey and me with them to stay at the Residence Hotel at Val d'Esquières, between

Fréjus and St-Tropez on the French Riviera. I remember sitting on a bed and cutting the pages of *Seven Pillars of Wisdom* for my father. Lawrence had been killed in a motorcycle accident in May and the first edition for the general public had just been published. My parents went on to Monte Carlo to meet the Marlboroughs, and Beakey and I returned by boat to England. We stopped off at Gibraltar and it took five days to get home. But Val d'Esquières had cast a spell on me, and after the war I knew I must go back there.

Not long afterwards my Aunt Iso wanted a governess for Sammy and Susie, and Beakey's more amenable sister Katty went to live with them. Beakey left when I went to school in 1937 but came back to us again in 1940. She was a good teacher, but re-engaging her after the war to teach my own children was one of the biggest mistakes of my life.

★   ★   ★

My parents loved practical jokes. Their great friend Porchy Carnarvon fancied himself as a rider although he had little reason to do so. My father sent him a telegram from Aintree, telling him that a jockey had found himself unable to ride at short notice and could Porchy possibly charter an aeroplane from Highclere and ride in the race instead. He flew up, only to discover that it was all a joke. Luckily he thought it was funny too.

A few years later Porchy got his own back. My parents had taken a house at Twyford for the racing at Ascot. The royal princes were there and joined in the games of bicycle polo, played on cheap 2s 6d bicycles bought for that purpose from a second-hand shop. One day Porchy had a row with my parents about something. The next morning before the party went off to the races he called Sammy and me aside for a private word. He said that he'd give us each a £1 note if when they were all out we would throw the contents of the lily pond into the drawing room. So we went and hurled goldfish and water lilies all over everything. It was enormous fun.

Unbelievably, when they came back, we weren't ticked off and were allowed to keep the money.

A more elaborate joke was played on Mrs Gerard Leigh, who lived in Thorpe Satchville and who was having an affair with Lord Titchfield (later the Duke of Portland). My parents found a dead fish in their pond and, having sewn it up in a canvas salmon-bag, got the valet to take a train up to the Portlands' fishing lodge in Scotland. He then put the fish on the train back south, at the same time sending a telegram, purporting to come from Lord Titchfield, to Mrs Gerard Leigh: 'Sending you down salmon'. (Salmon was a great treat in those pre-salmon-farming days.) Mrs Gerard Leigh rang my parents and said, wasn't it marvellous, Sunny was sending her a salmon, come and dine on Thursday. Of course when Thursday came, there was no salmon.

We children played practical jokes too. At the beginning of the war I was living in Milton in Wiltshire with my cousins Sammy and Susie. At a time when children were being evacuated from London, Sammy, then aged thirteen, went to the village's call box and rang the ladies living in the half-dozen big houses in the village. She said she was the Revd Smith from Newbury and was organising for crippled children to be evacuated to Milton; could they please come to a meeting at the Manor with Mrs Pease (her mother, who with her husband was at the races for the day) that afternoon at 2.30. She must have been convincing, because they all agreed to come.

We fooled around in the bushes at the front of the house and watched the women arrive, complete with hats and gloves, and ring the front-door bell. George, the butler, in his shirt sleeves with sleeve bands on, thought it was us and came to the door brandishing a broom which he pushed out from the door. The women told him they had come for a meeting, but George told them curtly that Mr and Mrs Pease were not in. When they got home, all the ladies started telephoning. We were sitting together on a sofa in the smoking room when the calls came. After several had been answered, my aunt looked up and said, 'Children, is this something to do with you?' And we had to admit it. But instead of being ticked off, Sammy was congratulated on her impersonation.

I do remember an embarrassing moment when my mother assumed there was a practical joke when there actually wasn't one. We were on holiday on the Isle of Wight in 1946 when one morning the cook announced the arrival of 'Lord and Lady Tryon'. Perhaps because of the name 'try-on' my mother thought it was Susie and me being silly, and she hurled a cushion across the room as the door opened – which hit a very surprised (and real-life) Lady Tryon.

★   ★   ★

Before the war my parents seemed to dine out almost every night. My father would come and kiss me goodnight in his white tie and tails and my mother in one of her grand dresses (some of which she gave me towards the end of the war when there was clothes rationing). As a mother, Myrtie was hopeless. I adored her when I was grown up, but she couldn't deal with children and couldn't be bothered with the sort of things we wanted to eat. She had breakfast in bed, went to lots of parties and rode and hunted, and always travelled with my father, however wild the journey.

But they were good parents in other ways. They took Sammy and me to Paris for a week to a large international exhibition when we were ten and eleven, and always took us to the Ritz for lunch before Christmas, where we were allowed lobster. They made a fuss of me on my birthday when I always dined downstairs with lots of silver on the table, and they would take me to the theatre two or three times every holidays. And, along with my aunt Iso, they would spend the whole of August every year with me and my cousins at the seaside on the Isle of Wight, from 1932 onwards. No nanny or governess came and we did everything together with them –

picnics, climbing hills and walls, paddling canoes, swimming and diving.

On the island we stayed first at Bembridge and later in a cottage on the Brooke estate belonging to Sir Hugh Seely. I remember a huge cedar that had been planted on the estate by Garibaldi (a Seely forebear had been a big supporter of his), which fired my early interest in the Italian revolutionary. I remember too that Irene Ravensdale, Curzon's eldest daughter and a former girlfriend of my father's, would bring slum children each summer to camp on the estate. We used to play games with them, even though we were shy with them and they with us, and we barely understood each other's pronunciation.

By the time I was ten my parents must have thought it time for me to go to a conventional school. In 1937 they let Beakey go and I was sent with Sammy and Susie to Burton Hill House School near Malmesbury in Wiltshire. Like my cousins I was a weekly boarder, and I spent weekends with them at their home, Milton Manor, near Marlborough.

My parents were pleased that the girls at the school came from a variety of backgrounds including the daughters of local farmers, doctors and vets. I became great friends with Di Erroll. She was being brought up in Wiltshire by her aunt, Lady Avice Spicer. Lady Avice's under-butler would fetch Di every week in a motorbike and sidecar, which we thought very stylish.

Di Erroll barely knew either of her parents, who had divorced in 1930. Her mother, Idina Sackville, was the legendary 'Bolter' and her father, who lived in Kenya, was the victim of a sensational murder there in 1941. All the reports of the murder were cut out of her aunt's newspapers, but when I rang up at the time and asked to speak to Lady Diana, Iso told me I should have asked for Lady Erroll. She had inherited the title from her father, although not his seat in the House of Lords. (When I asked my father-in-law why she didn't have a vote in the House of Lords, he said, 'We can't possibly have women in the Lords. What would we do about the WCs?')

We had been at the school only four terms when we were abruptly taken away. My father had seen an advertisement in *The Times* which announced that Lord Walsingham (who had been his Instructor at Sandhurst) was undertaking to educate other girls along with his daughters at Westmere in Norfolk, 'Protestants only'. That settled it. My cousins and I were off to a new school.

CHAPTER 3

War

I can recall exactly where I was when I heard Neville Chamberlain announcing on the radio that we were at war with Germany. It was the end of the summer holidays and I was in the schoolroom at Milton, looking out of the window over the rose garden and the field beyond. I thought a war sounded exciting.

Back at school in Norfolk, there were some immediate changes. Every day we had to do half an hour's lesson wearing gas masks, which were horrible to put on and hot to wear. We mixed a flour-and-water paste and used it to stick strips of muslin onto the downstairs windows. All the upstairs ones had muslin stuck solidly over the whole window to stop any flying glass in case a bomb fell nearby. We were set to making many-tailed bandages – the 'tails' were straps of material to hold these large bandages in place. We helped to dig an air-raid shelter in the garden and then we had to sit there to get used to it. It was damp and smelly. And of course we had the black-out when it got dark.

At meal-times we were waited on by fourteen-year-old girls from the cottages on the estate. They had just left school and Lady Walsingham wanted to train them so that they could get jobs. Lady Walsingham believed herself to be psychic. At the beginning of the First World War she had gone into a room and seen the people who were going to be killed. She was horrified when she discovered that we were using the wooden loo tops in the many bathrooms of the house to play planchette (it was a perfect place to play because you could lock the door). With another war starting, she was unnerved by any dabbling in automatic writing, seances and the paranormal, and our games of planchette were strictly forbidden.

Both my aunt and my grandmother took in evacuees. At my grandmother's they all slept in the attic, where they peed on the floor and the stains showed through on the ceiling below. At Milton my aunt decided that her evacuees must go to church (though she seldom went herself) and they must have hats to do so. Curtains from the housemaids' room were cut up by the local dressmaker and made into hats within a week. (We too always had to cover our heads when we went to church, wearing hats for services and knotting the corners of a handkerchief if we went inside a church at any time.) The evacuated children didn't stay long. The immediate bombing threat on London didn't materialise, and they were unhappy in the country.

I spent Christmas 1939 with my parents in a farmhouse in Lincolnshire, together with Masters, our butler, Mummy's lady's maid and Biddy, the housemaid. I slept in a large dingy room with brown lino on the floor, which also stored a vast amount of live ammunition. This could have ended in disaster when Masters, who had overslept and had to light the fire quickly in the sitting room below, threw some petrol onto the blaze to encourage it. Luckily we all survived.

My father had been elected to Parliament in a by-election in May 1939. It happened like this. Myrtie had a boyfriend called Arthur Hope (later Lord Rankeillour), who was an MP. In 1939 he was appointed Governor of Madras, so he offered his seat of Birmingham Aston to Flash. As a Member of Parliament, Flash could have avoided active service if he'd wanted to – but of course he didn't.

Flash's Regiment left for the Middle East in January 1940. He came into the sitting room in Lincolnshire and kissed me goodbye. He said he knew he would see me soon, told me to look after

Mummy and that he was going to take her with him to the station. I so wished to have gone on that drive to the station, but he was wise to take her on his own. I never saw my father again.

The next day we packed up and left. My father had made out an elaborate plan of numbers so that if he referred to a number in a letter, Myrtie and I would know where it was. I found it the other day. I don't believe it was ever used, but it was flattering to be trusted with it.

⋆　　⋆　　⋆

The Sherwood Rangers' destination was Palestine, to join the British Cavalry Division. They travelled with their horses by train down through France – at one point the train ran over a French soldier and cut him neatly in two – and arrived in the area of Marseilles, during the coldest spell in those parts for fifty years. The resourcefulness of the Regiment's troopers shines through in the following incident of Corporal Harrison and the sick horse (the details come from Martin Lindsay's *History of the Sherwood Rangers Yeomanry*).

The horse chose to go sick in the middle of France, miles from civilisation. The train clanked to a halt at a small country station. The horse was let down onto the platform and Corporal Harrison, a former stud groom at Welbeck, tossed out numerous bales of straw, then jumped down to keep the horse company. The train puffed on, leaving the pair behind.

Harrison led the horse into the waiting room, surrounded it with straw, locked the door and walked off to the shops, returning with several bottles of brandy. The brandy cure had to be persisted with and took some time. Outside, it was freezing. The travelling population, red-nosed and blue-cheeked, stormed the waiting room demanding admission. Harrison and his horse held the fort. The door was still locked.

After a time, both the brandy and the horse were exhausted.

Harrison racked his brains and remembered that one of the liaison officers between the British and French commands was the Duke of Gloucester. He commandeered the stationmaster's telephone and by sheer effort of will persuaded a chain of operators to connect him with His Royal Highness.

Harrison's explanation was brief and to the point: 'Sir, you remember when you visited Welbeck there was one horse with a wart on its nose?' The Duke had not forgotten. 'Well,' Harrison continued, 'I've got this horse here in the waiting room and it's got the colic.'

Within the hour a special carriage was hooked onto the next train. In the carriage were three veterinary officers from the Indian Army, equipped for any contingency. By the time the Regiment reached Marseilles, Harrison and the horse (thoroughly alive and kicking) had caught up with it.

At the end of January the Regiment embarked for Haifa. The sea was very rough and upset men and horses. Arriving in Palestine during the rainy season, their first action was a cavalry charge, with swords drawn, through the streets of Jaffa.

The wives of some officers, including Myrtie, ignored regulations and a couple of months later joined their husbands in Palestine. Myrtie shared a tiny house near Tel Aviv with her friends Anne Feversham and Ruth Wood, whose husbands, Sim and Charles, were based in Palestine with their own cavalry regiments. The High Commissioner of Palestine, Sir Harold MacMichael, took a dim view of these 'illegal wives', but they were tolerated until September 1940, when they were all obliged to leave. (Hermione Ranfurly, the author of *To War with Whitaker*, was an exception. With shorthand and typing skills she managed to get herself a job as secretary to Sir Harold and then General 'Jumbo' Wilson.)

But the war's intensity had now increased and getting back to Britain through the Mediterranean was very dangerous. The only alternative was to go east and get home by going right around the world. Myrtie, Anne and Ruth got to India, where they stayed some months with the viceroy, Lord Linlithgow.

Lord Halifax, then the British Ambassador in Washington, where he had been sent by Winston to get him out of the Cabinet, was allowed to fly his daughter Anne and daughter-in-law Ruth home via America. But Myrtie had a much longer and more complicated return journey, with endless changes of ship, and it was almost a year before she arrived back in early September 1941. We were surprised to get a cable from her (all in capital letters of course): 'Am returning with primrose cardigan.' We couldn't think why she was telling us that she was coming back with a yellow jersey. It turned out to be Lady (Primrose) Cadogan.

To meet her on her return, we were allowed to go to London with Aunt Iso and spend two nights at the Hyde Park Hotel.

★   ★   ★

My mother came back to Milton Manor, a beautiful house that I loved very much. (It was recently bought by Anne and Michael Tree's daughter and her husband, and Ed and I went to lunch with them there a few months ago. It was an absolute joy to see it again.) The centre of our lives was the 'schoolroom', off which there was a bedroom for the three of us. This bedroom, which was down a few steps, was over the scullery and had a low ceiling and was part of a later addition to the Georgian house.

The schoolroom was large and had big cupboards in which we kept most of our clothes. We had a table in there, which for tea was always covered with a cloth and matching napkins. We often had tea there on our own, with Sammy – the eldest – always pouring the tea. There was a wind-up gramophone, on which Susie and I would sometimes play a particular song over and over again until everyone told us to stop it. Mummy and Aunt Iso used to come up and spend time with us there. Iso would read to us for half an hour after lunch and we were expected to draw or paint at the same time.

Beyond the schoolroom was a bathroom with a separate loo, known as the children's bathroom but where the servants were allowed to have a bath between two and four o'clock in the afternoon, when we were forbidden to use it. Beyond that was the back stairs, covered in cork flooring which we thought far superior to the lino which most friends' back stairs had.

Uncle Geoffrey had fought in the First World War, so he was just too old to fight in this one. This did not prevent me having a terrific row with Sammy about her father not fighting in the war when mine was – I remember pulling a great handful of hair out of her. He was a racehorse trainer and, unlike most sports, horse racing was allowed to continue in the war on a restricted basis. We children helped to exercise the racehorses, when we weren't riding a pony called Pudding with a very hard mouth.

There were plenty of jobs to be done. One was churning milk into butter. My uncle was a very greedy man and, warned by the local diary that the evacuees would need a lot of milk so that cream and even milk would therefore be in very short supply, he had bought two Jersey cows. All the flowerbeds were turned over to vegetables and we gave any surplus fruit or vegetables to people in the village.

Other jobs included feeding the hens and cleaning up their eggs with a wet tea towel, while sitting in the smoking room, in order to sell them; visiting wounded soldiers in hospital (which I hated doing); helping to organise fundraising events in the village hall; and sorting out the huge boxes of clothes and blankets in the servants' hall which Lady Tweedsmuir had arranged to be sent to Mummy for onward distribution to the Regiment's widows. I used to climb inside the box and lift things out for Mummy to decide who was to have what.

As the war went on, my cousins and I took on further chores.

My parents' head housemaid until the war, Biddy, had taken over as cook when the (male) cook was called up, along with the kitchen maid and the scullery maid. We helped her preparing the vegetables, bottling fruit and washing the saucepans. We were taught how to clean the silver, using jeweller's rouge, to relieve the pressure on George, the butler. Aunt Iso went out several nights a week to work in a munitions factory, which she loved.

Meanwhile my cousins and I were still at school in Norfolk. We had left for a few months after the fall of France in 1940 and then returned. But all was about to change. In the summer of 1942 the War Office commandeered most of Lord Walsingham's estate for a battle-training area, not only our school, but the Walsinghams' house and farm and entire villages. In all more than a thousand people were evacuated with just three weeks' notice from several villages and 17,000 acres of land. (There was an unequivocal promise at the time that it would all be returned after the war. But the area is still occupied by the Ministry of Defence today.) Aunt Iso came to collect us and take us back to Milton.

So in September 1942 it was time for a new school. But I started at that school several weeks late because in the holidays I had had an operation which had long been pending. When I was born (weighing only 3 lbs 3 oz) I had a birthmark scar on my forehead and right eyelid. It greatly upset my mother. It didn't upset me that much, although other children sometimes used to ask what it was. Before the war I had been taken several times to the London Clinic to discuss it and have minor operations.

My mother now put pressure on me, using emotional blackmail. She said, 'Darling, you will *have* to have this done. Daddy so wants you to have it done. He's fighting. You can't let him down.' I was taken to Park Prewitt Hospital near Basingstoke to meet the legendary pioneer of plastic surgery, Sir Harold Gillies. Astonishingly – given the importance of his work at the hospital on badly burnt airmen –

he agreed to come to Newbury nursing home and operate on my birthmark. (We had a link to him because he had operated before the war on Aunt Iso when she had had her hunting accident.)

I had a horror of hospitals and general anaesthetics, and I only agreed if I could have it done with a local anaesthetic and a mirror rigged up above my head so that I could see them doing it. The operation went well, but unfortunately I got septicaemia afterwards. I had been allowed back to Milton to recuperate and while feeding the hens Sammy had thrown a bucket of corn over my head and my wound had become infected. I was rushed back into hospital and ended up having the general anaesthetic I'd been trying to avoid.

We had only one wireless at home and my mother had lent it to me in the nursing home. But I had left it on all night by mistake and had run the battery down. So my mother couldn't listen to what was happening in North Africa, where my father was fighting and where the desert war was reaching a critical point.

The new school was at Tackley, a few miles north of Oxford, where Brenda Loder lived, and I did lessons with her daughter and a few other girls. I was there for almost a year, and enjoyed meeting the exciting people that she entertained. As well as a number of generals, these included Lord David Cecil and Sir William Beveridge (when I asked Sir William what we could do to help his plans, he told me to get married and have lots of children).

Mrs Loder was High Church and she persuaded me against my better judgement to go and make my confession. I didn't like the local parson so I bicycled to Woodstock to make it there. I also remember bicycling to the nearby village of Kidlington, where I knew that no one would know me, and terribly shyly buying a minute lipstick (of which there was an acute shortage in the war). I took it home and hid it but I was never brave enough to use it. And then an extraordinary thing happened. I fell in love with a girl. For a short time, about six months, I was very keen on her and she on me. I hated myself for it and I've never been more relieved when she left to go to a music school.

★   ★   ★

As well as what my mother and others told me, there are two eyewitness accounts which help to describe my father's war. The first is the wartime letters back to his family of our great friend Myles Hildyard, *It is Bliss Here: Letters Home 1939-1945* (published just after his death in 2005). Myles was in the Sherwood Rangers throughout the war. The second source is *Alamein to Zem Zem*, a memoir of desert warfare by Keith Douglas, considered by many to be the finest English poet of the war. Douglas disobeyed orders in order to take part in Alamein and stayed with the Sherwood Rangers until he was wounded at Zem Zem in Libya.

Having arrived in Palestine as horsed cavalry, the Regiment converted to artillery in 1940 and took part in the defence of Tobruk and Benghazi and then converted to tanks, serving in most of the major Eighth Army tank battles in North Africa, including Alam Halfa and Alamein.

Flash always insisted on a religious service, if possible, before every battle and often preached the sermon himself. Impeccably dressed, he also expected a smart turn-out in his Regiment. Instead of the more usual short socks and sandals he insisted on long shooting-length socks and proper shoes, and he encouraged everyone to press their shorts by sleeping on them. 'Flash is only rivalled by Monty as a showman', Myles wrote in a letter home.

Flash nevertheless managed to get to Cairo fairly frequently for relaxation. He was a great friend of, and I suspect had an affair with, Mary Newall, the glamorous commandant of a volunteer ambulance detachment who always wore a large revolver in a leather holster. She later became the mistress of Walter Monckton, the head of British propaganda in Cairo.

Smart nightlife in Cairo required a black tie and stiff collar, and at one point Flash ran out of black silk evening socks. Myrtie rang Randolph Churchill, whom she knew was about to go out to Cairo, and asked if he would take out two pairs. Randolph said that he would be swimming ashore – it was a secret mission – so Myrtie suggested he could take them in his mouth. He agreed and Flash got his socks.

Flash rarely complained, although in a letter to me in September 1942 he mentioned the 'beastly desert sores' on his hands and 'the flies which are too awful'. In August, in the build-up to Alamein, he had dined with Churchill and other select company. He led the Regiment at Alam Halfa and Alamein, where he won the DSO. Soon after, in January 1943, in the desert near Tripoli, he had a very narrow escape. As Myles recorded, 'Flash got a direct hit from a high explosive very large shell yesterday. Bits went through his map case but he popped his head down in time.' Then on 23 March, at the Battle of Mareth in the Tunisian desert, he was killed outright when a shell burst alongside his tank while he was standing up shaving.

There were many tributes to my father, but one of the more unexpected came from Keith Douglas, whose initial hostility to the Sherwood Rangers officers in general and Flash in particular had gradually changed to frank admiration. Picking up a newspaper while on sick leave in Tel Aviv and reading of Flash's death, he reflected (*Alamein to Zem Zem* uses pseudonyms and Flash was 'Piccadilly Jim'):

Piccadilly Jim, with all his faults of occasionally slapdash and arbitrary conduct, had been a brave man and a colonel of whom we could be proud. Of whom, I discovered, somewhat to my own surprise, I had been proud myself. He was an institution: it seemed impossible that in a moment a metal splinter had destroyed him. He had embodied in himself all the regimental characteristics he had been at pains to create. That assumption of superiority, that dandyism, individuality, and disregard of the duller military conventions and regulations, had made the regiment sometimes unpopular – the Australians could not understand men who polished their badges for a battle – but always discussed and admired. We knew we were better than anyone else, and cared for no one. But the focal point of this confidence was Piccadilly Jim … killed as one might say, typically, while he was standing up in his tank, shaving under shell-fire.

CHAPTER 4

Education and MI6

My mother was with us at Milton when we got the news. A policeman came to the house one evening and Susie and I asked him why he'd come. To see my uncle, he said. But in fact he'd come to tell my mother that Flash had been killed. Two hours later, when I was in the schoolroom, Uncle Geoffrey came and asked me to go and see my mother in the drawing room, and I heard what had happened.

Myrtie took to her bed for a week with the curtains drawn and would see no one but me and Iso. As for me, I couldn't quite believe it for a bit. I think some part of me thought my father would still, somehow, come back. His letters continued to come for a few days and that felt so strange. It was only when the Regiment came back to England in December without him, to retrain for D-Day, that it finally sunk in that he really wasn't going to return. I felt shattered.

He was buried in the desert where he was killed, as was normal in wartime. Later he had a military funeral and burial at the Sfax War Cemetery in Tunisia. My mother wouldn't have a memorial service for him in London. She said lots of people had been killed in the war and she wasn't going to single him out. 'You can't make a fuss.' ('People like us don't cry,' was another mantra of hers. She had heard the King of Greece say this to his wife, when they had been getting on a boat together and she had been crying at having to leave their homeland.) My grandmother, however, was furious when I arrived to have lunch with her at the Guards Club not long after and my mother hadn't dressed me in black (not so easy with limited clothes coupons) but instead in a red coat.

And yet there were some things my mother did make a fuss about. When the Regiment returned from North Africa my mother rang the Ritz to book rooms for four of the officers. When told that the hotel was full, she said, 'I'm sure with Americans, who have never fired a shot in the war.' The hotel agreed that, yes, the rooms were occupied by Americans. So she said, 'I'm afraid you must turn them out for brave men who have been fighting in the desert.' The hotel complied and the officers got their rooms.

Three months before my father was killed, Myrtie had taken a call from her friend Anne Feversham, whose middle brother Peter Wood had been killed at the battle of El Alamein. Now Anne rang with news that her youngest brother, Richard, had had both legs crushed by a German bomb which had failed to explode. At least he was alive.

I heard the following conversation from my mother's end of the line: 'Darling, how awful. I just can't believe it. Poor you, I can't imagine what you must be feeling and such a short time after Peter was killed. When will you hear any more? I am so sorry, I don't know how to begin to tell you…'

When we asked her what had happened, she answered, 'Lady Feversham's little brother has lost both his legs.' The thought of this happening to anyone was more than I could bear. I had always hated seeing anyone ill. For several nights I prayed hard that God would let Lady Feversham's little brother die. Much later when I told Lord Halifax about this, all he said was, 'Isn't it lucky that the Almighty knows best.'

$\star$ $\star$ $\star$

In the summer of 1943 I left Brenda Loder in Oxfordshire where I'd been for a year, and Sammy and I, together with Margaret de Grey, Lord Walsingham's daughter, and Sarah Wilson, the daughter of Sir Arnold Wilson, were sent to Hillhampton House, a few miles outside Worcester. A Spartan Jacobean house, it had housed prisoners in the First World War and was now a centre for domestic-science courses. We cooked, sewed and cleaned; we scrubbed and blackened grates.

Out of doors in autumn and winter under a corrugated-iron roof we did laundry, which we then ironed with old-fashioned flat irons heated up on a solid hotplate by a fire underneath. We starched and ironed stiff collars. We always wondered whose. I hated it, but it did give me some useful skills. The only light relief was hitch-hiking or bicycling into Worcester twice a week to the cinema. I did French with the local parson, who was also teaching the son of George Hales, Flash's chaplain in the desert, so we had a link.

After six months all four of us got ourselves sacked. My mother was furious, but she did then allow me to do a secretarial course in Oxford at Miss Sprules' Secretarial Academy, which had been evacuated there from London. This involved French, shorthand and typing, and public speaking. This was much more fun, except for the fact that Miss Sprules herself was lesbian and I had to take evasive action from time to time.

It was there that I first fell in love with ballet. Together with a few friends I would go and sit at the feet of Margot Fonteyn, Robert Helpmann and Beryl Grey, who were rehearsing at the Oxford Playhouse because London was considered too dangerous – this was the time when the V-1 flying bombs were hitting the capital. We used sometimes to go and have coffee in the morning with these ballet luminaries when we should have been typing, and we got to know them quite well. Beryl Grey in particular became a lifelong friend.

I remember noticing when I came up to London in late summer 1944 that the V-1s or 'Doodlebugs' had a much more terrifying effect on people than the more conventional bombs of the Blitz.

People would lie down in the street if they heard a Doodlebug 'cut out'. But we were never allowed to do that or to take any sort of evasive action. 'People like us don't', my mother said. My cousins and I were never even allowed to go to an air-raid shelter. It was strictly forbidden.

'Darling, I didn't go to church today,' Myrtie said – that was all – when she telephoned me on Sunday, 18 June 1944. I was puzzled. What she had decided not to tell me was that the Guards Chapel had received a direct hit from a V-1 rocket a few hours earlier, during the morning service. The concrete roof had collapsed, 121 people were killed and 141 seriously injured. News of the tragedy was suppressed at the time, although rumours of the disaster soon spread across London. But I was in Oxfordshire and didn't hear them.

'Boy' Browning often came to Milton during these months. As a very young girl, my mother had fallen in love with him. But I hadn't heard of him until after my father was killed and he began to come over for dinner from Upavon, where he was training the Airborne Division for the Arnhem operation later in the year. One night Susie and I bravely asked if he would get his wife, Daphne du Maurier, to sign our autograph books. Iso immediately told us not to be a nuisance to General Browning. It was years later that it became clear that he had never told his wife that he was seeing my mother.

I was so mad about him that when I saw his picture on the front of *Picture Post* at a station bookstall I immediately jumped off the train to buy a copy and the train then left without me. My aunt met my bicycle at Savernake Station but not me. When I did get there I hid the magazine from my aunt at the back of my trousers. I couldn't possibly admit why I'd missed the train.

*　　*　　*

That summer of 1944 was our last at Milton, because in the early autumn Iso 'bolted'. A couple of months earlier a very good-looking man called Arthur Smith-Bingham, who had work in the area for the Claims Commission, had come to lodge with us at Milton. When he said he was going to take Iso to Dorset for the weekend, Uncle Geoffrey never complained. Then one day Iso simply left Milton and went to live in the Savernake Forest Hotel with Arthur.

It was Iso's house but, despite rows on the subject, Uncle Geoffrey went on living in it. The household immediately broke up, leaving my uncle in sole occupation. Sammy was already in the Wrens. Susie went to live with a dreadful great-aunt, our grandmother's youngest sister, Janie, in Edinburgh, where she smoked in bed and managed to set fire to a sheet. My mother and I moved to London. I was very sad to leave the house and the village. I never went back to fetch some of my belongings. I remember in particular a photograph book which I was sorry to lose.

My parents had bought 5 Clifton Place near Paddington before the war and we had lived there intermittently. But at the beginning of the war the house and all the adjoining ones had been commandeered, before being bombed flat in the Blitz. With nowhere to live in London we had then taken two rooms in Gloucester Place with Doria and Douglas Scott (his sister Henrietta, who was seven years younger than me, was not with us). Douglas slept with his mother in one room and I slept with mine in the other. Douglas and I weren't considered old enough to be allowed out, so out of boredom we used to stand on the balcony and try to spit on the heads of American soldiers when they came past.

On Sundays Doria's sister Irene (Lord Haig's youngest child, later Irene Astor) would take Douglas and me out to lunch at Flemings Hotel in Mayfair and afterwards to review her allotments running down the side of Hyde Park, where she would issue instructions. (When Mummy took me to stay at Flemings, you had to fill in your nationality. I put 'Irish' and all hell broke loose, Ireland being neutral in the war.) I also remember that wheat was planted for miles on the wide verges of the A1 road in Bedfordshire.

From Gloucester Place we moved, for the last months of the war, to the chauffeur's old flat at Bathurst Mews, behind our old house at Clifton Place. There were three minute bedrooms and two garages underneath. We used one garage as a drawing room and the second one became a storeroom. I suppose we were lucky to have anywhere, but it was very uncomfortable. Myrtie had one bedroom, Doria another and I had the third one. Like the kitchen, it only had a roof light, which dripped with condensation all the time.

Lighting the gas-fired hot-water cylinder with a match used to terrify me, when the gas caught alight with a boom. The solitary loo was upstairs in the bathroom, where we were only allowed a three-inch-deep bath. A red line around the bath marked the official approved limit – the baths in the Dorchester were the same. I complained to my mother that she never let her bathwater out. She said she'd always had a maid to do that. Jim Forrestal, the US Secretary of the Navy, was an admirer of Myrtie's and he often used to visit her here at Bathurst Mews. She clearly loved him, and he and his wife didn't get on, but she would never marry anyone divorced.

Doria worked in a munitions factory and Myrtie ran a Welfare Service for the Sherwood Rangers. They were both Air Raid Wardens. Now that I was properly back in London I applied for, and got, a job at the Foreign Office. The job turned out to be at MI6. The hours were 9 a.m. to 6 p.m., six days a week, with one day off a week but you couldn't choose the day, and one week's holiday a year. I was paid £5 a week. Flash had died virtually bankrupt and I had to pay Myrtie £3 out of that for my keep.

MI6 was at 54 Broadway, near St James's Park (conveniently for me, only a few stops along the Circle Line from Paddington). It pretended to be the Minimax Fire Extinguisher Company, but most London taxi drivers seemed to be aware of the building's real function. The Service tended to take only people from good backgrounds, as it was thought they would not be traitors (how wrong they were).

There were a number of people in MI6 with me that I knew or who became friends later, including Janet Marshall-Cornwall (later Middleton), Skip (Elizabeth) Lumley (later Grimthorpe), Billy Brooksbank's sister Crystal (later Pakenham, Salmond and Tweedie), Margaret Elphinstone (later Rhodes) and Minta MacMichael's sister Priscilla (later Raynes). Elizabeth Jackson, who married John Cowdray, worked in MI5 just across the park and the two organisations were very much connected.

Sir Stewart Menzies, the head of MI6, lived at Bridges Court in the Wiltshire village of Luckington, in the house next door to my grandmother's. I had met him before the war because I used to be taken to see his baby daughter Fiona (which I hated doing). On my first day at MI6 I ran into him in the corridor, as his office was only a few rooms away from mine, so of course we spoke. I had told my mother I was working for the Foreign Office, which we all had to do, and when I got home that evening she naturally asked me who my boss was. I had to say I didn't know – only to get a rocket from her at my ignorance after all she'd spent on my education. I was told to find out the next day for sure. I was in a torment, but I managed to avoid telling her and she finally gave up asking me.

I didn't have a great deal to do at MI6, although I used to do personal insurance for the spies – their watches, jewellery, etc. – which was all done through Stewart Menzies' own insurance company. If they were captured or killed, they were immediately transferred, as from the previous day, to the Pioneer Corps, so that their wife or husband would get a pension. I said: why couldn't they be in a better regiment? The answer was: nobody knows anyone in the Pioneer Corps!

For a short time I had a boyfriend called Leonard Byng. He was very rich and spoke marvellous French, but he had Fascist views and my mother made it clear that he was totally unsuitable. She believed he had been sacked from the Welsh Guards – the least fashionable Guards regiment. I went to his wedding to Mary Anne Stuart and then I went to the 400 Club several times with him while his wife was having a baby. He bought Lutyens's Queen Anne-style house, The Salutation, in Sandwich.

The long hours at MI6 didn't stop us dancing the night away, often till four in the morning – we made do with little sleep. I remember throwing thunderflashes into the crowds in Leicester Square with Johnny Dalkeith while we were waiting for the 400 to open. (Myrtie was shocked to think that a naval officer who would be a duke could do such things!)

Looking back it seems to me quite remarkable that you could get on the Underground in a grand dress (my mother's probably, since you couldn't get such clothes in the war) and the men in white tie and tails or 'patrols' (the military equivalent of a dinner jacket) and be quite accepted by the poor bombed-out people sleeping in crowded bunks down in the stations. Instead of any animosity, they'd remark cheerfully, 'You look as if you've been having fun!' And you could walk home in the black-out quite safely.

CHAPTER 5

The Halifaxes

Richard Wood was born in 1920, the third son of Edward Wood, 1st Earl of Halifax, Viceroy of India, Foreign Secretary and wartime ambassador to Washington. The Woods of Garrowby were Yorkshire landowners. Sir Richard Wood, the first Viscount Halifax, was Chancellor of the Exchequer in the 1840s, at the time of the Irish potato famine. The 2nd Viscount became obsessed with religion and by the idea of closer union between Canterbury and Rome. Both these interests – politics and religion – were passed on to later generations.

Politics was an equally strong element in the family of Richard's mother Dorothy. She was the daughter of the 4th Earl of Onslow and had grown up at Clandon Park, the Palladian mansion near Guildford (nearly destroyed by fire in 2015), although most of the winter would be spent in a grand hotel in the south of France with her mother while her father stayed in London on Government business. She liked politics, gossip and foreign travel, but wasn't very keen on the country or countryside pursuits. She disliked the hunting so dear to her husband's heart (she was always terrified that one of her sons would be 'brought home on a gate') and was a perfect nuisance to everyone on the few occasions she joined us out shooting.

Peter, the next to Richard in age, was four years older to the day than him, so Richard's early years were not unlike those of an only child. He saw much more of his nanny, Nanny Gaywood, than he did of his parents. (Richard always referred to her as Nanny and used her own surname; whereas as children we had all referred to people's nannies by their employers' surnames, i.e. Nanny Kellett, Nanny de Pret, etc.) When Richard's father was unexpectedly appointed Viceroy of India in 1926, he had hesitated before accepting. His father had been born in 1839, so Lord Halifax thought he would be unlikely to see him again. In fact he did.

He also knew his children would mostly have to stay in England: Anne 'coming out', Charles at Eton, Peter at the prep school where eventually Richard followed him. But at the beginning the whole family travelled out to India, including Nanny. There are pictures of Richard, splendidly attired, with a small sword, acting as his father's train-bearer alongside the equally youthful son of a maharajah. He also acted as his father's page at lengthy investitures held in the Viceroy's dining room, kept awake by an occasional tickle from his mother's feathered fan.

Thrilled by the impeccable drill of the 'Garden' Highlanders, who mounted guard every morning in front of Viceregal Lodge in Delhi, Richard soon recruited his own little army from messenger and servant boys. They acquired a small supply of wooden 'rifles' and at their peak rose to a strength of seventeen, drilled by Richard, their commanding officer. These boys also found themselves press-ganged to act as Richard's cricket team. None of this was probably good for his character.

Meanwhile, Lutyens's vast new palace for the Viceroy (today the official residence of the President of India) was finally nearing completion. Queen Mary, the wife of King George V, took a great interest in Lutyens's plans and wrote many letters to my mother-in-law about it.

When it was ready for occupation in 1929, Richard and Nanny were the first occupants – his parents were away on a long tour in southern India. The chief joy for a boy of nine was the great Moghul garden, with fountains and several acres of connected waterways. Round and round the watery network went his small boat, powered by a tiny battery.

Richard's Aunt Gwenny, his mother's sister, looked after Richard in the school holidays while his parents were still in India. She had married Rupert Guinness, 2nd Earl of Iveagh. When Rupert succeeded his father and gave up his seat in Parliament, Aunt Gwenny succeeded him, to be followed in turn by her son-in-law, Chips Channon, and then by his son Paul. She was somewhat shy and aloof – she and Richard never kissed each other and only shook hands till the day she died – but her youngest child, Brigid, was his favourite cousin. Back from India, Richard was also looked after by his father's sister, Agnes Bingley (known to all the family as Auntie Mum because she and Lord H had called each other Mr and Mrs Mum all their childhood).

The family came back from India in 1931, but Richard had been sent back the year before to go to prep school at St Cyprian's in Eastbourne. He fared tolerably well there, under the autocracy of the formidable Mrs Wilkes. His success on the cricket field was largely due to his father who, as soon as he returned from India, had a concrete pitch with matting and a surrounding net constructed in the field below the stables at Garrowby and engaged a professional coach to come up from Lord's for a fortnight every summer.

In 1933 Richard went on to Eton, where his elder brothers had gone before him. His brother Peter was in the same house. As Master of the Beagles, Peter was an ex-officio member of Pop and he rather unsportingly witnessed Richard's first beating, for 'idle fagging'. Richard passed School Certificate and matriculated in 1936, and in those days there was no further educational challenge. Cricket remained his main interest and, like his great friend Nat Fiennes, he got into the Eleven. Other friends included Peter Ramsbotham, Dick Ker, David Quilter, Geoffrey Jameson and Timothy Tufnell. In due course Richard was elected to Pop, becoming President of

Pop in Michaelmas 1939, his last half. His housemaster, John Hills, wrote in his final report, 'Even if Richard becomes Pope of Rome or Prime Minister, he can never hope to be as important again.'

Garrowby remained the centre of his life. The house itself was decidedly eccentric. Originally a small shooting box, it had been considerably extended by Richard's grandfather, the 2nd Viscount Halifax, whose additions included a set of gloomy attic rooms – to attract ghosts, of all things (it didn't work). In the words of Francis Johnson, the architect who remodelled the house in the 1980s for Richard's nephew Peter, and his wife: 'Garrowby was a very involved and difficult house, claustrophobic with narrow corridors and complicated parts that required a fairly numerous staff … It was a late romantic building of singular inconvenience. Three entrance halls in series, each with its own front door.'

But for Richard it was, quite simply, home. And in those pre-war years it did have plenty of servants: butler, footmen, cook, kitchen maids, housemaids and parlourmaids. Out of doors there were three keepers, one of whom was usually free to escort Richard shooting pigeons, rooks, or rabbits in a cornfield until he was old enough to go out on his own. While his father, sister and brothers hunted, Richard was never happier than when rough shooting. With cricket added a little later, Richard never wanted to go away during the holidays. In the late 1930s friends came to stay for a week in August to play cricket matches against teams within reach of Garrowby. One year friends asked him to join them skiing, but his father (then Foreign Secretary) refused, as he said he would otherwise never see his son in the holidays.

Attendance at Sunday Evensong in the house's chapel was obligatory for the whole family and no excuses were accepted. On many mornings, too, there was Holy Communion at 8 a.m., which everyone had to attend. Gentle tennis was a great favourite with Lord Halifax despite his withered left hand, and it was often played between Evensong and the first bell for dinner. The dressing bell rang at 7.45 and a five-minute bell at 8.10. Unpunctuality was only reluctantly forgiven. Before India, Lord Halifax had been as unpunctual as anyone else but as Viceroy he had had to behave like royalty and keep to the strictest of schedules. Thus trained, he was determined to impart this excellent habit to others.

★   ★   ★

The Second World War began as Richard was about to start his last half at Eton. His parents moved from their great mansion at 88 Eaton Square (to which they never returned) to a vast suite at the Dorchester, which was thought to offer more solid protection against the bombs that didn't arrive until many months later. All the family managed to assemble at Garrowby for Christmas 1939 before Sim, Charles and Peter left for Palestine in January, Anne and Ruth following them out there a couple of months later.

Richard was firmly told that the Army would not need him until August, so his father (who was Foreign Secretary) arranged for him to go as an honorary attaché to the British Embassy in Rome for a few months. At the Embassy he worked in the commercial department, in huts at the bottom of the large garden, trying to prevent goods needed by Germany reaching their destination through Italian ports. The Ambassadress, Lady Loraine, ticked him off for spending time talking to the secretaries. He learnt Italian but he was terrified of the social life, so he persuaded his cousin Brigid to come out and join him.

One night in the Embassy he was seated next to Mrs Keppel (the long-time mistress of Edward VII). She was deaf, and when Richard asked her, 'How old is Mr Hepple [the Third Secretary]?', she answered loudly, 'Did you ask me the age of Colonel Keppel?' Richard was mortified. Years later I met Hepple at the German Embassy and he got his own back by remarking, 'I heard that Richard was a cripple.'

Richard had to leave the country swiftly in early June, only days before the rest of the embassy packed up and left. Mussolini, who could see the way the wind was blowing, was about to declare war on Britain and France. He left in a flying boat which took off from Lake Bracciano, north of Rome, carelessly leaving behind a despatch case at the airport which contained some confidential letters that his father had sent him in the previous months. These letters were not complimentary about the Italians, and Richard used to wonder if they might perhaps have hastened Mussolini's decision a few days later.

There followed a few months' training as a private soldier at Strensall, just north of York, from where Harry the chauffeur used to fetch him in the dark in a car without any lights on. Back at Garrowby he combined farm work with patrolling up and down Worsendale with a 12-bore shotgun in case any German parachutists should land on the Wolds. By November 1940 he was at Sandhurst.

Meanwhile Churchill had decided to send Lord Halifax as ambassador to Washington. Christmas, spent with his parents in Yorkshire, was overshadowed by the prospect, particularly abhorrent to Richard's mother, of life in the Washington embassy. She had insisted on asking for a meeting with Winston, so that she could protest, after he had told Lord Halifax of his decision. But it made no difference.

Richard passed out of Sandhurst as an officer in February 1941 – there was a quick turn-around in wartime. He was surprised that he had liked the place. He had been amused by the mixture of contempt and superficial respect with which they were treated. 'Stop behaving like a bloody fool, SIR!' expressed it all.

Military exercises followed, at Chiddingfold on the Surrey/Sussex border, where he met his first girlfriend, whose father later tried to persuade him to marry her. He wouldn't, so she married a Pole in the Royal Navy who later became an admiral. Then there were more exercises at Tidworth in Wiltshire. In September his regiment, the King's Royal Rifle Corps, embarked on the SS *Franconia* for a long voyage around the Cape to Egypt, which they reached in December. Once ashore, they began to move westwards into the desert along the coast road. Richard was surprised by the cold and even more by the wet.

Soon their advance was checked by Rommel's 'reconnaissance in force' and they were pushed back towards Cairo. Richard grabbed a few days' leave to see Charles and Peter in Jerusalem. Then he was learning new skills and gunnery in command of a platoon of anti-tank guns. The battle of Gazala followed and Rommel's capture of Tobruk in June. An attack of acute jaundice prevented Richard from taking part in the battle of Alamein. He was recovering in Jerusalem when he read one morning in early November 1942 in the *Jerusalem Post* that Peter had been killed in the battle.

Later that month he rejoined the Battalion, preparing for the long push to drive Rommel out of North Africa. Late December found his platoon deployed in the desert in central Libya south of the coast road, not far from a well called Bir Zidan. On 30 December German Stuka dive-bombers attacked and hit the platoon's supply truck. They had almost finished unloading supplies from this truck when the Stukas returned. Thinking that lightning wouldn't strike the same place twice, Richard and his sergeant made for two large bomb-craters, created by that morning's attack. Richard's legs were crushed by a bomb, which for some reason failed to explode.

He remembers being offered a cigarette, which he didn't want, and a cup of tea, which he did, and then a shot of morphia. One leg was amputated above the knee, and the other leg below the knee, at an Advanced Dressing Station in the desert. Then a very slow ambulance drove him east for five days, before a small aeroplane took him on to hospital in Cairo. Because of the long journey the second knee had to be removed at the hospital.

Visitors flocked to see Richard in Cairo. His brother Charles had been on his way home by boat via South Africa, but came back to see him. Countess Sophie Tarnowska, who had founded the Cairo branch of the Polish Red Cross, was sent to him by his brother-in-law Sim, who was weary of the attention she was giving him. She became such a tireless visitor that Richard arranged a secret signal with the nurse who would come in and say that it was time for his dressings to be changed. The most awkward visitor, surprisingly, was General Alexander. Richard found he had to keep the conversation going himself.

In April 1943 Richard was flown out to Washington. Because of the war, the aeroplane followed a very roundabout route and the flight took four days, via Khartoum, Ghana, Brazil and Trinidad. Despite being in a wheelchair – American development of artificial legs was then some years behind that of the British – he was soon enjoying a busy social life. He met Kick Kennedy and was quickly charmed by her. George Marshall, America's top soldier, lent him his personal aeroplane for a week's visit to New York. When in May a high-powered dinner party was laid on at the embassy for Churchill, and Halifax suggested that his son should go out to the cinema, Churchill responded, 'Not at all. We'll make Richard an honorary member of the Cabinet for the evening.'

Richard returned with his parents to Britain in August by Clipper, a long-range flying boat which provided a very privileged form of luxury travel. At Roehampton Richard was fitted with a pair of short legs and soon progressed to longer ones. When his father returned to Washington, his mother – who disliked America in general and Washington in particular – decided to stay on with Richard at Garrowby. She had the good excuse of looking after Richard, even if he had no wish to be looked after.

At the end of January 1944 Lady Halifax reluctantly returned to America and, after some weeks on his own, Richard accepted

Anne's invitation to stay with her at Sleightholmedale on the edge of the North Yorkshire Moors. Her home, Nawton Tower, had been taken over as an orthopaedic hospital for children. Anne went to see Nye Bevan to ask for the return of her house, but he refused, so she rented Sleightholmedale. Sim was away fighting, and brother and sister grew close at this time, perhaps closer during these months than at any other time in their lives. Just before D-Day Richard acquired a black Labrador puppy. He called it Bir Zidan, after the place in the Libyan desert where he had lost his legs.

Kick Kennedy came to Yorkshire a few times that spring to see Richard. Then in May 1944 she married the Duke of Devonshire's heir, Billy Hartington, in a registry office, shocking not only her mother but many other Roman Catholics. She wasn't married for long. In September Billy Hartington was killed by a sniper near the German front. A few months later Kick went back to America, shortly before Richard returned there himself with his parents in late September.

Richard stayed in America until the following May. He enjoyed the social life in Washington that winter. Meanwhile someone had decided that he should visit American military hospitals to further the cause of Anglo-American relations, and before he left he had been all over the country. His fellow speaker was Willis Roxburgh, the Assistant Air Attaché, who along with his wife Joan later became lifelong friends of ours and their son is Richard's godson. Rox had flown on too many operations and had become 'bomb happy'. He needed a rest and a change. Richard would tell his audience about Monty and the desert, and then Rox would describe sinking U-boats off the Outer Hebrides.

CHAPTER 6

Marriage in Westminster Abbey

Richard and I first met in the summer of 1945 at the Dorchester where Sim and Anne – Myrtie's great friend – were staying. He was the very last person I wanted to meet. I couldn't bear to meet someone without legs. Myrtie protested that he had what she called 'wooden legs' (actually tin) and that he looked like everyone else. None of my arguments persuaded her otherwise, so off we went. Richard was wearing a ghastly American suit and, sitting next to him, I found little to talk about. Whenever I could, I turned to talk to Sim on my other side. I was very relieved when Richard announced at the end of dinner that he was going to meet Kick Kennedy in the Orchid Room.

Not long afterwards Myrtie and I were staying with Anne at Nawton Tower when Richard came over from Garrowby. Anne announced that she and Myrtie would ride over the moors and meet Richard and me by a stream three or four miles away. We would drive over to meet them and ride back in their place. I rode badly and was often scared. But I had always loved the moors: the exhilarating sense of space, the beauty of the hills and the ever-changing cloud shadows on the heather, the absence of other people. All these combined to produce the sort of 'heaven on earth' feeling which I later had on desert journeys in the Sahara.

I was riding Jinks, a little grey pony with a lovely soft mouth. He was easy to control, there was no jumping required and no galloping because of the uneven terrain. I felt really happy that afternoon. The moor seemed to have worked a sort of strange magic on both

Richard and me. From then onwards we got increasingly pleased to see each other.

I was at Garrowby that autumn and helped Richard pack up books and other possessions for his first term at Oxford. We drove there in his little black Ford Prefect car which he had had before the war. Lord Halifax had been Chancellor of Oxford University since 1933 and it must have seemed only natural for Richard to go there. In fact it was a mistake. After his years of fighting in the desert and then travelling all over America, he felt cramped by the restrictions of university life. Especially as he was quite unable to climb the walls to get back into New College after midnight, as his friends regularly did.

Permission to spend nights away was given by his moral tutor at New College, David Cecil, whom I had met at Brenda Loder's. But in those days such leave was rarer than it became later. (David Cecil's absent-mindedness was endearing – one morning when Richard called on him he had lost an important cheque. After a long search they found it in the wastepaper basket.) A contemporary and good friend was Tony Wedgwood Benn and in Richard's last term they ran the college's Junior Common Room together.

Richard also saw a lot of Edward Boyle, who had long been a friend of mine. I was frowned on by friends for dancing with Edward because he hadn't fought in the war (he had been at Bletchley, but of course none of us knew about that then). Edward and his sister Ann were very clever. She could read at the age of three, and Edward at two and a half, having taught himself from *Little Black Sambo*. Their very tiresome mother had a long-standing boyfriend of about her age called Jack Brunner Gold. He was a marvellous architect and built superb houses at Sledmere for Richard Sykes's employees and a moorland house for Sim.

Ann and Jack fell in love, and when she was twenty-one and without telling her mother she ran away with him to a Registry

Office and they married. He must have been about ninety when he died, and Ann rang to tell me. When I asked about the funeral she said they weren't having one (they later had a 'memorial picnic' in Kew Gardens) but she asked if I would come to a party in his bedroom the next day to see him. I declined. A year or two later I tried to ring her and got no answer. She had dropped dead in the night.

In December 1945 Richard wrote to me from mid-Atlantic on board the *Queen Mary*. He was on his way to Washington for a final Christmas there while his father was still ambassador. The ship was crowded, with almost 12,000 American GIs returning home. They sailed through fog and snow, and then hit some rough weather. As Richard walked on deck between the American soldiers and lurched from side to side, they assumed he was a drunken Brit. But the actor David Niven, who happened to be with Richard, soon put them to shame by letting them know that Richard had lost his legs in the war. (Although he was younger than her, Myrtie had known Niven well when he was a child on the Isle of Wight.) When Richard reached Washington he wrote that he had seen Kick, adding 'I am still single!'

Richard was one of only two friends (Myles Hildyard was the other) that I asked to my mother's wedding to Billy McGowan in February 1946. She had Andrew Scott to give her away, and Andrew and Doria had the wedding reception in their home. I wasn't surprised that she remarried – she hated being unmarried – but I was shocked and surprised at her choice of husband. She herself had always been dismissive of him. He had been in the Black Watch and was transferred to the Sherwood Rangers, where some of the men used to say: 'Don't send me out with Mr McGowan, Sir.' He had been badly wounded in the war, had lost an eye and had a stiff knee, and he drank too much. His father had been given a peerage after making a lot of money in 'trade' (ICI), so that damned him too and his mother was described by Myrtie as 'like an old

Scotch cook'. (She sounded like one, but in fact she was perfectly charming.) To cap it all, they lived in a flat in Mayfair, which was then thought very ostentatious.

Perhaps I would have resented whomever had taken my father's place, but there were two people who Myrtie might have married that I shouldn't have minded. The first was Rolie Cubitt (Lord Ashcombe). He was married but he didn't get on with his wife Sonia (who was Mrs Keppel's daughter).

The other was Tommy Dugdale (Lord Crathorne). He was also not very happily married to someone who had been divorced, but divorce was a big taboo for Myrtie. Tommy was great fun and had always treated me as if I was a grown-up. At some point he and Myrtie decided it was too dangerous for them to go on seeing each other. When Myrtie died he wrote to me, 'I hope we did the right thing all those years ago.' To which I replied, 'I am sure you did the right thing, but how I wish you hadn't.'

★   ★   ★

I had no desire to live with my mother and my new stepfather, nor did they want me to. So I decided to take up Sim and Anne's offer to live with them at Nawton Tower, their house in Yorkshire that had been commandeered in the war but was now restored to them. This meant giving up my job in MI6, which I loved and where I would otherwise happily have stayed. At that time you had to give two years' notice at MI6 unless you were leaving for a 'career' job. Fortunately Antony Head, a newly elected MP and a very close friend of my parents, was prepared to pretend that he wanted me as his secretary at the House of Commons, a job which counted as a career. So I was able to leave.

Richard's sister Anne played a large part in my life. As a great friend of my mother's, I had known her since she was twenty-five and I was seven. But now she treated me as a complete grown-up. I had a lovely time. They seemed to have plenty of servants, I remember having a huge bedroom and my own bathroom, and having breakfast in bed. After wartime London, this was heaven.

The arrangement suited Sim and Anne too. They had married in 1936 and had had a daughter, Clarissa, two years later. But they were not getting on. Anne had had many boyfriends, including Bob Laycock, who was not thought grand enough by Lord H, and the Duke of Kent, whom he thought would take Anne away to be part of the Royal Family. Both Sim and Anne had amorous interests elsewhere and they wanted someone else in the house. As well as helping Anne with the flowers and doing some typing for her, I acted as a sort of go-between, with each confiding their secrets to me.

At Garrowby Richard and I used to go out in the pony cart and sometimes ride together. The head groom, Atkin, made everything possible and I grew very fond of him. Sometimes we spent the evenings in Lady Halifax's small sitting room reading to each other – a lot of Disraeli and the Brontës – or playing whist in the housekeeper's room with Nanny and Mrs Lowe, the butler's wife (Lowe was still in Washington with Richard's parents). Looking back, I can see how unexciting and lazy it sounds, after the hectic activity of the war. Perhaps that was exactly what one needed.

If I was seeing more of Richard that spring of 1946, so was Kick, who had bought a small house in Smith Square. I remember that at one dance where I hadn't had many partners, I said to an older man, 'Why is it that Kick Hartington gets so many partners and I get so few?' To which he replied, 'She's an attractive American widow and you're just a debutante.' Richard thought about marriage to her as a real possibility and she also seemed to have it in mind, even though she had presented him with a book on Catholic doctrine in which a mixed marriage (i.e. marriage with a non-Catholic) was described as 'life in the very vestibule of Hell'. Still, that hadn't put her off marrying Billy Hartington.

Lord and Lady H couldn't bear Joe Kennedy. They also hated women being richer than their husbands, and Lady H didn't like Americans. So it's odd that they would have been perfectly happy if Richard had married Kick. And on top of that, she was a Roman Catholic.

Another rival for Richard's affections was Sim's niece, Caroline Worthington, whose father had been accidently shot and killed, early in the war when people were jittery. He had driven back to camp in the dark, drunk, and had failed to stop when challenged. Her mother had then committed suicide. Caroline was in love with Richard and I behaved badly to her, but she has never held it against me. I saw her with much pleasure only a few months ago.

That year the visitors' book at Garrowby became full of the alternating signatures of Kathleen Hartington and Diana Kellett. Years later Richard brother's Charlie cut these pages out of the book – a silly act of vandalism, you might say, to a venerable old volume – to remove the evidence of Richard's indecision. And eventually Lady Halifax was driven to cancel one of my visits because of 'the difficulty of getting housemaids'. Anne made the journey to Oxford to encourage Richard to make up his mind. She had never much liked Kick and she loved me, the daughter of her great friend Myrtie.

Richard proposed to me by post from Oxford, and the engagement was in the papers at the start of what turned out to be his final term. Lord Halifax said it was unromantic to be proposed to by post. I asked him how he had done it. He said it was in the Waiting Room at Berwick-on-Tweed railway station and he'd simply said, 'Lady Dorothy, will you marry me?' I said, 'I don't think that sounds very romantic!'

I have a letter of 31st October 1946 from Richard, two weeks after we got engaged, which reminds me of the constraints on telephone conversations that still prevailed at that time. Richard wrote: 'These telephone talks are wonderful and make all the difference … but I almost go mad at that *very* pompous operator who says: "Come on, caller, say your goodbyes now." Still, I suppose it *is* his job!'

★   ★   ★

My first Christmas at Garrowby was daunting. My mother said I must give my prospective parents-in-law a Lenare studio photo-portrait of myself. I duly did, but I was very embarrassed – I was only nineteen and very shy. There was a Servants' Ball and since I was engaged I had to lead off the dancing with Harry the chauffeur. Another tradition was charades, at which I was later rather a star, but it was intimidating to begin with. There was an obligatory chapel service before breakfast on most days after Christmas, followed by a substantial formal breakfast at which one had to go around the table greeting everyone individually: 'Good morning, Lord Halifax', 'Good morning, Aunt Mary', 'Good morning, Father Talbot', and so on. This was quite a trial. I never ate much at breakfast and I didn't like getting up early.

After Christmas I stayed on at Garrowby and Richard continued to work at his university studies. Then came a bombshell. One day after church Richard walked into the drawing room and announced, 'Father, I'm not going to marry Diana.'

'Have you told her?' Lord Halifax asked.

'No, but I'm telling her now,' Richard replied.

I was there in the room all the time. Lord and Lady Halifax went off that afternoon to their other house, Hickleton, instead of dealing with the situation. Richard then took to his bed, and Nanny said I was being horrid to him. I didn't know what to do. I rang up Sim and, despite the severe petrol rationing, he drove over and took me back to Nawton Tower.

Looking back, I now think this crisis was related to the war and the effect on Richard of his injuries, a type of post-traumatic stress disorder if you like. But at the time no one would admit that it was anything to do with the loss of his legs. In those days, that would not have been said.

About a week later I came back to Garrowby and Richard had changed his mind – again. He had in the meantime received an early wedding present of a very handsome box of poker chips from a general who had been in India with the Viceroy (and who had wanted to marry Anne but was considered unsuitable for her). Richard thought the poker chips were lovely. He said that he couldn't bear to send them back, so he would marry me. I should have said, Well, I'm not marrying *you*.

It was soon decided that Richard would not return to Oxford, and I volunteered to go and pack up his things at New College. The thing I baulked at was carrying his spare pair of tin legs across the quad. But he told me, you'll have to. If you can't do that, I can't marry you! He also had some wine, rather a rarity then, and he asked me to give it away to one of his friends. The first friend of his I ran into was Tony Benn. I gave him the bottles, saying that Richard *particularly* wanted him to have them. He looked a little surprised – I didn't realise that he'd always been a teetotaller.

Our wedding was planned for mid-April 1947, but before that there was another important development in our lives: Richard was persuaded to put himself forward for election to Parliament. One afternoon in February when Richard was alone at Garrowby, a neighbour, Sir Richard Sykes, had appeared from his snow-bound estate at Sledmere (1947 was an exceptionally cold winter). In the course of a couple of hours he persuaded Richard of two things: first, that Richard really was a Conservative (about which Richard himself had recently had some doubts, having voted Socialist at the end of the war) and, second, that Richard should stand for the local Buckrose constituency.

Richard Sykes had filled the hall in Bridlington with all his local friends and relations and, petrol being severely rationed, few others came. So Richard, greatly to his surprise, was chosen as the candidate, though he was not formally confirmed until after we got married. Such a potentially safe Conservative seat would nowadays attract scores of applicants, but then there were only two others on the list besides Richard: one had been the MP until defeated in 1945 by a Liberal, and the other was another defeated ex-MP who was Chairman of the Association. When the East Riding seats were reduced from three to two, Richard's constituency was called Bridlington.

*　　*　　*

The only person I had to dinner on the night before my wedding was Catherine Macmillan, who married Julian Amery three years later. She had been at the secretarial college in Oxford with me and we saw a lot of each other at parties in London. When the 400 closed, Catherine said she felt that the end of the world had come.

We were allowed to have our wedding in Westminster Abbey because Lord H was High Steward of the Abbey and because in the Nave – which was better than the Choir because everybody could see what was happening – there were practically no steps for Richard to negotiate. Apart from one or two in small side chapels, the next couple to be married in the main body of Westminster Abbey was Princess Elizabeth and Prince Philip.

Though I later came to like him a lot, I was very relieved that Father Ted Talbot was unable to take the service, so that in his place we could have Canon F. L. Hughes, my father's chaplain in the Sherwood Rangers, then Monty's chaplain and Chaplain-General to the Forces. He gave us invaluable advice for life: always to put each other first (I repeated this advice in the address I gave at my granddaughter Leo's wedding five years ago). Another piece of luck was the frostbite that prevented my stepfather from giving me away (he'd got snow in his shoe on a walk in the park, but hadn't realised because of a war wound to his leg).

Instead I was given away by James Howard, my grandfather's first cousin, whom I had known all my life. His daughter Bidger (Virginia) was one of my bridesmaids. The Howards had lived near us in Leicestershire as children and later we used to stay with them frequently at Anmer Hall, and Bidger came with us to the Walsinghams' school. She married Dick Ker, Richard's friend at Eton.

On my wedding morning Lord Halifax made both Richard and me go to Holy Communion at St Paul's, Knightsbridge. I protested that I ought not to see Richard on my wedding morning – he said not to look. But I did stand up to him in one respect. He wanted me to keep my veil on when I walked out of the Abbey. He'd made Anne do that. When I asked why, he said it was to show that I was still a virgin. So I said, it would be a bit difficult in the vestry, wouldn't it. I won that battle and thereafter we were always great friends.

There were 750 guests. My mother had been worried that we wouldn't be able to fit everyone in and wrote to the Dean, who replied, rather dryly, that he was sorry that there was only room for a mere 750. Naturally a wedding of this size was expensive and most of my trust money went in paying for it. The invitation itself was very simple – a single, small piece of paper. It couldn't be engraved, there was no copper available for that. I refused to have my stepfather's name on it, only 'Mrs William McGowan'.

Clothes and food rationing were still very much in force. To get the bridesmaids' dresses and the pages' uniforms we bought clothing coupons off gypsies for two shillings and sixpence a coupon. The wedding cake was an elaborate four-tier affair with a coat of arms made of material stuck on both sides. Getting enough ingredients for it was a major operation. A great many people contributed currants for the cake and the tenants at Garrowby helped a lot. As for alcohol, fortunately in those days very few of the girls drank.

The American Ambassador, Lewis Douglas, signed the marriage register at the end of the service as a witness. I wanted James Howard to sign but Lord H said it was important to have the Ambassador sign it instead. Douglas entrusted Oliver Green-Wilkinson, Richard's best man, with a stack of silver dollars to give to the bridesmaids and pages, but Oliver lost them.

The reception was held at nearby Ashburnham House. My father-in-law wouldn't allow any speeches. He simply caught hold of the tallest man in the room, Anthony Gibbs (later Lord Aldenham), and instructed him to propose the health of the bride and bridegroom. So we avoided the usual boring speeches.

The whole thing was extraordinarily speedy. We were married at 2 p.m. and left Ashburnham House at 4.45. From the reception we went to drink champagne with my stepfather and Myrtie at Ennismore Gardens, and then tea at Kingston House with Richard's parents. There we picked up our little car, stuffed with all sorts of things everyone thought necessary – including Richard's special saddle and a spare pair of legs, all my jewellery, evening clothes with stiff collars for Richard and five evening dresses for me – and we set off on our honeymoon to Ireland.

CHAPTER 7

An Irish Honeymoon

We had chosen Ireland because you couldn't get foreign exchange of any sort for travel in Europe. We reached the Bay Tree at Burford for our first night and the Adelphi Hotel in Liverpool for our second. Most of the Adelphi's windows had no glass and were still boarded up – the war had ended less than two years before.

We were met in Dublin off the ferry by C.O. Harvey's son Peter, who warned us that our car must always give way to horse-drawn traffic. Thanks to Lady Halifax, C.O. had a job in charge of the personnel in the Guinness brewery. He had been with them in India and was something of a boyfriend of my mother-in-law's and his son was her godson. Inevitably Richard's Guinness connections would loom large on our Irish tour. We had lunch with both Iveaghs and a swarm of Guinnesses at Farmleigh, where the Iveaghs lived for part of every year (their grandson later sold it to the Irish Government). I remember in particular Paul Channon, Chips's son, who later became Richard's PPS, and his cousin Benjamin Elveden and his sisters. At the Shelbourne Hotel in Dublin, Beakey's gentler sister Katty was the manageress of the hotel. I was embarrassed at her seeing Richard and me in bed together.

We set off for the west of Ireland from Dublin, our little prewar Ford crammed with luggage. I had packed four or five very grand evening dresses and my jewellery – our parents had said I would need them. Richard's saddle was specially adapted to hold his knees in place. His father had been determined that Richard should carry on with as many of his old pursuits as possible. He himself had been born with a withered left hand, which he concealed with a long cuff and a leather glove. When Richard had first arrived in wartime Washington his father had said to him, 'I've had one hand all my life and I've managed. I'm sure you will manage without legs.' He never mentioned the subject again.

On our way to Adare in Limerick we tracked down my step-grandmother Jesse Kellett in Tipperary. She was living in an ugly modern bungalow a few miles from our former family home at Clonacody. This was the only time in my life that I met her, and she had no idea we were coming. On a table beside her armchair was a silver-framed photograph of my father. When I saw her sitting looking at him all the time, I felt terrible that he'd been so horrid about her.

In the pretty village of Adare we stayed at the Dunraven Arms and went one night to dinner with Dicky and Nancy Adare. His father, Lord Dunraven, had been born in 1857 and was very deaf, and I was embarrassed at having to shout at him to make myself understood. Not many things sound very interesting when you've repeated them three times. Their house, Adare Manor (now a luxury hotel), was enormous and hideous. In the 1830s the Earl of Dunraven of the time had decided to replace a classic Georgian house with a Tudor Revival mansion, but at least its construction had provided local people with work during the Great Potato Famine.

Richard got rather drunk at dinner. On the way home I was so alarmed by his driving that I decided there was nothing for it but to push him out of the driving seat and drive instead. I hardly knew how to drive at that time and didn't pass my driving test until the following year. But we got back safely enough. A couple of days later Richard went riding with Lord Dunraven's daughters and the son, Thady, a charming dwarf-like boy with a normal body but very short legs, who afterwards got polio at school. Thady later married his nurse and was the last Earl of Dunraven.

From Adare we drove southwest through beautiful country to Tralee and Castlegregory on the Dingle Peninsula. Tralee was filled with horse traffic of all sorts and carts loaded down with seaweed, the collection of which seemed to be the town's main livelihood. (I remember Lord H saying that his father used to deal in seaweed, so there must have been money in it.)

Our next stopping place was further north, the village of Cong in County Mayo, where we stayed in Ashford Castle on the shore of Lake Corrib, a Guinness residence that had become a hotel. In the little diary that I was keeping at the time I wrote: 'It is a ghastly sham castle and the inside is horribly over-decorated, but the gardens and country around are heavenly. Our room looks out over an enormous lake – with wooded islands – and mountains beyond. We had a fire in our room and it was still flickering on the ceiling when we went to sleep.' The following day we went fishing on the lake. Richard caught a trout, which we had for dinner in our room. A blissful day. I took a photograph of Richard's hands which I still have on my dressing table.

We then made for Enniskillen in Northern Ireland. At the Customs no one stopped us, so I told Richard to drive on. At which point men rushed out from several angles. They poked and prodded and unpacked all the luggage, and even unrolled my stays. They kept asking for proof of where everything had been bought. By the time we reached Enniskillen all the shops and in particular all the chemists were closed, so there was no chance of buying something that it was illegal to sell in southern Ireland – contraceptives.

*   *   *

We crossed back into southern Ireland and could have stayed in Sligo but I wanted to get to the Renvyle peninsula. Renvyle was on the Atlantic, the mostly westerly point of Connemara, and was described by Augustus John as 'the most beautiful landscape in the world'. We had more than a hundred miles to drive and it was late when we set out, through some very wild and bleak country. We finally arrived at our hotel at one o'clock in the morning. We banged and rang, hooted the horn and threw stones at a window, but no one came. So we settled down to sleep, very cramped, in the car. At 6 a.m. the manager, who had got up to shoot rabbits, saw us and let us in.

The manager was the son of the poet and politician Oliver St John Gogarty, who was still alive but living in America. Over glasses of Tullamore Dew, the poet's son filled us in on local history. His father's house had stood on the site of the hotel and had been burned down by the IRA during the Civil War. The house had been rebuilt and had become a hotel.

In an old V8 Ford with very little glass in the windows, so that the rain came in from every angle, Gogarty drove us to a little whitewashed cottage. There we were introduced to Michael, who was going to show us the local country in his pony trap. While he was harnessing the big grey Connemara pony, we talked to his wife by an open peat fire in the whitewashed kitchen. She told us that all her sisters had emigrated and married Americans. The local poverty was palpable, the smallholdings seldom larger than an acre or two. On our drive Michael kept pointing at tumbledown houses, whose owners had only recently emigrated. In spite of all this, and the cold, it was a lovely drive, with the sea and the islands and the mountains all around, and I couldn't have enjoyed an afternoon more. We had tea by a peat fire in our sitting room.

Fishing on Tully Lake was less successful. On the way there our car got stuck in a peat bog, but we dug it out with the help of a woman who appeared from nowhere. Eventually we pushed off into the lake in a rowing boat from a tiny stone jetty. We were soon busy bailing out the peaty lake water from the bottom of the boat with a small saucepan. We caught nothing. Paddy, the hare-lipped ghillie, said it was too cold. It was hard to disagree.

On the Sunday we got up early and went to Holy Communion in the Roman Catholic church at Tully Cross. All the women sat together on the left and all the men on the right. I sat on the right with Richard, a lone female among the men and the boys. The service was in Latin and was the first Roman Catholic service I had ever been to. I wrote in my diary: 'I was impressed by the devoutness of them all but I understood nothing of what was going on & the Latin and the chanting together sounded extraordinarily like a droning of bees.'

Our time in Ireland was almost over. After church we drove back to Dublin, staying once again at the Shelbourne. The next day we had lunch at the Guinness brewery with Bryan Guinness (who had become Lord Moyne after the assassination of his father in Cairo) and other directors, and were then taken on an exhaustive, and rather exhausting, tour of the famous brewery. Two days later we left.

We smuggled a number of things through the Irish Customs in Richard's tin legs. We knew that Richard's nieces, who had been our bridesmaids, wanted alarm clocks and for some reason you couldn't buy them in England at the time. Scent was also almost impossible to get hold of in England, as were camera films. All these went inside Richard's legs. Another thing you couldn't buy was men's hats and my stepfather wanted a trilby. He had a much smaller head than Richard, but the only way to get it through Customs was by perching it on Richard's head. It looked silly, but Billy got his hat.

CHAPTER 8

Yorkshire and Politics

As soon as we returned from Ireland we moved into Welburn Cottage, which belonged to the Shaw family who lived in the big house near Kirbymoorside and whom we knew well. I loved the North Riding, having lived there with Sim and Anne, but the cottage itself was very basic. We shared a bathroom with the couple to whom we paid £3 a week. She worked for us and he for a local farmer. They had the use of an earth loo outside the drawing room. To cook there was an oil stove.

We had no fridge until the following year when Richard gave me one for my twenty-first birthday. Oliver Green-Wilkinson was staying with us and the three of us went to York to go to the cinema as a birthday treat. In the cinema Oliver went to have a word with the organist playing the cinema organ. This man suddenly stopped playing and announced, 'We are very honoured tonight to have the Honourable Mrs Richard Wood here. It's her twenty-first birthday. Will you please sing "Happy Birthday" for her.' If I'd then kept quiet no one would have known where I was, but I couldn't help saying, 'Oliver, blast you!' and everyone turned to stare at me.

The cottage had no curtains of any sort – there were shortages of almost everything at the time. But, for the bedrooms, my mother-in-law had large damask tablecloths dyed and made up by the village dressmaker with old blankets as backing. My parents-in-law had been to the USA just after we married and had brought back paper curtains which we hung in the drawing room. Our bedroom windows wouldn't open at the bottom and Lady H feared that her son might be burned alive in his bed. So she bought us an axe to break the windows open. She made us swear to keep it by the window-sill in the bedroom and not to chop up logs with it.

Our married life had a rather extraordinary beginning. Richard seemed to be often ill and certainly depressed, and before very long he announced, 'I'm going home to Mummy.' 'Well, you'd better go!' I said. But I never thought that would be that. At the age of nineteen, and with divorce considered impossible by both our families, I just assumed all would be well in the end. Meanwhile I was asked out to dances, including a lovely ball at Sledmere, and I thoroughly enjoyed myself.

As I've already mentioned, I think Richard was suffering from a type of post-traumatic stress disorder, although it had no name in those days. Some feeling of loss, and nostalgia for his pre-war life, was only to be expected. Moreover, his mother had spoilt him – not surprisingly, perhaps, as her middle son Peter had been killed in the war and Richard himself had been severely wounded. And his father couldn't deal with it at all; because of his withered hand, he couldn't bear anyone to have anything wrong with them. After a couple of months Richard returned and we resumed our life together.

For the sum of 10 shillings (50p) a week we kept a couple of ponies stabled with the Shaws and we soon planned a series of summer rides around the constituency. The weather was kind to us and we stabled the ponies each night with various politically sympathetic farmers. Richard had never particularly liked riding as a child, but now he took to it. He could ride where he couldn't walk and the constituents thought it a good joke. The rides got a good press and were even compared by some with Cobbett's *Rural Rides*.

These rides were the main political activity in the summers before the 1950 election. In the winter Richard's agent for the constituency, Jack Sykes (not to be confused with Sir Richard Sykes, the local grandee), got together a concert party which toured the remote villages, whatever the weather. Sykes had a reasonable voice and would sing, together with his wife and a few other girls, and in those pre-television days this simple entertainment generally filled the village hall. A silent Charlie Chaplin film might then be shown or a propaganda film, followed by some words from Richard as the Conservative candidate to reinforce the message. Sykes had recruited a dustman from Bridlington called Jack to introduce Richard. Jack's words never varied. He always *sounded* as if he was saying: 'I have no great pleasure in introducing the Horrible Richard Wood.'

The constituency of Bridlington in the East Riding had a few towns: Bridlington, Hornsea, Filey and Withernsea – apart from Bridlington none of them were big – and a mass of small villages. It was thought important to form as many local branches as possible in the villages. Soon after Richard was formally adopted as a candidate someone rang to tell me that I wasn't on the Voting Register – I was too shy to admit that I was only nineteen. Sometimes political heavyweights would come and lend their support. When Harold Macmillan came to speak at Bridlington he insisted on going into a pub beforehand to have a stiff drink. I was surprised at how nervous he was. His daughter Catherine was a great friend and I had assumed that her father would be very poised.

In the summer there were endless garden fetes. I remember an occasion when as the candidate's wife I had to judge babies. I was warned that the mothers of the ones not chosen would hate me, so I chose the ugliest in the hope that there wouldn't be any jealousy and they'd realise that I was an inexperienced teenager. At another garden fete lots of women stood behind a curtain showing just the lower half of their legs, for Richard to judge who had the best ones. The prize was a pair of stockings (silk and nylon stockings were almost unobtainable). My legs were in fact the best but I didn't get the stockings. Richard said he could not give something so valuable to his wife.

Even more tedious were the Chamber of Trade and other constituency dinners: tinned soup; meat which was cold, so it could be cut more thinly (because of meat rationing), submerged under thick gravy; ice cream, covered in hundreds and thousands; lots of sweet white wine, but plain water almost impossible to get; coffee with milk always put in first. And husbands and wives were always seated next to each other so that the latter were not uncomfortable.

★   ★   ★

When Richard was elected, an MP's salary was only a few hundred pounds a year. Petrol used in the constituency was not repaid, and MPs had to meet their own telephone costs, buy their own House of Commons writing paper and envelopes, and stamp their own letters. MPs were given free first-class return railway tickets to London, but their wives had to pay for their own. And MPs had to pay for their own accommodation in London. Fortunately Richard's father gave him an allowance of £1,000 a year and early in our marriage he became a director of Yorkshire Conservative Newspapers, which owned the *Yorkshire Post* and the *Yorkshire Evening Post*. For this he received an annual salary of £200. Even so, we were not well-off.

We might have been better-off if I had been clever about property. I had inherited from my father's mother a number of houses in London, including a large one in Hampstead. In the late 1940s this house was let to Hastings Banda, later the long-running President of Malawi but then a young doctor writing very offensive letters to Churchill and other Conservatives. Lord H believed that this unfortunate connection could be a liability to Richard's political career and advised me to sell my houses. It was also thought that Labour's plans for leasehold reform were going to greatly reduce the value of such houses. So I sold them all, at the worst possible time.

It was Sir Jameson Adams who had persuaded the *Yorkshire Post* to take Richard on as a director. Preferring to be known by everyone, from porters to the royal family, simply as 'The Mate', Adams was a naval captain who had been Shackleton's second-in-command on his first attempt to reach the South Pole. Scott had then asked him to go to the South Pole with him, but he had refused as he didn't like Scott. A friend of Edward VIII, he never had any money but still contrived to hunt twice a week. For many years he ran the appeals for the King Edward VII's Hospital for Officers (now King Edward's Hospital Sister Agnes). The Mate died there in the early 1960s and we missed him greatly.

When we were first married Richard declared that he never wanted to go abroad again, but I passionately did and an opportunity soon arose. In the early summer of 1948, BLESMA (the British Limbless Ex-Servicemen's Association) was due to hold a joint conference in Biarritz with their French counterpart, Les Amputés de Guerre. As a trustee of BLESMA, Richard was encouraged to attend. He was very reluctant, but Myrtie told him that he that must go and he must take me too – her daughter would never stay with him if he refused to take her abroad.

In Biarritz we stayed in great comfort in the hotel that had been patronised by Edward VII, and Richard decided that he did like going abroad after all. But the trip started badly. On the ferry we met a friend who told us that Kick Kennedy had been killed. Richard was desperate. When we got to the hotel the hall porter gave us the details. The small aeroplane carrying her and her lover Peter Fitzwilliam from Paris to the south of France had crashed in a storm in the Cevennes mountains in the Ardèche, killing all four occupants. It was a sad and terrible tragedy. A year later we made a pilgrimage to the place where Kick had died. Richard wanted to go up the mountainside to the spot where the plane had crashed, but that was impossible.

After Kick's funeral at Chatsworth the old Duchess of Devonshire (Debo's mother-in-law) found Richard's letters to Kick and returned them to Lady Halifax. Two decades later, when Kick's brother Bobby was assassinated just before the 1968 US presidential election, Richard wrote to Kick's mother. She wrote back:

HYANNIS PORT
MASSACHUSETTS

September 5, 1968

Dear Richard:

Thank you very much for your letter
which I know came straight from your
heart, and my heart responded with
affection and gratitude.

I remember your friendship with our
dear Kathleen, and I know what high
regard and admiration she felt towards
you. I recall one evening when you
went to the movies together. You were
entitled to a front place at the ticket
office due to your war injury and to
your father's eminent position, but you
insisted on standing in the regular line,
much to Kathleen's surprise and edifica-
tion.

I remember her telling me about the fun
she had when she helped your mother make
jam in the country during the war years.
I recall, too, when we lost Joe. The
first words that his father said to me
were "We must be brave and carry on like
Lord and Lady Halifax."

HYANNIS PORT
MASSACHUSETTS

And so, dear Richard, your note with
your recollections brought me joy.

I have not been in London very often
lately as my husband has been ill
during the last seven years, but when
I go again, I should like very much
to see you.

My love, dear Richard, to your dear
mother and to you,

Very sincerely,

Rose Kennedy

Mrs. Joseph P. Kennedy

*   *   *

Emma was born in February 1949 at Welburn Cottage. It had been arranged that we would borrow the flat belonging to Richard's cousin Brigid in Elizabeth Street for the birth, but Emma arrived a week early. No one we knew had a baby in hospital in those days. When I was a child and the stud groom's wife had a baby in the hospital in Melton Mowbray I assumed that no one must love her. Indeed you never said you were having a baby or appeared in public if you were. When my mother-in-law had been having children they shut their house in Eaton Square and took one just outside London so that she wouldn't be seen. I remained very thin, so I had been able to carry on with normal life most of the time.

Only the district nurse was in attendance when Emma was born. Afterwards I was very glad to accept Anne's offer of the greater comfort of Nawton Tower for a week or two. But I had to be carried into the house by the doctor as one wasn't allowed to stand for a fortnight after having a baby. The first Monthly Nurse was on drugs so we got rid of her and she was followed by someone super for a month. After a few false starts we found a very old-fashioned nanny who had been with Richard and Virginia Sykes, was paid £3 a week and had no days off apart from her month's holiday a year.

Not many weeks later we set out on our second foreign journey. Travellers were only allowed to take abroad £25 each. Simple hotels were cheap, but we knew we'd have to be very economical. In Venice we went back each night to sleep in the car and we walked everywhere, not easy for Richard. But what a joy it was to eat different food – many types of food were still rationed in England or simply unobtainable. In Rome we stayed in a very scruffy B & B where you couldn't have breakfast, so we walked to a tiny trattoria at the bottom of the Spanish Steps where we would have bananas and Coca-Cola. I hadn't had a banana for seven years, so it was thrilling. Later in the day we'd have steak (also unobtainable in England).

On the way home I wanted above all to see Val d'Esquières again, on the French coast west of St Raphael. It was where I had stayed with my parents before the war and it was a sort of dreamland for me. Staying at the wonderful Residence hotel was out of the question at £6 a night – a few days later, on our way home, we rashly sat at a table at the Baumanière at Les Baux and realised we couldn't even afford the starter.

At Val d'Esquières we found a tiny inn, the Bastide, where we spent two or three nights. It was run by a patron whose wife did the cooking, their son waited on us and their daughter cleaned the rooms. Over the years we returned to Val d'Esquières many times.

A few years later we slept on the beach for a week, under the stars without a tent, swimming in the sea and cooking very simple meals on a driftwood fire. No one else ever came onto the beach except for a few gypsies at the very far end.

Back in Yorkshire we began to prepare to move to Flat Top House later in the year. This was not our first choice. Lord H had offered to buy for us one of several houses – I remember one in particular, a super place, a Queen Anne house with eight bedrooms, two cottages and 250 acres, all for £7,000. This was Westow Hall, bought just a few years later by Christie and Skip Grimthorpe, and now lived in by their younger son, Danny Beckett. But Lady H vetoed them all: they were too far from Garrowby. In the end we compromised. Flat Top House was as far away from Garrowby Hall – a few miles – as it was possible to be while still being on the Garrowby estate.

When, some years later after my father-in-law had died, she came to live with us in London I grew to love my mother-in-law, but at this stage in our lives I found her barely tolerable. She frequently appeared without any warning, often accompanied by Nanny Gaywood or with one of her house guests. She would also come over and plant our garden, until I began to hate roses. Richard did little to foil these invasions.

Flat Top, which Lord H had bought from Richard Sykes in the Depression, was a brick-built late Georgian farmhouse on the side of a hill with a wide view over the Vale of York. Before we moved in, it was in a primitive state with double outside loos and only one loo and bathroom inside. It had virtually no garden and just a rough lane leading up to the house. A farmer farmed the land and kept the farm buildings in a disgusting state. There was a shed for tractors which we later turned into a cottage. Over time we made numerous improvements.

We were a little over a mile away from our nearest village, Bishop Wilton, up a very steep hill. The postman had no van or car and did his deliveries on foot to all the farms within about four miles of the village. He had been in the Navy and thought nothing of carrying parcels uphill in the rain. The post came on the Sundays before Christmas and on Christmas Day. There were two daily deliveries to the village, so I used to go down every afternoon when Richard was abroad, in the hope of getting another letter. In London there were three posts. You could post a letter in the City in the morning and it would be delivered in central London in the afternoon. One day not long after we'd moved in we received a postcard addressed to: Mrs Wood, c/o The Right Reverend Bishop Wilton, York. Nothing else. Yet it got to us.

Lord H wouldn't let his children go to church at Bishop Wilton because he disapproved of the services taken by the parson, Mr Fawcett. Moreover Fawcett's wife had left him and taken their son, but he wouldn't divorce her because he would have had to give up being a parson. I liked Fawcett and he was one of the reasons I was prepared to live at Flat Top. He became a great friend and always used to come to lunch on Christmas Day.

★   ★   ★

The first rebuilding of Flat Top was still going on at the beginning of 1950 when a General Election was announced for the end of February. Richard's main opponent was the Liberal candidate, George Wadsworth, who had won the seat from the sitting Conservative MP at the 1945 Election. Wadsworth indulged in some dirty tricks during the election, asking how his 'cripple' opponent could possibly represent the constituency. It didn't help him.

In that pre-television age, live meetings were all-important and the candidate would have to make half a dozen speeches a night in town rooms and village halls. At one stage in the election Richard lost his voice. His brother-in-law Sim recommended the whites of two eggs, broken into a cup. Richard swallowed this with some difficulty, but it did the trick. Polling day was long: you had to leave at seven in the morning and you got back at about eleven at night after visiting all the polling stations. We took club sandwiches with us, made by Hilda Slater, to eat with Richard Sykes in remote places. The day itself was quite fun except for the endless cups of tea pressed upon one. Richard's victory was announced at noon the following day, to our great relief.

A few days later Wadsworth asked us to dine at his house. His motive was clear. He asked Richard if he would nominate him as a Conservative Party candidate for the next election. In the chicken on my plate I was surprised to find several small pellets. Mrs Wadsworth told me that her husband had been unable to catch the bird in time for dinner and had therefore got out his gun and shot it.

When Richard was elected I knew I wanted to be with him in London, leaving Emma in Nanny's reliable hands. But when Edward was born we realised that this wasn't working, as Nanny was incredibly difficult and my mother-in-law was pressing us hard to get rid of her. Beakey had written to us from Ankara where she was employed by what she described as a very uneducated councillor in the Embassy. She longed to leave, so we decided to employ her as Emma's nursery governess, helped as a nursery maid by the fifteen-year-old daughter of a local farmer. Beakey came for a year and stayed for twenty.

When we moved to Flat Top we also employed Hilda, whose father worked on Lord H's Home Farm. In the war she had been in the ATS, where she had had all her teeth taken out. She never had false teeth but was able to chew everything with her gums. She was not a good cook but we liked her very much. She used to bring us breakfast in bed and clean and iron. She only had two afternoons off a week, Wednesday and Saturday, alternating with Wednesday and Sunday. We turned a huge store on the ground floor into a flat for her, with a bedroom, sitting room and shower room.

Once again Lord Halifax offered to buy us a house, this time in London. And once again this was thwarted by Lady Halifax, who wanted us to live with them. Before the war the Halifaxes had lived in an enormous house at 88 Eaton Square (a fact now recorded by a blue plaque), which Lord H had inherited from his father. But during the war they lived, when in London, in the basement of the Dorchester with a number of others, including Duff and Diana Cooper and Baba Metcalfe, all in a big 'dormitory', because the hotel was considered to be one of London's safest buildings.

After the war my mother-in-law thought a mansion flat would be preferable, and they moved into one in Kingston House in Knightsbridge. Richard and I had a bedroom between their two bedrooms. (Richard never remembered his parents sleeping together or even sharing a bathroom.) We used their dining room as our sitting room, except when Winston, who didn't want to dine downstairs in the communal dining room, came to dinner, when we had to move all our things out, including a budgerigar and typewriter.

When our next child was due in August 1951, Richard was determined that I had the baby in Yorkshire in case it was a boy, so that he would be able to play cricket for Yorkshire. (Alas, Edward barely played cricket.) Richard and I were entirely alone at Flat Top both the night before he was born and the night after. Beakey had taken Emma to Bembridge to be with my half-sister Fiona, born to my mother and stepfather after we married and just fourteen months older than Emma. Hilda was on holiday, and even the gardener had been sent away. Luckily our GP had nobly promised to come back from his fishing holiday in Scotland to deliver the baby, and he arrived just in time. Afterwards he went on to the local villages to let them know that Richard had a son.

STONE TROUGH BOOKS

51 WALMGATE, YORK, YO1 9TY

E : georgeramsden@btconnect.com   T : 01904 670323

W: stonetroughbooks.com

Norma Martin
1 March '18
Invoice
_____

Diana Holderness's book
2 copies"   £ 36·00
_____

Your cheque rec'd
with thanks.

1. One sent to Maurice Ray

GEORGE RAMSDEN

CHAPTER 9

'I always Kiss the Queen but You Can't'

I had been presented to the Queen on my marriage at the beginning of the 1947 Season by my mother-in-law. Lady H had been a Lady-in-Waiting to the Queen before the war and knew her well. She told me, 'I always kiss the Queen, but you mustn't copy me' – in case there was any doubt! In theory you were presented when you 'came out' and again after you were married, but there had been no Courts during the war. My presentation, at a Garden Party at Buckingham Palace, was less formal and I wasn't all dressed up in feathers. For a number of years, however, we would drive into Buckingham Palace at the start of every Season and 'sign the book'. You told the man at the gates, 'We are coming to sign the book' and were shown to a side door at the front and in a thick leather-bound book wrote your full name, not just a signature.

Richard and I were lucky enough to go to both George VI's funeral and to the Queen's Coronation the following year. At the former they wanted to fill empty seats caused by invited guests who were unable to come. Richard's father, then Chancellor of the Order of the Garter, could nominate replacements, so we were asked to St George's Chapel Windsor for the King's funeral.

This was a great honour, and it was a sombre and moving occasion. But unfortunately my mother, always very fashionable, had persuaded me to wear a plaited black mask, rather than a veil like everyone else. I felt acutely embarrassed. Moreover we had arrived for the funeral service in our conspicuously small Hillman, a glaring contrast to all the other large and shiny chauffeur-driven cars. As we left in our car, Harold Macmillan was heard to remark, 'Who on earth is that?'

For the Coronation, MPs were asked if they'd like a seat in the Abbey or four good seats on a stand outside. With our children not yet five and two, we opted for the Abbey. We occupied two places near the roof of the South Transept, amazingly reconstructed for the occasion. The ushers were almost all friends. We were entitled to buy our chairs (or for us, stools) for £8 each. R decided we couldn't afford £16. Apart from the Queen herself, the heroine of the day was the gigantic Queen Salote of Tonga. She moved about in an open carriage, taking no notice of the appalling weather. London loved her.

Richard wore knee breeches and decorations. The next day *The Times* listed all the women from duchesses down to me as an Honourable and how we were dressed ('The Hon. Mrs Richard Wood had a dress of gold *lamé*, with a fitted bodice and a full skirt, and a blue fox stole. She wore a diamond tiara.'). I had borrowed both the stole and the tiara from Patsy Lennox-Boyd and the dress had been adapted from a sari belonging to my mother-in-law, at the cost of £3. After the service we had no time to change before catching the train – third class – to York. No one commented on what we were wearing and surprisingly we weren't embarrassed. When we got home we found the children thrilled with the black-and-white television which we had hired for twenty-four hours, with Emma asking if we could keep 'that lovely thing'.

People were very snobbish about television in those days. The general idea was 'We've got one for the servants,' but then our friends would sneakily look at it themselves. Lord Halifax was President of the Halifax Building Society (possibly just because of his name). When he retired as President the Society gave him a television. He thanked them of course but he had absolutely no use for it and gave it to Nanny Gaywood.

My father-in-law was a curious mixture of economy and generosity. His economies were well known. Garrowby had a lovely drawing room which they seldom used, preferring to sit in what they called the hall. Richard and I were never allowed to sit in the drawing room or hall when we were there alone but always in Lady Halifax's very small sitting room, to save logs. There was no central heating. Before we could go in to dinner Lord Halifax would go around the entire room, often on his hands and knees, switching off every lamp from the plug in the wall. He continued to do this when old and lame. I remonstrated with him but he said it was a necessary economy. I was also with him when he tipped a porter sixpence. He said, 'He'll be very grateful to carry Lord Halifax's bags.' I wasn't so sure!

Another unexpected economy, because he was a very smartly dressed man, was a sudden enthusiasm for plastic collars – detachable white plastic collars in place of the traditional starched ones. They could just be washed, he said. He got me to order four more – he said the size didn't matter. He wanted to give them to other peers.

Yet he could also be very generous. He had offered to buy us a house in Yorkshire and in London, but Lady H vetoed both as she wanted her youngest son to live near or with them. He gave me diamonds and offered to buy me a ball dress to be painted in, but I refused as I liked my own.

In the early 1950s he had me painted by the fashionable portrait painter Sir James Gunn. Gunn was very choosy. He said, Well, bring her. So I was brought and he looked at me and said, 'Yes, I'll paint her. But I want £2,000 and a chandelier.' A fortune in those days! When I pointed out to Lord H that he'd never had Ruth painted, he said, 'I will, if she wins the Derby.' She didn't, but Charlie eventually did, with *Shirley Heights* in 1978.

In the early years of my marriage Lord H used me as a go-between with his daughter Anne. He was irritated that Anne wouldn't tell him anything. Would I find out why Anne wasn't having another baby? Anne's daughter Clarissa had been born in 1938 but there had been no children in the years since, and in particular no son and heir to inherit Sim's earldom.

I think his children were rather frightened of him. I wasn't. And I teased him, which they didn't. We'd go to exhibitions together, to the cinema and other amusing things. Once we went to some all-in wrestling. I remember him spitting in the street on our way there. I said, 'Really, Lord Halifax, you can't do that,' and he replied, 'But Papa always did.' When we got on the bus, there was a notice saying No Spitting. At the wrestling he said he wanted the best seats, so there he was right at the ringside (which he hadn't expected), dressed in striped trousers, black jacket and homburg. He loved it. He had a marvellous sense of humour.

He could behave oddly. He had learned to drive relatively late, in America, and he said that he had passed his test by bribing the instructor with a bottle of whisky. The Americans had presented him with an enormous Cadillac, which he brought back to Britain. In those days the road in Belgrave Square was made of wooden blocks, rather like parquet flooring, and over the years these blocks had become greasy with oil. Driving the Cadillac, Lord H had skidded and knocked down the area railings of a house in the square. But he didn't tell the house's owners. The next day he suggested I went with him to look at the railings. No, he said, there's no need to tell them. That was strange.

He maintained his firm Anglo-Catholic faith to the end of his life (he called his own faith 'Catholic', so to us all the Pope's followers became 'Roman Catholics' to indicate the difference). I have already described the importance of the services for the family at Garrowby. And his farm workers would be given the day off if they went to church on important saints' days.

★   ★   ★

In the election of October 1951 Richard substantially increased his majority and the Conservatives took over the Government from Labour. Derry Heathcoat-Amory became Minister of Pensions and chose Richard as his PPS. There were strong connections between their families and Derry's brother Billy had been Richard's colonel in the Western Desert (indeed Billy had once reprimanded Richard for sharing some scarce whisky with his men rather than keeping it for the officers).

Derry was very able – he later became Chancellor of the Exchequer – but he was also modest and had a delightful sense of humour. He had had a very narrow escape from death in the war. Wounded in Holland, he had been in a local hospital when it was overrun by the Germans, who then began systematically killing everyone in the hospital beds. Derry realised what was happening, pulled a sheet over his head and lay dead-still. Assuming that he was already dead, they left him alone.

If Richard was pleased with his boss, he was less delighted with the duties of a PPS, for which he felt ill-suited. If Derry wanted a 'pair', Richard would have to walk round and round asking Socialists if they would pair with him. Sometimes in order to get one he had to offer to drive the MP back to his lodgings, which were usually a long way out because the Government didn't pay for them. Nor did Richard like the necessity of spending time in the Library in order to get the latest 'gossip' to pass on. Maybe he just wasn't very clubbable. Before the 1955 election he moved on twice, as Derry's PPS, first to the Board of Trade and then to the Ministry of Agriculture.

But one consolation for an MP was a long recess every summer and an opportunity for travel. In 1952 we drove through Belgium to stay with Sammy and her husband Charlie Toller and their baby, and my godson Mark. Charlie was then a captain in the 10th Hussars, stationed in West Germany at Iserlohn on the edge of the

Ruhr where Richard's old friend Roly Gibbs was also stationed, and we all went to see the Mohne Dam. From there we made a sweep through southern Germany, Switzerland and France down to the south coast. We often slept in the car. The Hillman had been doctored by Antony Head's ex-chauffeur, who normally worked on Rolls-Royces. He had managed to make the front seat lie more or less flat against the back one. It cost £12 to have it all done.

In the summer of 1954 a long-planned expedition took us first to Venice by train and then down the Yugoslav coast by boat to Split and Dubrovnik, before crossing to Greece. In Athens Charles Peake was the British ambassador. He and his wife Catherine were very old friends of the Halifaxes – Charles had been Counsellor at the British Embassy in Washington when Lord H was ambassador. Their son Joh Seb Peake was a great and long-standing friend of ours, and remained so until he died of cancer in 2002.

The highpoint of our trip was an open-air production of the Greek tragedy *Hippolytus* in the ancient theatre at Epidaurus. It was attended by most of the royal families of Europe – the Peakes had been close to King Paul and Queen Frederica (King Constantine's parents) until the issue of Cyprus made social contact difficult. All the royals that evening were wearing a sort of uniform – dark trousers, short-sleeved white shirts and red cumberbunds – including Brigid's husband Fritzi, the Kaiser's grandson. I think perhaps Queen Frederica thought it would encourage the young royals to marry each other.

Our ritzy holiday continued with a train to Venice, where we joined the Iveaghs. Seeing the sights with the Guinnesses, generally from a gondola, was very comfortable and a far cry from our last visit to the city.

At Flat Top we built a little chapel out of an old forge. Religion played a large part in our lives. If Richard's father and grandfather were strong Anglo-Catholics, my father had been an equally staunch

Southern Irish Protestant. (In the war Flash removed all the Roman Catholics from his Regiment – except one.) In the chapel at Flat Top Richard and I would say Evensong together, reading the Psalm for the day and the Lessons and we would often sing hymns. Wherever we were, Richard would read Matins and Evensong every day – if he was in a car or a train he would read them to himself, with the help of a little leather-bound volume, *Services of the Church*.

Richard and his family had strong links with the Anglican monks at Mirfield and he often went there for retreats. Once or twice I went on a retreat with him (but not at Mirfield where women were not allowed to stay). We had separate bedrooms and couldn't talk, and I didn't enjoy that. Richard would make his Confession and every now and then I would too, but I hated doing it. Looking back I can see that we were both rather stubborn about our different religious traditions and found it hard to compromise with the other's practices. Eventually Richard got a bit 'lower', but I never got 'higher'. Jonathan Graham, who used to pander to my Protestant views, was a monk who became a friend. He used to come with us electioneering and frequently stayed at Flat Top.

One of the pets we kept, which some found odd, were lizards. I'd had them since I was a small child, as had my mother when she was young. Like me, she adored them, so we'd leave them with her when we went abroad. When one died she tried to replace it, but realising I would recognise that it wasn't the one I'd left with her, she had to tell me. I often kept them on my jersey. We had two called Anthony and Clarissa, and before that a couple called Harold and Dorothy, after our prime ministers and their wives. We fed them worms, which themselves had been fed on bran. They were the most friendly creatures, almost like a dog. And the dogs didn't mind them. When, later, we had cats we no longer had any lizards or we wouldn't have had cats. Sadly they never lived long. I gave up having them in the end because their lives were so short and I was so unhappy when they died.

*   *   *

Despite his wartime experience as a speaker in America, Richard was surprised to be asked, along with a Labour MP, to tour the USA and Canada in early 1955 to speak on political subjects to a variety of audiences. But he accepted. We crossed the Atlantic from Southampton to New York in great comfort in a vast cabin with adjoining sitting room on the French liner SS *Liberté* (originally a German ship, the SS *Europa*, which had been transferred to France as part of war reparations).

We were soon summoned to the captain's table, which included Alfred Hitchcock among others. When we reached New York, Hitchcock photographed me against the background of the Statue of Liberty. He promised to send me the photograph, but sadly he never did. While he was photographing me I should have been in the Lounge checking out our luggage, and by the time I got there the Steerage passengers – many just with a tied-up bag on a stick, like Dick Wittington – were queuing up. To my huge embarrassment an announcement was made: 'There is a first-class passenger here to check out, so will you take her first please.'

In New York the head of the British Information Services, the sponsors of the tour, asked me about my father: 'How is Flash? He's my best friend.' As my father had been dead for more than ten years, we moved the conversation swiftly on. From Washington, trains took us all over the south and west, to Cincinnati, Kansas City, Santa Fé, Denver and other cities. San Francisco was one of the few I was at all sad to leave.

Coming from an England where practically no one had central heating, American houses, hotels and trains seemed wildly overheated, and the nylon carpets gave one electric shocks when you shook hands. Moreover the unfailing conversational stamina of our companions was itself hard to endure. Before we left Britain,

Lord H had given us £600 in case we wanted to stay in hotels and be independent, instead of staying with the local British consul. I was rather sorry when Richard insisted it was much better to be sociable.

Richard enjoyed this trip more than I did. I didn't relish being packed off to women-only lunches, and it all got too much for me when we stopped in Calgary on our journey back across Canada on the Canadian Pacific Railroad. Richard went off to a meeting and I was surrounded by a group of hospitable, well-meaning but very inquisitive Canadian ladies. Where had I come from? Where was I going? Where was I staying? My brain went numb. I couldn't answer any of these questions. So finally they asked me a very simple one: where did I live in England? I couldn't even answer that. It was clearly time to go home! From New York we returned to Britain on the *Queen Mary*. The sea was calm and I spent much of the time in blessed sleep.

* * *

By the time we returned it was clear that a General Election couldn't be far away. Winston's strokes in the early 1950s had been miraculously hidden from almost everyone by Christopher Soames, his son-in-law and PPS. Richard knew nothing about them at the time and doubted that many outside the Cabinet knew any more than he did. But it was only a matter of time before Winston retired, and in April 1955 Anthony Eden became Prime Minister.

The election was in June. A lot of people in the Holderness villages and elsewhere turned out to Richard's meetings in the open air, which were a lot more fun than those in cold village halls. The Conservatives were returned with a comfortable majority. Few predicted the troubles that lay ahead.

At the end of the year Anthony reorganised his government. He telephoned Richard and said, 'I wonder if you would join this little government of ours as Parliamentary Secretary, War Pensions.'

Richard thanked him and said yes, but Anthony stopped him: 'No, ask Diana first, and ring me back' and gave him his private number. I was encouraging. Richard was depressed by the offer, but confirmed his acceptance. Anthony had always been incredibly good to us both – to me as a silly girl of seventeen and then, among other things, insisting that Richard be offered the job as Honorary Colonel of their Regiment if he, Anthony, retired from it.

Around this time Richard had happened to meet Winston in the lobby of the House of Commons and had thanked him for signing his wedding present to us – four volumes of *Lord Chesterfield's Letters*. Richard's diary notes that Winston replied, 'I was glad to do it, my boy.' (Richard adds, 'But I am sure he had little idea what he had done.') Later – needs must – we sold these leather-bound books, also signed by Clemmie, for several thousand pounds.

That August Richard and I left for a holiday in Assisi and Umbria with Oliver Green-Wilkinson and his (then unmarried) sister Felicity. Oliver, an old friend who had been Richard's best man, was then the Anglican Bishop of Northern Rhodesia. By now we had a well-established routine of camping on many of these summer travels. Outside Perugia we camped in a lovely field belonging to a super Italian family. We gave them a box of chocolates and some Chesterfields, in exchange for eggs.

Oliver was keen that Richard should get into a good position to admire the evening *passeggiata* on Perugia's main street and have a good view of the young bloods and pretty girls. The police were unenthusiastic as our car mingled with the walkers on its way to a vantage point. But Oliver was determined that Richard should not be obstructed. His grasp of Italian was slender but his constant repetition of '*Mio amico molto mutilato nel guerra*' usually got us through.

On this holiday we sometimes had to drive up to Oliver's hotel on early mornings for Communion – an arrangement I never liked.

My parents in America in 1934, with Cecil Beaton and Loelia Westminster.

With my parents on their way to a meet of the Quorn, 1930.

My parents travelling across Afghanistan on their way to India in 1935 in two Hillman Minx car

Lord Carnarvon and his home, Highclere. He was a great friend of Flash and Myrtie, who went big-game hunting with him in East Africa.

At my grandparents' house, Trewsbury. I'm on top, my cousin Susie is at the horse's head and her sister Sammy is behind the mower.

Michael de Pret, my first love.

With my father at Val d'Esquières in the
South of France, 1935.

With Anna Beakey, my nursery governess.
Later she became a very mixed blessing.

Lord H (then Lord Irwin) when he was Viceroy of India in the late
1920s. His train-bearers were the son of the Maharajah of Bharatpur
and Richard.

Milton Manor, where I lived in the war with the Peases.

A school photograph, Westmere, Norfolk, 1941. Top row, second from left, M. de Grey, Rosemary Nettlefold at the end of the row. Middle row: K. de Grey (first left), me (in the middle), Bidger Howard, Sarah Wilson. Bottom row: Susie Pease (third left), then Anne Fletcher and Caroline Tremayne.

Richard and the other members of Pop, Eton College, 1939. His friends included David Quilter (first on left in top row), the Hon. Julian Holland-Hibbert (fifth in third row), Peter Wake (extreme left, sitting), Geoffrey Jameson (extreme left, standing), Roly Gibbs (third from left in fourth row), Mike Chinery (first on left in front row), and Nathaniel Fiennes (fourth on left in front row). Richard is second from the left in the front row.

Chamberlain, Mussolini, Lord Halifax and Count Ciano in Rome at the opera (which Lord H hated), January 1939.

With my father in Lincolnshire, December 1939, our last Christmas together.

Flash, on the right, with Winston Churchill in North Africa.

Officers at rest, Palestine. From the left: Joe Goodhart (with no hat), Flash and Donny Player.

India, 1941. From the left: Myrtie, Sir Arthur Hope (later Lord Rankeilour) and Anne Feversham. Forced as 'illegal wives' to leave Palestine in September 1940, Myrtie and Anne could not get directly back to Britain and had to take a very roundabout route back home.

Tommy Dugdale in the war. After my father was killed, I hoped my mother would marry him.

Sim Feversham, Hermione Ranfurly and Donny Player in wartime Jerusalem.

Caroline Worthington and Richard learning to walk without legs, Yorkshire, late 1943.

Kick Kennedy in the 1940s.

Our wedding in April 1947 at Westminster Abbey. From the left: Sonia Gunston, Elizabeth Jackson, Sammy Pease, Richard and me, Oliver Green-Wilkinson, Susie Pease and Diana Drummond. The pages: James Daly, John Hills and Martin Dunne. Sitting in front: Clarissa Duncombe, Susan Wood and Caroline Wood.

Oliver Green-Wilkinson at our wedding, with Bidger Howard on the right and Susie behind.

My stepfather Billy's sister, Nan Daly (who was later murdered). From the left: her son James, Martin Dunne, John Hills.

Charlie and Ruth Irwin in conversation with Lord H at our wedding.

Getting to know people by riding around his Yorkshire constituency in 1947 after Richard had unexpectedly become the Conservative candidate. The riding often scared me.

Sinnington point-to-point, 1946. From the left: me, Clarissa Duncombe, Sim and Anne Feversham, Eric Dawnay and Charles Irwin.

Emma's christening at Kirby Underdale, March 1949. From the left: Lord H, Myrtie, Myles Hildyard, Sammy Pease, Diana Drummond, Richard and me, Anne Feversham, Nat Fiennes, Clarissa Duncan and Lady H.

Susie and Archie Kidston's wedding. From the left: Serena Sheffield and Camilla Belville were bridesmaids. The children: Reggie Sheffield, Fiona McGowan, Mark Toller, Emma, James Pleydell-Bouverie and Laura Sheffield.

Richard on the beach, then deserted, in the South of France on which we slept and cooked in 1950.

Richard with my half-sister Fiona at Flat Top.

An aerial view of Flat Top House. The barn buildings are below, with the cottage just visible on the other side of the drive.

Nanny Cross with Emma and Ed at Garrowby. She had been Sammy and Susie's nanny and had often looked after me.

The family above Flat Top, with Richard's much-loved terrier, Rags.

CORONATION OF HER MAJESTY
QUEEN ELIZABETH II

By Command of The Queen
the Earl Marshal is directed to invite
Hon Richard and Mrs Wood
to be present at the Abbey Church of
Westminster on the 2nd day of June 1953

Norfolk.
Earl Marshal

Our invitation to the Coronation.

Emma and Ed inspecting the portrait of me by James Gunn.

From the left: my cousin Sammy, Gran (Mrs
Albemarle Cator) with Sammy's son, Mark
Toller, and Sammy's mother, Iso Smith
Bingham, at Estcourt House in 1950.

Richard breaks the ice to swim in the pool
Flat Top on Boxing Day. Ed is looking on

With Billy Brooksbank at a Garrowby
Christmas.

A Garrowby Christmas with Charlie
Halifax.

It was even worse when Oliver said one evening after dinner, 'Now you must fast and not drink water until you've received Communion in the morning.' It's very hard not to drink water when you're camping. Richard obeyed. I didn't.

We had a less friendly experience with some Italians on our way home. We had stopped to spend the night in the town of Como, at the southern end of the famous lake. We parked the car across the road from our hotel and had dinner at a nearby outside restaurant. Towards the end of dinner a tram came along the street and hooted loudly, apparently at our car. A dozen youths lifted our car bodily and moved it nearer the pavement, out of the tram's way. A helpful intervention, or so we thought. But when we looked more closely, two of my cameras (one of them a cine camera) and Richard's race-glasses were missing. There was a little chink of window open and a slender Italian hand had managed to get through it. The police made copious notes but admitted there were lots of camera thieves in the town.

As soon as we returned, Richard became involved in a cross-party conference on the future of Malta. The question was whether or not Malta should be offered some sort of political integration with Britain, with the right to send a few MPs to Westminster. The high-powered Labour contingent included Attlee himself, Nye Bevan and Dick Crossman. Deliberations in London were followed by a week on the island, where the whole group were entertained by Bob and Angie Laycock. Bob, then Governor of Malta and famous for his service with the Commandos in the war, had been a suitor of Anne's – until Lord H decided he was not sufficiently aristocratic – and his two brothers had been in the Sherwood Rangers with Flash.

Richard returned from his week on Malta with a lasting affection for Nye Bevan. His politics were impossible but his charm was irresistible.

The King and Queen wanted to meet Nye and they asked my

parents-in-law to dinner with Nye and his wife. When dining at Buckingham Palace one had to wear a ball dress without sleeves, but of course Jennie did not know this, which caused comment. And Nye wore a black tie (rather than the required white tie and tails), which was also commented on. Years later when Richard was on the board of the Friends of Covent Garden, Jennie Lee wanted to take her nephew to the ballet there. Ken Davison, then Secretary of the Friends, rang Richard and said he was not to wear a black tie, as he always did, 'because it will upset Jennie'. So Richard went in a suit. The nephew told me he was so disappointed not to be allowed to wear his dinner jacket but he understood that Richard never did.

CHAPTER 10

Friends Throughout a Long Life

Early on in our marriage Richard and I decided quite independently of each other that if one of us liked something, the other would to make an effort to like it or at least get used to it. (Probably because that was how my parents had lived. Richard's had behaved quite differently.) I had hated shooting, but Richard was a good shot. So I walked across the moor, often carrying two guns and a cartridge bag and with Richard's hand on my shoulder to steady him. Eventually I liked shooting even more than he did. He liked opera and I didn't; I liked ballet and he didn't. But before long we were both able to enjoy what the other enjoyed. I drew the line at the *Ring Cycle* but I would catch the Tube to Covent Garden, meet Richard in the Crush Bar, have dinner with him and return home. I never became enamoured of cricket, however, though I usually used to go with him because he loved it.

By the late 1950s we were going to Covent Garden as often as three times a week. We always wore evening clothes for both the ballet and the opera. Because Richard had lost his legs he was allowed by Bert Postlethwaite, the Commissionaire, to park his car right outside the Opera House, and we had first option for booking tickets and a reserved table in the Crush Bar for smoked salmon sandwiches in the interval. The Orchestra Stalls were our favourite seats – we thought it quite extravagant to pay £5 for them. If Richard had a 10 o'clock vote, he usually managed to return before the performance ended. Our stalls were easy to reoccupy without disturbing anyone.

Lord Halifax took a rather different view of ballet. He said of his two remaining sons: 'One likes something immoral [racing] and the other something immodest [ballet].' But he did agree to come to the ballet once, though only if we took a box. He then bagged the best place and none of the rest of us saw very much.

In the mid-1950s we began to make various improvements to Flat Top. An extension, the so-called Nursery Wing, was added to the house. Not long after, a simple summer-house with a hipped roof was built. It was useful to eat out in and see people when we didn't necessarily want them in the house. Not long after that, Richard, with help from me and the part-time gardener who carried the earth away, dug out quite a big swimming pool. It had no filter or any means of cleaning it and was filled by water diverted from a spring. Richard later decided that he must swim in this pool at least once in every month of the year. There is a photograph of him swimming in it on Boxing Day – and apparently enjoying it – all of us hoping that he would not get stuck under the rather solid ice.

Meanwhile, a couple of miles away, a long-planned project of my father-in-law's was realised in 1956. He wanted a crucifix at the top of Garrowby Hill (the highest point of the Yorkshire Wolds). The Church objected to a crucifix, but he didn't want a plain cross. So he got permission for it if it was a memorial to King George VI, and a 25-foot-high wooden crucifix was built. Beneath it are the words: GEORGE, KING SERVANT OF HIS PEOPLE. Michael Ramsay, then Archbishop of York, came to dedicate it.

In London that summer we went to a very smart ball at St James's Palace given by the Duke of Norfolk for his daughter Anne: white tie, knee breeches, decorations, ball dresses and tiaras. We were partnered into dinner – in my case by Lord Hambleden. As we were leaving the ball, Bernard Norfolk caught hold of Richard and asked him to go and have some conversation with the Princess Royal. Very reluctantly he went over to talk to her. The Princess Royal was very shy and not easy to talk to, so no one was in any hurry to relieve Richard. Meanwhile, having agreed to leave, I had got my coat and walked to our car. After waiting more than half an hour in the Mall, I wrote furiously in lipstick on the car windscreen, 'I HAVE GONE HOME.' I took a taxi home and had to wake up the caretakers for some money to pay for it.

A few months later the Norfolks gave another ball, once again for Anne, this time at Arundel Castle. For some reason I was very disorganised and I'd forgotten to pack a stiff collar, evening shirt and even pyjamas for Richard. A footman borrowed one of Bernard's collars but it was much too big for Richard. I remember Margaret Douglas-Home, Alec's sister-in-law, who was running the ball for Lavinia, saying to me, 'It's tiaras tonight. But I didn't tell you as I knew you wouldn't have one.' Actually I did have one but hadn't been told to bring it, so I was rather cross. At the ball, which was great fun, Richard picked up Caroline Somerset (Beaufort) and took her to lunch at Wiltons. But he then thought better about taking it any further.

There would not have been any divorcees at either of the Norfolks' balls as the Duke of Norfolk was a keen Roman Catholic, but disapproval of divorce was not confined to Catholics. At my staunchly Protestant school in Norfolk, children had to leave the school if their parents divorced. I remember one girl having to leave in the middle of term, as Lady Walsingham said the school and the parents had to be in agreement for the sake of the girl. And wartime made no difference. During the war the King wanted to ask some of the officers stationed at Windsor to shoot with him. The colonel sent in half a dozen names. The answer came back that they were all acceptable except for Sir Jock Gilmour, because he was divorced. Sir Jock was furious and said, 'I suppose I'm good enough to shoot the King's enemies but not his pheasants!'

Such disapproval of divorce continued into the 1960s. Up until

1955 you couldn't get into the Royal Enclosure at Ascot – considered a pivotal fixture of the social calendar – if you were divorced, nor would you be invited to Royal occasions. In addition it was very difficult to be adopted for Parliament if you were divorced. When Anthony Eden married Clarissa Churchill in 1952 after his divorce from Beatrice (Sim's step-sister and first cousin), Richard received many letters from High Church people telling him that he must 'hound Eden out, as we cannot have a divorced Prime Minister'.

Like divorce, gambling was also disapproved of and private gambling clubs were illegal until the law changed in the early 1960s. But John Aspinall, who Myrtie knew, used to run private gambling parties in the late 1950s, in smart houses which he would rent for very large sums for a few days at a time before moving on to another house. We had been to a Charity Ball at which Lavinia Norfolk was president and I was chairman. When we left, Myrtie suggested that Lavinia, Richard and I should go with her to one of these parties. Lavinia said that as a Duchess she couldn't come and Richard said as an MP he couldn't either. It was difficult to get in, you had to ring the bell a certain number of times. Once inside, there was marvellous food and huge sums of money being gambled on poker and roulette. Getting out wasn't easy either. It was important that we weren't seen and we had to leave at different times.

I made the mistake of telling Lord Halifax about the party. He then told a man called Tony Pepys, who had been with them in Washington. Not long after, I had a telephone call: 'This is the *Daily Mail*. I understand that you were at Mr Aspinall's the other night. Can you tell me more about it?' I was shaking all over. I thought – an MP's wife and Lord Halifax's daughter-in-law, to be caught doing this! When I found out it was just a tease, I was so angry. I never liked Tony Pepys after that and we didn't give him a present when he married Bernard Norfolk's sister Rachel.

★   ★   ★

In the same month as the ball at St James's Palace, July 1956, Nasser had ramped up international tension by nationalising the Suez Canal. But it was in the last week of October, 'the most momentous week of my short career', as Richard wrote in his diary, that the bombshell fell. This was the announcement, which 'staggered us all', that Anglo-French troops were being sent to occupy the Canal. Richard was deeply dismayed. But he knew that he must support the Government, and Anthony in particular. We never forgave Anthony Nutting (Anthony Eden's protégé) for resigning, and later when bathing in Lake Geneva with Selwyn Lloyd, and finding myself next to Anthony at lunch, I found it very hard to speak to him. I didn't like him anyway, as he hadn't fought in the war.

It was a profoundly divisive time, not least for Conservatives. Best friends wouldn't speak to each other. For some reason Walter Monckton believed that Richard was against Suez and so asked us to a drink in his grand office in the House of Commons and started to try and persuade him, only to learn that we were all on the same side.

With the failure of the Suez expedition and the illness of Anthony Eden, a new prime minister was only a matter of time. Richard and the other Parliamentary Secretaries were addressed by both Butler and Macmillan. Harold said that before Suez he had been 'looking forward to retirement and to shooting the few pheasants on my estate'. Richard noted that 'it was an impressive performance but few were taken in by this expression of noble detachment.' Still, we were both pleased that it was Harold rather than Rab who succeeded Anthony.

When Harold formed his government in early 1957 Richard was disappointed by his lack of promotion. Harold rang Richard to say: 'I am not quite ready to move you yet. I do hope you don't mind [as Under Secretary (War Pensions)] looking after these dear people for a bit longer.' This lull encouraged Richard to put his name forward for a Parliamentary delegation to visit Africa during the summer recess. But before that, I had gone on a short but eventful holiday to Italy.

Before she married, my sister-in-law Anne had had a terrific affair with Ralph Grimthorpe who owned the Villa Cimbrone. Sim and Anne now borrowed it off him and asked Richard and me out there. I went reluctantly without Richard because in June Parliament was still sitting. The villa (now a hotel) is a wonderful house with spectacular views, standing on a rocky outcrop on the Amalfi coast. Lots of famous people had stayed there – Winston, Greta Garbo, T. S. Eliot and many others. I went twice more later on with Richard, although you couldn't drive to the house which was half an hour's walk down to the square and then on down to the beach. But somehow Richard managed it.

It was a huge house with innumerable bedrooms. Anne used to go off with her lover David Bethell to a different room every night. When David's wife Ursula, who was only twenty-six, complained about this to Sim (then himself having an affair with Pam Baring), he advised her, 'Well, get yourself a lover.' I loved it there, but I used to cry every night without Richard. My cousin Susie, having married the millionaire Archie Kidston and mindful of all we had given her in her impoverished days, had presented me with a return first-class sleeper to Naples, as I was scared stiff of flying. But Anne persuaded me to fly back with her and Sim, with the promise of giving me one of the Purple Hearts which Derek Parker Bowles had got for her. Before they were banned, you could get Purple Hearts on prescription if you were scared of something. They were very effective.

Now it was Richard's turn to go abroad without me. In Richard's case it was to lead a mixed-party Parliamentary delegation to Central Africa. On his first evening in Salisbury Richard stayed with Evelyn and Molly Baring at Government House and had dinner with

Michael Lycett and his wife Mo, who had been a Cairo girlfriend of Richard's in 1943. They were in the process of adopting a child. They wouldn't reveal the child's identity but they told Richard he knew the parents. The whole story is a strange one.

Lord Yarborough, who had commanded the Sherwood Rangers at the start of the war with my father as his second-in-command, had two daughters, Diana and Wendy. Her parents didn't like Diana, and when in 1952 she married a pilot officer and went to live in Africa they cut her off without a penny. Diana had two daughters, disliked them and put the elder into a children's home – her husband wouldn't let her do the same with the second. At the same time Michael and Mo wanted to adopt a child and decided, knowing the family, that Marcia (the elder child) would be ideal. They told Richard they were bringing her back to England to be re-christened as Anthea and asked Richard to be a godfather.

But at Benghazi airport the plane crashed. Mo managed somehow to break the porthole glass and threw Anthea and her Bible out onto the tarmac. Mo herself died, but Anthea survived with a broken arm. Michael then flew to London. He rang me in Yorkshire and said could he bring Anthea and himself and a friend's nanny to stay. Anthea was terribly disturbed. When I went to say goodnight to her, she clung to me, saying, 'Don't leave me, don't leave me. Not another Mummy leaving me!' That was awful. Michael did once take her back to Rhodesia and one day he saw her real father on the other side of the road. But Michael hurried Anthea away without explanation. I believe she barely knows her sister.

In 1959 Michael married Diana's sister, Wendy, and together they brought up Anthea, but she called her Aunt Wendy and not Mummy, and Michael took complete charge. He has recently died at over a hundred. Anthea runs a bookshop and has never married. She is in touch with the Yarboroughs, and I am in contact with her from time to time and like her very much.

Richard enjoyed his travels around Northern Rhodesia (later Zambia), Southern Rhodesia (Zimbabwe) and Nyasaland (Malawi), and in Lusaka was able to stay with Oliver and Prue Green-Wilkinson. In Lusaka other members of the delegation went off to look at wild animals, but Oliver insisted that Richard should spend time with the Christians rather than the lions! At one of Oliver's mission stations the unfortunate priest had filled the chalice with white-ant poison rather than wine and had killed several communicants. Less serious was the report given to Richard at a school: 'Emma Zimba has been dismissed because of misconduct. She has been conceived, which is the main reason why she has left.'

Among his fellow MPs he found that Jim Callaghan was a good companion. Towards the end of the trip Richard was amused one evening to have a late-night visit from Callaghan, who came in his pyjamas to Richard's room to discuss something. Callaghan had asked, 'as my name's not Driberg', if he could come in for a chat. Afterwards, they became good friends. When he admired Richard's red felt braces, Richard gave him a pair. I was sitting in the Commons gallery one day and happened to see Callaghan come into the chamber. He saw Richard and tweaked his braces to show Richard that he was wearing them.

The other friendship made on this trip was with Charles Fletcher-Cooke, a clever and amusing barrister and fellow Tory MP. A couple of years later we went to his wedding to Lady Avebury, somewhat reluctantly as we suspected that marriage was just not his line. This was confirmed when a young male friend of his was caught driving in his official car and Fletcher-Cooke lost his job as a Home Office minister. The Home Secretary Henry Brooke seemed only too ready to abandon him to his fate, while at the same time excusing the adultery of George Jellicoe, the other junior minister in his Department.

At the end of Richard's trip I went to meet him at Orly Airport.

I was rather proud of having flown to Le Bourget, terrified though I was of flying, and hiring the smallest Citroen, a *deux chevaux*, and finding my way around Paris and its suburbs in time to meet him at Orly. We then allowed ourselves a few days' luxury at the Trianon Palace hotel at Versailles.

★　　★　　★

The Ministry of Pensions was not the most lively department of government and Richard sought variety and some relief by dashing around the country visiting regional headquarters and local offices and listening to their problems. These journeys were lent a certain gravitas by the fact that in those days if he was on official business even a very junior Minister would be met, and seen off, by the stationmaster, often in a top hat, at the more important stations.

Back in London, frustrated pensioners occasionally besieged the office. When Richard's boss, John Boyd-Carpenter, was dining at his house in Eaton Terrace, an artificial leg, thrown by a disgruntled amputee, sailed through the open window of his dining-room and narrowly missed him. Certain gatherings had to be attended. The annual British Legion service in the Albert Hall was quite enjoyable. But the Spiritualist assembly, also in the Albert Hall, was a great trial. Inane and obviously bogus messages came from the dead loved one to an expectant parent, wife or some other relation.

In Yorkshire I took notes for Richard and wrote the necessary letters afterwards at his monthly surgeries in the constituency, always held in Bridlington and then either in Filey and Driffield or in Withernsea and Hornsea. It was important to do it, even if many of the problems presented were trivial and others clearly insoluble. One man said the Devil was stopping him going upstairs. He kept pulling the man back. One woman claimed to know all about the Resurrection because she herself had risen from the dead. I had to stop myself from laughing when Richard's laconic response to this revelation was simply: 'Yes, I see.' Another regular caller seemed to be quite sensible except for her certainty that God was in some way interfering with her Hoover.

One constituent asked if we could get her husband out of Broadmoor. When Richard asked what he was there for, she said, 'He murdered his best friend, that's all.' Richard said, 'That was rather bad luck on the best friend.' But, she said, her husband was such a nice man. It was a good excuse to go to Broadmoor, which was fascinating, but we couldn't help her husband. He was clearly by then a completely harmless mental case. Broadmoor was a hundred per cent better than any of the very many prisons I have been to – from English prisons to South American, West Indian and Egyptian ones. I had been fascinated by Broadmoor ever since reading Angela du Maurier's *Treveryan* as a child.

Our neighbour Richard Sykes was very much a feature of our Yorkshire lives. He had played a central role in getting Richard elected to Parliament, he was president of the constituency association, and he generously lent his beautiful house, Sledmere, for a number of constituency functions. Very early in my marriage I had played gin rummy at Sledmere and had lost £5 to Andrew Devonshire. I did not work and had no income (I wasn't yet twenty-one, when I would have access to a small Trust). I couldn't think how I could tell Richard that I'd lost £5. He said I must send Andrew a cheque and never gamble again. I did both. Andrew never acknowledged it, but of course to him £5 was nothing. I was always very fond of him.

Richard Sykes was very peculiar but I loved him because he was nice to me and I've always loved older men (he was exactly my mother's age). He played the organ beautifully in the hall at Sledmere and he could be very charming. He adored his wife Virginia, it broke him when she died of appendicitis. His mercurial temperament may have been shaped by feelings of inadequacy as the son of a famous father, Sir Mark Sykes (of the Sykes-Picot Agreement), who had died when Richard was only fourteen. He had died of Spanish flu and many years later his grandson Tatton allowed him to be disinterred in order to help medical research.

When Richard Sykes was staying at Wentworth Woodhouse in his early twenties, the other guests had made him an apple-pie bed. He was so furious that he threw all the valuable oil paintings in his bedroom out of the window into the garden and he left in the middle of the night. And years later, at a ball at Sledmere, Virginia Sykes had let people leave their coats in his dressing room. Wanting to go to bed, he threw all these coats down the stairs in a heap.

Tony and Jane Bethell were also great Yorkshire friends. In the war Tony had lost a leg below the knee and at the end of the war at the age of twenty-two he had married Jane Pleydell-Bouverie. He ran the estate he had inherited from his father Adrian, who had been married to Myrtie's great friend Clare Tennant but who left him to marry Lionel Tennyson. Tony let the house to nuns who ran a girls' school, where both their daughters went to school (Sarah, the younger, is still a friend of Emma's). Tony and Jane lived in the former Vicarage. He was MFH to the Holderness Hunt and Richard asked his permission to use Holderness as his title. We stayed there a lot for constituency things, often driving the fifty or so miles to dine with them. We went every year to the New Year's Eve dance they gave, along with Kate and Tony Philips, Billy and Ann Brooksbank and Charles and Elsie Chafer, and many others. It was a bottle party where we were told exactly what wine to bring – we wondered why others didn't copy that idea.

★   ★   ★

In 1958 Harold made good his promise to Richard and moved him from Pensions to the Ministry of Labour, where the Minister was Iain Macleod. The work there was more to Richard's taste and much more varied. In a short time he achieved considerable success in getting employers to make more apprenticeships available. Once again his instinct and preference was to get out of London as often as he could and meet people, rather than gossiping in the House of Commons Smoking Room, helpful as the latter would clearly have been to his career.

The same year saw the tragic death of my friend Jeremy Cubitt, the son of my mother's boyfriend Rolie Cubitt and the uncle of Camilla, Duchess of Cornwall. Jeremy had married in 1952. He then worked in prisons and used to bring prisoners back to sleep on the drawing-room floor, always feeling that he could somehow change their lives. He realised that his wife, not surprisingly, didn't like this. To make things harder, Jeremy then decided that he'd like to be ordained. But his bishop told him he couldn't be ordained if he was divorced. At the same time he knew that there was no way that Diana would agree to be a parson's wife and that it would be cruel not to allow her to divorce him.

At a party Jeremy told me all this. He was in a terrible state and he felt trapped. He went to see his father, who was in a meeting at the Savoy. He waited and waited to see him, but the meeting went on and on and Rolie's secretary wouldn't fetch him out of the meeting. So Jeremy went to the top of the Savoy and threw himself off. A lot later the secretary told me how terribly guilty she felt.

Jeremy had been a great friend of mine and Archie Kidston's all our lives. We both wanted to go to the funeral. By then, suicides could be buried in consecrated ground (although the act of suicide was not decriminalised until 1961), but it was still very unusual for outsiders to attend the funeral service. Myrtie consulted Rolie, who said we were both allowed to send flowers because we had been such friends of his. Presumably others could not.

CHAPTER 11

Minister of Power

Harold Macmillan had revived the Conservative Party and his stock was high when he called the General Election for October 1959. He was returned with a majority of a hundred seats and Richard increased his own majority to over 17,000. But perhaps inevitably it is the *faux pas* from election meetings that one still remembers. At a packed meeting in the village school at Hunmanby the chairman told the electors: 'Mr and Mrs Wood are always only too ready to interfere in other people's business.' At the end she asked for only one more question, because 'Our Candidate is ready to pass on.'

Harold made Richard the Minister of Power. He wrote to him: 'You see, the miners are the difficulty… What I really want is a gentleman to look after them… they like the Colonel much more than the Sergeants.' Before long Richard had gone down his first coalmine and in 1960 I went down the mine at Easington Colliery under the North Sea with Paul Channon, Richard's PPS. Paul told me he knew how much I'd object to having tea afterwards with only the wives, but he'd been unable to persuade them we should all be together. Several coalmining visits followed, where I usually joined Richard. His affection for the miners quickly grew. He was popular with them too.

The impressive thing about the miners was their sense of community, like a village in the best sense. They all helped each other and depended on each other. They had a bond, which soldiers on active service of course have too, but that rarely exists in normal civilian life.

At Kingston House my parents-in-law had a daily woman, Mrs Merrin, whose father was a miner in the West Riding. They had such a small house that her father and two or three of her brothers used to do the day shift and the other brothers the night shift, as there was not enough room in the house for them all to sleep at the same time. She bore no one any grudge about this and was delighted, when Richard became Minister of Power, to think that he would be looking after the miners.

I wanted to go down a mine which would require some crawling. It was narrow and there wasn't much room to breathe but I was glad to have gone. I realised they would never have sent me anywhere dangerous. Clearly Richard couldn't do it, so they suggested I bring a companion. I took Myles Hildyard with me. They were surprised I hadn't brought a woman.

Myles was one of my very oldest friends. I had known him since I was twelve and he twenty-five. He had joined my father's regiment, the Sherwood Rangers, just before the war and had been with him in Lincolnshire and then in Palestine and North Africa. He had hero-worshipped Flash, but because he dressed poorly and rode badly my father was rather intolerant of him at first.

Untidy he may have been, but Myles was certainly brave and he had had an extraordinary war. Some of the Sherwood Rangers (but not Flash or his second-in-command and great friend, Donny Player) had been sent to Crete in 1941 and Myles was among those captured by the Germans. With a friend, Michael Parish, he managed to escape into the mountains. Eventually they reached the coast but had no money to pay for a boat-journey. Surprisingly the boat-owner allowed Myles to write him a cheque. After several more dramas, they reached the Turkish coast and Myles was able to rejoin the Sherwood Rangers in North Africa before Alamein. Myles and Michael were both awarded the Military Cross.

When Myles's cheque eventually arrived back at his local branch of the Westminster Bank in Newark, the manager telephoned Myles's parents to ask if it should be honoured. His parents had no idea if their son was alive or dead, so this was the first sign that he had survived the Battle of Crete. The story goes that his mother fainted on hearing the news.

Much of Myles's life revolved around the ancestral home of Flintham Hall, which he had inherited from his father, Judge Hildyard, in the mid-1950s. Flintham has been described as 'perhaps the most gloriously romantic Victorian house in England' and Myles had always loved it. He restored many of the rooms to their Victorian splendour and transformed the gardens and the woods.

Myles never married. He said he would probably have done so if his mother hadn't been so set on him marrying one of the Duke of Portland's daughters – which oddly enough Lord H had also hoped his son Charlie would do, but neither wanted to. During the war Myles had fallen in love with a young officer in the 11th Hussars. Jimmy was not in the least homosexual, so this turned out to be a very one-sided affair, though they were great friends. But this didn't stop Myles showering Jimmy with gifts. He gave him Desert Orchid, the legendary horse which won almost everything, he let him and his wife Anne and four children live in a Georgian garden house at Flintham and he paid for the education of their children.

Myles was a brilliant letter-writer and used to write to me, sometimes twice a week, and he often came to stay with us both in Yorkshire and in France. For his seventieth birthday party he had the garden designer Mary Keen sitting next to him. He knew I was cross because I always sat next to him at his parties, as I did at his ninetieth birthday party in 2004, less than a year before he died.

★ ★ ★

Just a month before the 1959 election my parents-in-law had given a great party at Garrowby for the tenants on all the estates, to celebrate their Golden Wedding anniversary. Lord H had to receive his guests in a wheelchair. He had broken his hip a couple of months before, falling over a tub in the garden that my mother-in-law had moved while weeding. He had been flown to London and it was the first time he had ever been in hospital or had an anaesthetic. At the party Lady H, her right arm in a sling, used her left hand to greet the guests.

Lord Halifax died on 23 December 1959. A particular regret for Richard was that he had not gone to see his father that October. He had returned to Yorkshire the day after he had been made Minister of Power. His mother, avid for details, had come over to Flat Top, but Lord H was less mobile. Richard was very tired but he could have volunteered to go over to Garrowby. He could not forgive himself for this thoughtlessness.

There was a requiem mass for Lord H at York Minster and also at Westminster Abbey. At York there was a note informing potential communicants that you had to give twenty-four hours' notice if you wanted to take communion (as stated in the rubrics of the 1662 Book of Common Prayer). The result was that nobody did. He hadn't wanted anyone to make their communion because he knew they wouldn't have been fasting at 11 o'clock in the morning. A requiem mass, which he had wanted, was not a service most people were familiar with. A memorial service in Westminster Abbey would have been better.

A surprising invitation arrived early in 1960 from the Polish Government, suggesting the visit of a British Minister to Poland. Harold decided that Richard should go and that I should go with him (I suspect this was because of his disability but that was never said). The precedent of allowing me to accompany Richard was followed for all of his subsequent ministerial trips abroad (though I declined one or two of them simply because I was so scared of flying). We were both very grateful to Harold, and later to Alec Douglas-Home and Ted Heath for continuing with this.

When the Polish trip came up, I had been going to give a talk about the Psalms in the constituency. I didn't want to let the organisers down but I remembered that our friend and neighbour Billy Brooksbank was something of an expert on them. He agreed to take my place – on condition that I brought him back a bottle of vodka, then almost unobtainable in England.

We flew to Warsaw in March. In our room at the Grand Hotel, with a 'wardress' sitting outside, Richard and I talked in whispers, convinced that the room was bugged. It was the first time we'd ever seen a duvet. We decided that they must be poor because they couldn't afford blankets. Meanwhile the need for an interpreter made light conversation with our hosts difficult.

We were taken to inspect a power station and coalmine near Katowice. There were few cars on the road and lots of horse-drawn carts but not a single tractor. On the way we stopped to see the portrait of the Black Madonna at the Jasna Góra monastery, a place of pilgrimage for many thousands of Poles. There we were shown a book signed by Hitler, Himmler and others.

At the coalmine Richard signed the visitors' book a few pages behind Khruschev. That evening we were taken to a production of *Il Trovatore* in the modest mining town of Bytom, not unlike Rotherham. We were told that the Silesian Opera Company put on a nightly performance in this unlikely place.

At most stops we were plied with vodka and brandy, there were short speeches and presents were exchanged. At our final dinner in Warsaw it was made clear to Richard that the main object of getting him to Poland had nothing to do with coal or power. It was an attempt to get Britain to increase its imports of Polish bacon. On his return Richard did try to persuade the Cabinet to improve the quota for Polish bacon, but he was overruled by the Minister of Agriculture.

★ ★ ★

Inevitably, Richard had problems with his legs from time to time. He insisted on kneeling in church when praying or receiving communion at the altar rail, which meant swinging his legs sideways. On one occasion one of his legs fell off while he was bowing to the altar. Another time, on a visit to a coalmine at Darlington, I had to do a running repair when a leg became unhinged. Most dramatically, one of his legs fell of when, as Minister of Power, he was showing the Queen and Prince Philip around an iron foundry in Wales. Even though it was an iron foundry, they couldn't mend his leg and it had to be tied back on with wire for the time being.

I always made it clear that Richard had lost his legs in the war, rather than in any other way. If anyone stared at his legs, I would glare back at them. If someone asked, 'Minister, will you be able to …', I would answer, 'Yes, of course.' I could never bear wheelchairs and I would never have a stair-lift, it had to be a proper lift. The Halifaxes gave us one for Flat Top and it was housed in a built-in cupboard in Richard's dressing room and went down on two small tracks to the dining room on the floor below. We later hung a full-length picture of Ed to conceal the tracks (these days Health and Safety will not allow such hidden things). Richard always walked with a stick. He should have been taught to carry the stick in his left hand because when shaking hands he always had to swop the stick over. I tried to get him to change but he said it was too late.

General de Gaulle came on a state visit to London that April. After the *Marseillaise* had been played he spoke for twenty minutes without a note in Westminster Hall and was rousingly cheered at the end (this was before he had said No to our joining the Common Market). That evening Richard and I were asked to a gala performance of ballet at Covent Garden in de Gaulle's honour. Everyone was in white ties and tiaras, a glorious sight. We dined with Peter and Iona Carrington and Arthur and Pam Onslow at the Berkeley, where no one seemed even remotely surprised by our attire. In the interval at Covent Garden, Lord Scarbrough, the Lord Chamberlain, wanted someone young to meet de Gaulle. Richard declined because of his lack of French. He thought I would be relieved, but in fact I was furious. I would have loved to have talked to the General.

After Lord H died and my mother-in-law moved to Kingston House from Garrowby for the last time, I got the flat ready for her before we went back to Flat Top. I filled the fridge, put flowers in the rooms, drew the curtains and turned down her bed. I was lucky, it was a turning point, vastly for the better, in our relationship. So much so that I remember that I burst into tears when we were in Singapore in the early 1970s and we got a letter from Myrtie telling us that Lady H was moving from London to a cottage next door to Garrowby. By then she was terribly deaf and Charlie thought she might get run over in London, and she suddenly decided she liked Yorkshire more than she ever had.

Of course we wanted our own flat in London. After a bit of walking around I noticed a row of houses in Eaton Place that was still derelict. They had been commandeered in the war and later used to house homeless people, but even fifteen years after the war they were in a terrible state. A developer had just bought them to turn into flats. For £12,000 we bought a flat on two floors with a small garden behind.

The flats were in the very early stages of renovation, so we were able to choose the cornices and mantelpieces, do up a bedroom, bathroom and sitting room for Lady Halifax and develop a flat for a couple to occupy. The husband had a job but his Luxembourg wife was not only charming but a marvellous cook and cleaner. We spent our first night at 14 Eaton Place at the end of August 1960.

When the children were older Lady H bought the flat upstairs and moved there, where she had a housekeeper with a strange story to tell. Iris Roberts, a very nice woman, had a teenage daughter, Judith, whose father was never mentioned and Lady H was convinced she was illegitimate. But one day Iris said to me, 'I'll tell you about my husband, I've never told anyone else.' He had been a Russian. One day he and Iris were walking along a beach on the south coast when he suddenly said, 'I must just leave for a bit, but I'll be back.' He never returned.

Within two days the police came to see her and told her she must change her name. Think of a name with the same first letter, they said, so she chose Roberts. She had to have a new birth and marriage certificate, new everything. Lady H had Foreign Office contacts and said she'd find out what had happened. Iris was thrilled at the prospect and told Judith, but the latter begged her not to, as she said they might be in danger and she was just trying to forget he ever existed. Iris felt she couldn't inflict this on her daughter, so Lady H never investigated. It seems possible that he was an anti-Soviet Russian who had tried to lay a mine on a Soviet ship which had at that time docked at a British port, and he had been caught by the Soviets.

★　★　★

Despite his new responsibilities Richard managed to fit in a considerable amount of shooting and I always loaded for him. John and Diana Astor had a shooting party at Meikleour in Perthshire, where I admired the amazing Meikleour Beech Hedge, planted in 1745 and said to be the tallest and longest hedge in the world.

In Yorkshire we shot at Bolton Abbey for several years, where the grouse moor was let to a syndicate by Andrew Devonshire at a ridiculously low price. Billy Brooksbank, Chandos Temple, Tommy Crathorne, Kenneth Parkinson and Ian Watson were all members of the syndicate. Once when Richard was shooting there on a day when Billy Brooksbank wasn't, Billy and I decided both of us would load for him using three guns. On another day when loading for Billy, who was an ace shot, I contrived to load a lipstick as well as a cartridge into one of the barrels of his gun. Luckily the lipstick came out at the other end, as I didn't know I'd done it.

Amongst many friends and neighbours who shot at Garrowby were Richard Stanley, James and Mary Bowes-Lyon, Derek Parker Bowles, George Howard, Nico Collin, Joe Goodhart, Debo Devonshire and Bobo Roxburghe (a friend of Myrtie's and the most superb shot).

When in the early 1950s Elizabeth Jackson was about to become John Cowdray's second wife, she had rung Richard to ask for his approval of her marriage to a man who was divorced. She was my friend, not Richard's; we didn't then know John and Richard didn't think he should have an opinion. He prevaricated. He didn't want to go to their Church of Scotland wedding, where divorced people were allowed to marry, but I persuaded him that he must. However, there was a three-line whip in the House of Commons so he had to dash from the church to vote and couldn't join me at the reception in the Savoy. When I shook hands with John and kissed Elizabeth at the reception, her face fell and she said, 'Oh, isn't Richard here?' I explained, but I don't think she ever believed he had come to the church.

John had lost an arm in the war but as well as being a famous polo player he was, incredibly enough, a first-rate shot, always assisted of course by a loader. He was tremendously generous and also completely unspoilt by his wealth. However, he wouldn't have people to shoot unless they could shoot well.

Julian and Catherine Amery used to stay at Cowdray to shoot. I remember Julian once asking for claret at breakfast. The butler went and asked John (who always had breakfast upstairs with Elizabeth) for the key of the cellar, and brought up a bottle. Julian finished the whole bottle and then shot admirably all day.

Catherine and Julian lived in a huge house on the corner of Eaton Square with Julian's mother, an arrangement which Catherine hated. Julian's mother was always in bed on the floor below Julian and Catherine's rooms, with the door open – still suffering, it was said, from the shock of the hanging of her elder son John. (He had been an ardent admirer of Hitler, had joined the Nazi cause and had broadcast propaganda for the Germans during the war. After his capture in 1945 he pleaded guilty to treason in a sensational trial at the Old Bailey and was hanged that year.)

One day Baba Metcalfe had gone to their house for dinner and was early. Julian wasn't back from the House of Commons, and Catherine walked stark naked into the library where Baba was sitting, never noticed her there and helped herself to a large drink. In the same library only a few weeks later we went to a cocktail party where Julian, as was his wont, had asked every grand person he could think of. I took a step back at some point and Julian declared, 'Diana, you have just trodden on the King of Albania!'

I was rather nervous about launching a vast oil tanker, the *Serenia*, on the Tyne in October 1960. We travelled from London in a special train, and Myrtie, Peter (then Irwin), Fiona and Emma all came. (Edward was considered too young, having only recently started at his prep school, Sunningdale.) But all went well and I was given a magnificent diamond bracelet for my pains. (Later I launched another tanker on the Tyne for BP, the *British Dragoon*, and was given a diamond crescent brooch.) I expected to have the chance to talk to some of the men who had built her, but I wasn't allowed to. I had to make a speech at the huge lunch afterwards. Iona Carrington told me that when she'd launched a ship – at about this time, when Peter was First Lord of the Admiralty – all she'd got was a little bit of wood from the ship. Clearly you were much better rewarded if the ship wasn't military!

The Conservative Party Conference was held that year in Scarborough – since thought too small a place for such a gathering. We asked Edward Boyle, Richard's cousin Paul Channon and Ted

Heath to stay. The first two came by train to York. Richard met them but then drove into a big flood in Stamford Bridge. Paul did his best to push the car out but neither Edward nor Richard were able to be much use. The water flooded the boot, and back at Flat Top we spent a lot of time trying to dry out endless ties of Paul's with the image of Winston Churchill, intended to impress the Conference. Ted wanted to spend as much time as possible at the Conference. He had not realised how far our house was from Scarborough and must have thought it a poor base for a serious politician like himself. When he got back, he would walk about the garden in striped trousers and a black coat. Ted didn't have much idea about the country, and stangely enough we later we found that Anthony Eden's son, Nick Avon, had even less.

At the end of the year we had gone to a grand dance, and loving dancing I had spent most of the evening and far into the night with someone we both knew. Richard went home early and, clearly suspecting what I had been up to, spent part of the night with Sim's girlfriend Pam Baring, who had been staying with us. We both had short but intense affairs. I think the reason why we survived so happily was that we always discussed it all and had no secrets from each other. That was crucial. My friend had asked me if I would go away and sleep with him. I asked Richard and he said yes, but luckily the friend decided it would be disloyal.

The lasting result was not only that we never kept anything from each other, but also that sadly I never dared to dance again.

★   ★   ★

In 1962 Richard took over from Anthony Eden as Honorary Colonel 4th Battalion KRRC (now the Royal Green Jackets). Anthony was very fond of Richard and had always said that he wouldn't give it up unless Richard agreed to succeed him. Richard loved the role and always went to their annual Camp with them. It gave him great pleasure and he gave a great deal to it. He didn't relinquish it until 1989, when he handed over to Lord Nicholas Gordon Lennox who had finished being Ambassador in Madrid. Among Richard's commanding officers were Keith Loudon-Shand, Nick Eden, Tommy Wallis, John Cornell, Bill Pirie, Tony Berry, Nigel Mogg and Christopher Miers.

The venue for the Camp varied from year to year. One year it was at Westmere in Norfolk on land which had belonged to Lord Walsingham and where I had been at school until the War Office had requisitioned it in 1942 (the land is still owned and used by the Ministry of Defence today). We were allowed to drive everywhere in the Battle Zone. Going back was fascinating. It hadn't changed at all. Time had stood still.

Perhaps surprisingly, the Battalion still had a portrait of Kaiser Wilhelm II hanging on their walls. The Kaiser had inspected the regiment in 1891 and had then presented them with a portrait of himself. We got this picture copied and gave the copy to Brigid's granddaughter, also called Brigid, to whom we were both godparents and who was the Kaiser's great-great-granddaughter.

That same year, 1962, Joy Maitland, Lady H's first cousin, died. One of her brothers was trampled to death by an elephant. The other died at sea when Joy was with him and he was thrown into the sea in a sack, like the Count of Monte Cristo. Lord H didn't really approve of her because she never married (he thought people should), she was a doctor working in the East End (he thought women shouldn't be professional), and she was plain. But we loved her, as did both Lady H and her sister Gwenny Iveagh. She was godmother to Richard's brother Peter, who had been killed in the war. So instead it was to Richard that she left the money that would have gone to Peter and her huge flat in Westbourne Terrace, on two floors and with a garden. We sold it for £3,000 and used the money to completely transform the farm buildings at Flat Top.

Towards the end of 1962 we first heard about the scandal that would burst upon an unsuspecting nation the following year – the 'Profumo affair'. Richard and I were asked to dinner at Eaton Terrace by Charles Peake's widow Catherine to meet Osbert Lancaster, a most engaging character who, sitting next to me, remarked, 'Of course it's absolutely dreadful about Christine Keeler.' At the time none of us had the remotest idea what he was talking about. But Osbert Lancaster's newspaper, the *Daily Express*, had been aware of the rumours for some time. The next year the scandal broke in full. It rocked the government, shocked the country and affected our own lives too.

CHAPTER 12

Under the Stars, from Alexandria to Tunis

Richard was Minister of Power during the winter of 1962-63, the coldest winter of the twentieth century. There were huge snowdrifts and the snow brought down power lines and cut off villages all over the country. While Richard tackled power cuts, gas rationing and coal shortages, some journalists decided that I was fair game too.

Press interest began when I went to King's Cross to meet Edward off his train from Yorkshire in early January. He was on his way to the beginning of term at his prep school, Sunningdale, which sadly he loathed, though the headmaster, Charlie Sheepshanks, and his wife Mary were friends and did their very best (Mary is a great friend whom I still see often. We travelled together to St Petersburg, Rome and Paris. She writes books and is great fun.) I think the trouble really lay with Beakey, who almost possessed Ed, and when he was unhappy at school wrote to him almost daily, although we asked her not to.

It turned out that there was no train to meet – the engine had been diverted to bring much-needed coal to London. But while I was waiting for the train in the Morris Minor that Richard had free as a Disabled War Pensioner, a reporter coolly got into the car beside me and began asking questions – how I kept warm and so on. In a temper I answered, 'We burn logs from my brother-in-law's estate,' and a short piece appeared in the paper the next day. After that, reporters kept coming around to our flat.

One evening a man rang the doorbell and asked if Richard was at home. He said he'd been in the war with him and he'd love to see him. He didn't look like a reporter, so I let him in. But he was from the *Daily Mirror*. I happened to have just bought some long black woollen pants from Jaeger and the press wanted to photograph me in them with black fishnet tights underneath. I was going to say no, but to my surprise Lady H said, You must do it. So I did. The next day the picture appeared on the front of the *Daily Express* and in other papers, sometimes combined with a cartoon.

By 1st February *Time Magazine* had caught up with the story. They published the same picture of me in the Jaeger pants and explained to their readers how the British were reacting to the extreme cold:

> Every sort of blizzard gear was worn, but the most spectacular outfit was sported by Diana Wood, 35, pretty wife of Britain's Minister of Power Richard Wood. When an outbreak of power failures brought a storm of complaints to the Power Ministry, Mrs Wood helped raise at least some temperatures by posing for the *Daily Mail* in her cold-weather costume: a turtleneck sweater, fish-net stockings, and skin-tight, black woollen knee-length panties.

★   ★   ★

Bill Astor was an old friend of Myrtie's and she and Billy often stayed at Cliveden, not least during the Profumo scandal. Billy once told us that he liked Christine Keeler, to which Myrtie responded, 'Nonsense, William, you know you don't.' To thank Myrtie for all her help at elections Bill had given me a cheque for £25 in 1945 to buy a coat for his marriage to Sarah Norton (at St Martin-in-the-Fields, where all Astors were married). Many years later we published Sarah's book about her time at Bletchley, *The Road to Station X*.

In March 1963 an article appeared in *Paris Match* about Jack Profumo at Cliveden with Bill Astor, Christine Keeler and Dr Stephen Ward. Jack vigorously denied having any relationship with

Christine Keeler. At the end of April Harold Macmillan invited his senior Ministers to Chequers for a meeting. Afterwards Peter Carrington asked Jack and Richard back to dinner at Bledlow and on the way there Jack declared to Richard, 'I am going to sue *Paris Match* for printing those lies.' Richard and Peter absolutely believed that he was innocent.

At the beginning of June we were on holiday in France – Parliament's Whitsun recess was quite long in those days – when we read in *Le Figaro* that Jack had resigned from the Government after admitting telling lies to the House of Commons. This was a huge shock.

The Government was damaged by the Profumo scandal and some urged Harold to retire without delay. In the event he was struck down by prostate trouble on the eve of the Conservative Party Conference that October and, despite complaints from Ministers who objected to an earl being Prime Minister, he was succeeded by Alec Douglas-Home. Richard happened to be shooting at Bolton Abbey on the day that Alec was summoned to the Palace. He immediately returned to London and was called to Downing Street.

Alec was having some trouble forming a Cabinet. Iain Macleod and Enoch Powell had refused to serve under him. Freddy Erroll was doubtful and was threatening to resign unless he was made Minister of Power, so Alec had given him this. In return, Alec was offering Richard the office of Secretary of State for War and a hereditary peerage. Richard refused both and instead accepted to become Minister of Pensions. When he came back to report this, I was so angry I slapped him in the face. I said that it was the one job I'd have loved. He would have been particularly good at it and his Regiment would have been thrilled, and why did it matter if he was in the House of Lords.

I had never shared Richard's affection for the House of Commons.

Looking back he regretted the choice he had made, but at the time he saw removal to the Lords as the effective end of his political career. He had enjoyed his four years as Minister of Power and still felt he had much to contribute there. He hoped, too, that in due course he might progress to be Foreign Secretary, like his father.

So for Richard it was back to the familiar Ministry of Pensions offices in John Adam Street, but this time as Minister. His Parliamentary Secretaries were Margaret Thatcher, whom Alec said had to remain, and a brave submariner, Lynch Maydon. Richard reported that at their first meeting Margaret had answered all his questions, sometimes at great length. She had then supplemented all of Maydon's somewhat inadequate answers, until eventually Maydon's patience and natural courtesy had deserted him. 'Margaret,' he said, 'you're being perfectly maddening.'

A friend suggested to me that I didn't like Margaret because she was a grocer's daughter. That's not it at all, I replied. I didn't like her because she had absolutely no sense of humour. Peter Morrison, later Margaret's PPS, was shooting with us in Yorkshire at the time she had been mooted as Conservative leader. I had raised heated objections at lunch, to which Peter responded very firmly, 'Diana, I am afraid you'll have to put up with it.' That didn't mean that I didn't think she was jolly good.

I was always Richard's secretary and early on he was chairman of a committee to deal with redundant Yorkshire churches for the Archbishop of York. There was a lot of printing to be done for it and sent out to the members. In those days there were only two photocopiers in the whole House of Commons and a notice required secretaries to give way to MPs. During my work Margaret came in and I moved over. She remarked, 'I have got to print out programmes for Mark's Christmas play.'

Once again Richard took opportunities to travel around the country when others might have spent more time at Westminster furthering their careers. One trip on which I joined him was to Orkney and Shetland. At our arrival at the hotel in Lerwick we were delighted by the response to our request for the key to our room: none of the rooms had a key, we were told. The sea was too rough to get to Orkney. I was glad to have seen Shetland, but visiting Pension & National Insurance offices and meeting the people that ran them was not exciting.

Alec put off the 1964 election as long as he could and probably reduced the size of the Conservative defeat to a handful of seats. But we knew that a second election would almost certainly lead to a comfortable Labour majority. So we began to prepare for a major expedition in 1965 along the desert coast of North Africa. Richard had long wanted to go back to where he had been wounded. He was convinced that the map he had left in his truck would still be there (in fact all those battle things had been removed only a few months before our trip by an enterprising Libyan who then sold them profitably). I had always wanted to go to the desert in the footsteps of Flash, who had loved it, both on journeys before the war and when fighting there. Richard had liked it too. We enjoyed travelling alone together.

First of all we needed a suitable vehicle. We wanted to be completely independent and have something we could comfortably sleep in (or more usually, outside of). So we bought a self-drive motor-caravan. It was rather like an ice-cream van. Parking it at Eton for the Fourth of June, I heard Di Erroll come past and comment that frightful people were now coming to Eton. I didn't show my face. Richard was less squeamish, but I couldn't bear our friends to know we'd got something quite so hideous.

It was, however, thoroughly practical. It could sleep four, just. It had a simple fridge, which had to be exactly level to work properly. It had no loo, which a later one did have. And it only carried seven gallons of water, which made it difficult to stay for long in one place, particularly as Arabs always asked for some.

We told the constituents that we should be away for a long time, but we took a basic radio in case a General Election was announced. Lady H remained convinced that we'd be blown up by one of the landmines that were still dotted around the North African desert. Myrtie thought we'd break down and Richard wouldn't be able to walk and I'd be raped by an Arab.

✻   ✻   ✻

We crossed the Channel with Emma (aged sixteen) and Ed (fourteen) towards the end of August 1965 and made our way through France and Switzerland to Italy. We camped every night, whatever the weather – on our own, never in a campsite, asking permission if that seemed appropriate ('wild camping' it would be called today). In France we made good use of the admirable public wash-houses – with a roof and a water supply but no walls – still at that time a particular feature of French villages and towns.

Ed flew home from Rome, and with Emma we met Anne and Lady H and stayed at Positano, going to Paestum and Pompeii. The Amalfi coast was very much Anne's 'kingdom'. Pompeii was almost devoid of tourists and Anne knew the man who ran it, so it was complete perfection.

Then we said goodbye to everyone and Richard and I were on our own. At Naples we put the caravan on a boat. Our cabin had a good bathroom and while I had a bath I left Richard in charge of my Carmen Curlers (then a very new thing). He didn't know the power was DC and not AC and, unnoticed by him, they overheated, the plastic melted and I had no means of curling my hair. Via the Corinth Canal, we reached the Greek mainland. At the port of Piraeus we watched in agony as the caravan was once again swung aboard a boat on a primitive crane, for the journey across the Mediterranean to Alexandria.

We were greeted at Alexandria by two men from Esso (a bonus

from Richard's contacts when he was Minister of Power). It took a long time to get permission to disembark as Wood was the surname of a Jew who was wanted by the Police, and without the Esso men Richard might well not have been allowed to land. They helped us with some preliminary shopping and some petrol. Petrol pumps would be few and far between in the desert. The AA had produced a very basic list. And then we drove westwards out of the city, hoping eventually to reach Tunis, our ultimate goal in Africa, by the end of October.

That first evening we reached Alamein, where we camped for the night. In the morning we found the name of Richard's brother Peter inscribed, not very skilfully, among the list of those whose bodies had never been found. I had asked Lord Halifax if he minded about this and he said why should he, Peter's spirit was with the Almighty.

Driving from Alexandria to Alamein was magical. I adored the desert – I knew I would – but seeing the rolling and ever-changing sand, and the brilliant turquoise of the Mediterranean, produced a feeling I wanted never ever to lose. I loved the emptiness and the heat, and the way that the desert alters all the time. When there was nobody anywhere and no lights at night, it was wonderful. On one night drive I thought we were driving down long avenues of trees, only to realise that there were none anywhere. We both felt this. It was strange.

But the extraordinary thing was that sometimes when you thought you were miles from anywhere, people would suddenly emerge. You couldn't see anyone for miles and then all of a sudden there could be someone there. It was almost creepy. Although the high motor-caravan kept much cooler than a car, most of the time we slept outside under an awning.

At Sollum near the Egyptian border we tried to dispose of our remaining Egyptian money and ended up at the Sollum Hotel buying up most of the beer that they had. I saw a waistcoat and trousers I wanted, but by then had little money. I haggled with the Egyptian but he would not give way, so all I bought was the waistcoat – which I still have. A strange figure sat drinking beer outside the hotel. He was so like a character from Somerset Maugham that we gave him that nickname, as we passed and repassed him many times on our way west. At our first meeting he had asked us for a lift. Rather ungraciously we refused. The thought of sharing camping with him was appalling. We were convinced that he was an ex-soldier from the Afrika Korps, intent (as Richard was) on visiting his old haunts. But much later when we met him again he told us he had been on the Russian front, doubtless not to offend us.

The Libyan customs were difficult and said we had to be inoculated. In those days I refused to have a needle stuck into me (even at the dentist), so I was in a total panic. Richard managed to talk them out of the inoculations in the end. It was an enormous relief to get through. At Tobruk we found the large war cemetery very moving, with the graves of soldiers, sailors and airmen from all corners of the world – British, Australian, South African, Indian, Greek, Czech, Polish. As we left Tobruk we saw Somerset Maugham thumbing a lift at the police post and shortly afterwards he sailed by in a fast car.

After Tobruk we began to drive through Cyrenaica. It was glorious country, particularly the Jebel Akhdar ('Green Hill'), a mountainous plateau with trees and valleys, quite unlike anywhere else in Libya. It was here above all that the Italians had tried to colonise North Africa. Indeed you could still faintly see 'DUCE' written on the walls of some farmhouses, even though all the Italian place-names had disappeared. We stopped to swim in the sea and rest for several days near the ancient Greek ruins of Apollonia. Like so many places along this coast, the ruins seemed only half-excavated, with so much more still to be done. It was a total joy to have it virtually to ourselves.

In Benghazi we collected a welcome bundle of letters from the British Embassy. The British Army had a training garrison of Green Howards just outside the city and we went to a service at the garrison church. Richard had gone with the Roman Catholic Colonel to Mass early. The next day the Colonel's wife met us at the NAAFI – it was a great bit of luck to be able to shop there – where we bought everything that we possibly could. We had largely been living on reconstituted dried food and tinned butter brought from England.

Further west, and visible for miles, a huge structure known as Marble Arch straddled the road. It had been a familiar landmark in the war for soldiers on both sides. Richard recorded the legend behind the arch in his diary:

> Marble Arch marks the legendary meeting place of the runners from Carthage and those from Cyrene, who set out from their respective capitals to establish, where they met, the boundary between the two domains. The Carthaginians, two brothers called Philean, had run so much further than the Cyrenians that the latter accused them of cheating, and agreed to the establishment of the boundary only on condition that the Carthaginian brothers would submit to death on the spot. The two Philean brothers nobly called the bluff and gave their lives for Carthage. Two thousand years later Mussolini commemorated the legend by building the Arch, which he opened himself, to mark the completion of the great Italian road in Libya, the Via Balbia. The Libyans have removed the Italian inscription and replaced it with Arabic, but the inside of the Arch contains two irremovable bas-reliefs, in praise of Mussolini and colonisation generally.

In 1973 Gaddafi had the Arch, a symbol of the Italian colonisation, blown up with dynamite.

We now turned inland and began to look for the place where

Richard had been hit by a bomb in December 1942 and lost his legs. Eventually, helped by a tall Arab dressed in white, Richard was sure that he had found Bir Zidan, the large well where the Battalion had spent that December day. Rather optimistically Richard hoped he might find the remains of the old truck that he'd been busy unloading when the Stukas struck. We did find a wheel, a rusty spring and a number of petrol tins cut in half – fairly reliable evidence of Army occupation. But that was all.

We then had the notion of changing course, leaving the coastal road and exploring southwards into the great desert of southern Libya. We did go quite a long way south and reached some impressive oases, with tall palm trees and vast dunes. One day when we stopped for lunch I gave in to an irresistible urge to go and roll in a huge mass of billowing sand. But before too long we decided that continuing in this direction was tempting but foolish. After some light rain – likely, we were told, to be the only rain of the year – the caravan got stuck and we needed the help of some passers-by to dig ourselves out. This confirmed the wisdom of our decision to head back north. Petrol was also a major problem.

Back on the Libyan coast, we spent several days at Leptis Magna, camping near the old harbour. The whole point of old Leptis had been its port, since natural harbours were almost non-existent on this coast. Now it's completely silted up and the focus of modern excavation is some way away. At about two o'clock in the afternoon the Libyan workers and guards would go home at the end of their day's work and we would have this vast city, and the sea to bathe in, to ourselves. As in other places, there seemed far more reconstruction still to do than had been done, but some of the carving of the pillars and capitals looked as if it had been finished only yesterday.

In Tripoli we passed the royal palace which King Idris never occupied. He preferred the climate of Tobruk, so that his ministers had to travel almost the whole length of Libya whenever he wanted to see them.

Although Idris was apparently popular, this may have contributed to the coup that would bring Gaddafi to power just a few years later.

At the British Embassy in the city we collected letters and had a bath. Three letters from Lady H contained cuttings about changes in the Conservative shadow cabinet. A letter from Ed had news of the end of his fagging days at Eton. One from Emma described her visit to Venice and her early impressions of the Principessa Colonna. The Principessa ran a very expensive finishing school in Florence. Cindy Fletcher, who later lived with us, was there too – she married Houston Shaw Stewart who became a great friend. Also staying at this establishment were two of Hughie and Elizabeth Northumberland's daughters who had been at Cranborne Chase with Emma and Cindy. The girls were taken to almost every art gallery and church in the city and learnt quite good Italian.

We found my father's grave in the war cemetery outside the Tunisian city of Sfax. I was very disappointed by the location of the cemetery. It was a most unpeaceful place, with a cement works behind it. I always thought that if Richard could be made head of the Commonwealth War Graves Commission I would move Flash's grave to somewhere nicer. But when Kenneth Rose asked the Duke of Kent, a great friend of his, he said the head of the Commission always had to be a general – so that was the end of that idea.

The Roman amphitheatre at El Djem, north of Sfax, was the next wonder, astonishing us by its huge size and survival. With just a few houses nearby, its isolation makes it even more impressive. Apparently it had survived almost intact until the seventeenth century, when some of its stones were carried off to build the Great Mosque at Kairouan, our next stop. Apart from the amphitheatre there was a recently discovered Roman villa with magnificent floor mosaics.

In Kairouan a youth in his late teens attached himself to us and gave us a guided tour of the old city, which we would have happily dispensed with though he did it with some charm. As we got back into our motor-caravan he played a little trick that was so neat it compelled admiration. The back wheel of his bicycle had suddenly gone flat. We had some money ready but waited to see what would happen. As Richard engaged the gear to drive away, he appealed to me: 'It is not for me, but it will be difficult without money to repair the wheel.' It was well done. We left him with admiration, if not affection, in our hearts. Whether if we had bought a carpet and earned him his commission, he would have bothered to remove the valve from the tyre, we will never know.

Carthage was now a suburb of Tunis and although it has some impressive remains, not least the Baths with their perfect symmetry and position by the sea, we found it much less exciting than other places. This was probably because there were a lot of tourists there and even camping on the beach we weren't entirely alone.

Before we could drive onto the boat to take us to Marseilles we had trouble with the caravan's insurance. The situation was looking bad. In desperation I said: 'But Monsieur is a Member of Parliament. He would never do what was wrong.' This appeared to do the trick, perhaps helped by the fact that when they asked why my passport said The Hon., I replied, 'Because my father-in-law is a lord'. The man got up from his desk and said, '*Enchanté, Madame*'.

On our way back through France we had a superb and long-awaited dinner and night at our favourite hotel, La Baumanière, where we slept in the room the Queen had occupied and were brought breakfast in bed by a footman in striped trousers and black coat and waistcoat. We had time to visit Les Baux once again, still in those days desirably empty. Looking at photographs of it all now, I often wonder how Richard managed to climb and walk everywhere there as he did. Back home in early November, this memorable expedition came to an end. But we were always determined to go again and see the rest of Tunisia, Algeria and Morocco.

CHAPTER 13

Wild Turkey

When Ted Heath replaced Alec as Leader of the Opposition in July 1965 he asked Richard to interest himself in developing countries, under Alec, who had become Shadow Foreign Secretary. We realised that we were not likely to be back in Government for some time and we began to think about another ambitious trip abroad for the following year.

Meanwhile Richard kept himself busy supporting or opposing Private Members' Bills. The Labour MP Leo Abse introduced a Bill to make divorce easier, basing it not on the well-known offences of adultery, desertion and so on, but on the irretrievable breakdown of the marriage. Richard was against this change because he believed that nobody should be divorced against their will. I remember that Nick Ridley, who wanted his wife Clayre to divorce him, got very angry with Richard for his opposition to the Bill. He came around one night and interrupted us in the middle of a dinner party to try to persuade Richard to change his mind. In fact rather later Richard did change his mind. He came to believe that the sooner a marriage with a completely hostile and disinterested partner came to an end, the better.

On the other hand he supported the Private Members' Bill introduced by Humphrey Berkeley to decriminalise homosexual acts in private between consenting male adults over a certain age. He hoped it would end the vicious blackmail which led to the downfall of prominent people. He was the only senior Conservative to vote in favour of this change. The Home Secretary Roy Jenkins gave the

Bill his support and a modified version of it later passed into law. This was a necessary reform, but the triumphant and malicious 'outing' of public figures which followed in later years did sometimes make Richard question his original enthusiasm for this change in the law. He maintained his opposition to the abolition of the death penalty.

Our old friend Mothy (Timothy) Tufnell certainly made little attempt to hide his sexual preferences. In St-Tropez he missed few opportunities to extol the charms of pretty boys and he was not averse to stroking a waiter or two and pinching their ears. Richard and I both went a long way back with Mothy. His mother had been a friend of my parents, and Richard and he had been friends since their first half at Eton.

Mothy's father had never worked and had spent his days in White's, so Mrs Tufnell, needing to earn some money, had started an estate agency, which in those days was not something that women did. (It was successful and Mothy worked there after the war.) In the war Mothy was a Grenadier and was awarded an MC.

Towards the end of the war he got married but it only lasted three years. In those days, as it was illegal, few people knew who was queer and who was not. Myrtie had never realised about either Mothy or Myles. But one day she had dined with Mothy and on going to the loo she saw his bed made up with pink satin sheets and turned down on both sides, so she then told Richard he would never get on in the Government unless he stopped seeing Mothy. We took no notice. He was a great friend and in any case we both had a number of male friends who were homosexual.

In late spring 1966 we flew out to Germany for the funeral of Brigid's husband, Fritzi (Prince Frederick of Prussia). When, just after the war, Brigid had told her mother that she was going to marry the Kaiser's grandson, Gwenny Iveagh went to bed for a week. It's too awful, she said, you can't. But the marriage proceeded and they had five children.

Fritzi was nice and we loved him, but he was very good-looking and he did have a roving eye. When Brigid complained about the girls he'd pick up at parties, he said Get yourself a lover, which is exactly what she did, and she then left him on the day that her mother was buried, so they hardly spoke to each other in the front pew of the church. Miserable without her, Fritzi went off to Germany and a few weeks later he was discovered to have drowned in the Rhine.

At his funeral in Hohenzollern, Fritzi's family, as you can imagine, were not exactly pleased with Brigid. We were presented to the German Royal Family, who was incredibly snooty, and we curtseyed or bowed. Richard and I felt very guilty. I had sat next to Fritzi at the lunch at Aunt Gwenny's funeral and he said he'd love to see us, he had a lot of things he wanted to talk about. But we did nothing about this before he went off to Germany, where he had dined with his sister-in-law, left the table and did not return.

Among the Opposition team in Parliament, Margaret Thatcher had been given responsibility for monitoring affairs in the coal industry. In October 1966 there was a tragic collapse of a coal-spoil tip down a hill and onto a school in the village of Aberfan in Wales, with the loss of many lives. Some fingers were pointed at Alf Robens, the Chairman of the Coal Board, whom Richard had appointed just a few years earlier because he believed it was appropriate for the miners to have a Socialist chairman of their board. Richard declared in the debate in the House of Commons that the Aberfan disaster was not the fault of Robens. Margaret was furious. Right or wrong, she believed that Richard should have made political capital out of the incident and used it to attack the Labour Government. She felt that Richard was being insufficiently 'political'. She was right about that.

Lord Halifax owned mines in the West Riding and Richard always made friends with the miners there when he was Minister of

Power. When his nephew Peter Irwin stood for the Dearne Valley constituency Richard canvassed with him, and the miners would always shake hands with him, if not with Peter. One evening a rather grand girlfriend of Peter's was canvassing and a miner opened the door in his vest. 'Oh, I'm so sorry!', she exclaimed, 'I see you're dressing for dinner.'

★   ★   ★

In August we had set off once again in the motor-caravan to drive across Europe, this time to Greece and then to make a wide sweep through Turkey, a country much less visited by Western Europeans fifty years ago and where, for example, driving insurance cover was virtually unobtainable. Emma and Ed were to come with us as far as Izmir before returning home.

To help us in Yugoslavia, in case that were necessary, Fitzroy Maclean had got us a letter from his friend, the Yugoslav Ambassador in London. It was very official-looking, with an impressive eagle embossed at the top of the letter. We made good progress through Yugoslavia before camping one night beyond Skopje. In the darkness, bedside the Vada river, we dined peacefully and Richard enjoyed a long talk over a bottle of Slivovitz with a young man. They got on so well that Richard decided to show our official letter to him. It had a disastrous effect. The young man thought (rightly) it was official and connected it with his Government. He spoke no further word before vanishing into the night.

Years later we planned to go to Libya with Fitzroy and Veronica, but the latter absolutely refused. She said wild camping would be dangerous under Gaddafi, Fitzroy was lame and Richard had no legs. We couldn't carry them and she didn't want to be imprisoned. I'm sure she was right, but it was a pity. It would have been special fun to have done it with Fitzroy.

In Thessalonica a little incident took place which restored our faith in human nature. Emma and Ed had gone into a small ironmonger's shop to buy a screwdriver. They failed to get one and they also left behind a purse with most of our remaining money – which we only discovered many miles later when we came to pay for some petrol. We drove all the way back to Thessalonica on the very slender chance of finding the purse. When we got to the shop, the owner rushed out to present us with it. Whenever my faith in human nature runs low, I remember the ironmonger of Thessalonica.

We pushed on to Turkey and down to Gallipoli, having obtained special permission from the Commonwealth War Graves Commission to camp on that hallowed ground. We spent several days there at the beginning of September. Richard's diary describes our first night on the peninsula:

> Opposite our platform under the trees is the island of Imros, from which the Gallipoli landings were mounted. More distant, and to the right of Imros, is the taller, more shapely island of Samothrace. The huge sun was just setting between them when we arrived. Ed prepared an encampment on the beach for himself and Emma and lowered his belongings with the aid of a rope. Emma prepared an excellent meal which we ate with the aid of a torch hung in the tree above us, until the nearly full moon rose and made artificial light unnecessary. A hunter came up the road with his gun and dog, and a little caravan of four primitive bullock-carts went down just before dark. Otherwise we saw no one. The children bathed before bed on the beach. D and I slept in great comfort on the top of our little cliff.

In the morning a creepy man came and stroked Ed before giving us a big fish. Thinking to keep it cool to eat in the evening, we put it in a bucket of sea water. But this had just the opposite effect. It had gone bad and made us all quite ill. Something to remember not to do.

At Eçeabat we made a closer inspection of the swift-flowing water of the Dardanelles. Observing the ferry-boats sliding sideways in the strong current, the children abandoned their ambitions to swim across to Asia!

Arriving by ferry on the Asian side we set off on the short journey to Troy. We didn't spend long there. The hawking of souvenirs was intense and the nine superimposed cities on this famous site are an archaeological jumble, at least for the amateur. We were soon on our way again. A couple of days later we were at Izmir. We collected letters from our Consulate and put Emma and Ed on the plane to Athens. That morning Richard had found a scorpion in his sleeping bag – against my wishes he let it live because he decided that it had left an obvious victim entirely unharmed.

At the ancient Roman theatre of Aspendos we ran into Freya Stark – dressed more for a garden party than a dusty journey – with Richard's cousin, Mark Lennox-Boyd, and Liz Bridgeman. Freya Stark's great charm was her complete naturalness and her assumption that everyone shared her knowledge and passion for out-of-the-way places. We swam with them in the old harbour at Side. The harbour was silted up and very shallow, but we all swam through a gap in the mole and the open sea was blissful. After lunch they took us to see their rooms in a small house with a well by the door, down a dusty street. In Freya's bedroom her table was covered with silver-backed hairbrushes and a silver-gilt dressing case that wouldn't have disgraced Queen Victoria.

Still driving east we took a very rough road to Uzancaburc with its imposing Roman ruins. But the chief charm was the friendliness of the people. After posing with them for photographs they took us to a little café where a score of men were busy with some game. Portraits of Ataturk and others gazed down from the walls. As Richard's diary records: 'Soon a few of the bolder spirits began asking questions: what was my job? My dictionary could not manage "Member of Parliament" nor "Politician", but it could do

"Statesman", so I settled for that. Everyone looked either impressed or aghast. I could not decide which.'

After reaching Tarsus, on the coast, too late in the afternoon to allow a search for signs of St Paul, we turned north for the Cicilian Gates, the pass through the Taurus Mountains. The next day we found ourselves driving among the strange volcanic cones which the Early Christians had used as dwellings or places of worship. We inspected a number of them, including the so-called Dark Church with its amazing paintings on the walls and roof.

We were now running out of time to get back to Istanbul by the end of September. The long drive back there via Ankara, which we skirted around, was a nightmare. Driving at night we had to swerve to avoid a jet-black donkey wandering by itself in the middle of the road. The corpses of dead animals were a common hazard. The road was full of large lorries belching black smoke and buses which drove straight at you. Derelict buses, lorries and cars were a frequent sight at the foot of gorges.

We recovered our equilibrium in Istanbul, where Richard's BP contacts made it easy for us to see some of the glories of that city, including the Topkapi Palace. Our route back home then took us via Bulgaria, where we were compelled to stay in an official camping site with the gates firmly locked for the night – I was scared and wished we hadn't come to a Communist country – and Yugoslavia. In Sarajevo we survived a problem with the caravan's brakes. The foot brake failed completely at the top of the mountain and we got down using the hand brake around every corner. We had a strong drink of relief at the bottom, looked at the place where the Archduke had been murdered and got the brakes mended. We were soon crossing northern Italy towards France.

Once in France we headed for a rendez-vous with Emma near Blois. Emma was spending a few months in the house of Madame de Sellier du Pin, learning French and seeing the chateaux along with a couple of other English girls. Emma's French had certainly improved but she was finding Madame's house rather creepy and life there rather dull. Weekends were enlivened by the visits of Madame's 23-year-old nephew Geoffroi. There was, however, a tragic sequel to Emma's friendship with him.

In the letters that Emma used to write to him after she was back in England she would begin 'Darling Geoffroi' without thinking about it. Then just after she had got engaged, Geoffroi came to stay with us for a weekend. As Emma took him to the train, she told him she was engaged to Nicholas Brooksbank. About a week later she came into our bedroom in floods of tears with a bundle of Geoffroi's letters that Geoffroi's mother had posted back, telling her that Geoffroi had killed himself. Emma's letters weren't love letters, they were just chatty, but perhaps the French read something different into 'Darling' and certainly Geoffroi had seen them quite differently.

When we got back from Turkey, for some reason we gave Ed our camera films to get developed. He used to send his off to an old-fashioned company by Trafalgar Square, for which he had worked for one summer holidays, and they would develop them and post them back. Ed was a bit careless with the packaging on this occasion, and the envelope was returned by the developer with a great hole in it. No films had apparently arrived. Knowing how much we would mind, Ed went into overdrive and wrote to the Postmaster General. To his, and our, utter amazement, the Postmaster General, then the Labour minister Ted Short, wrote back, apologising for the failure of the postal service. And the letter was actually signed by Short – Ed licked the signature and it ran!

A couple of weeks later, not only did the photographs arrive at Eton developed, and at no charge, but they were also brought by a Post Office official, together with a supply of sturdy envelopes for Ed to use in future. The Post Office man stressed that, should such an unfortunate event occur again, Ed should fill in a form at the Post Office. Ed's somewhat Left-leaning housemaster got wind of these happenings and called Ed in, telling him he must always go through the proper channels, as his grandfather would have told him. No, Ed replied, his grandfather had told him you should always go to the top. The housemaster remarked, 'Wood, you arrogant bastard!' We were delighted to have our photographs.

★   ★   ★

Our first trip the following year, a week in May for Richard and me in Bermuda, all expenses paid, sounded attractive. But the reality was not. It turned out to be a very dull Anglo-American conference, funded by an American organisation and preceded by a couple of days in Washington. Richard and others did at least have an hour with LBJ in the Oval Office at the White House, and I was introduced to Bobby Kennedy. At the conference in Bermuda Teddy Kennedy was one of the American contingent and was treated like royalty wherever he went. Richard was tempted to send himself a telegram ordering his immediate return and might have done so had the conference been longer.

In the summer Emma took up the position of Social Secretary at the British Embassy in Athens, where the Ambassador, Michael Stewart, and his wife Damaris were known to Catherine Peake. So she was unable to join Richard, Ed and me when in August we set out, once again in the motor-caravan, to France and Italy. Our goal was the far south of Italy and Sicily. On our way south we camped for several days in the French Alps before reaching the south of France, where we were struck by the pace of building development and the number of cars and also the litter thrown everywhere, which Richard and Ed insisted on collecting into bags, even after midnight, before we could camp. From Nice Ed flew home, and Richard and I set off for Italy.

We headed for Apulia, the 'heel' of Italy, and searched for peaceful places to swim in the sea. At the town of Vieste we found the seaside paradise we were looking for. The great castles and cathedrals built by the Normans were everywhere, even though the long siesta that seemed to prevail in this part of Italy – from noon until 5 p.m. – often made sight-seeing difficult because we needed to find somewhere to camp that was absolutely level, for the caravan's gas-powered fridge to work, while it was still daylight. In Alberobello we were delighted by the *trulli* – the dry-stone huts or little houses with a conical roof.

We reached Sicily by ferry as darkness fell. As soon as we had found a place to camp for the night, Richard strode across the sand for a swim. It was a disaster. He came back covered in black oil which he then thoroughly rubbed off onto our only big bath towel, which we had no means of washing.

Sicily has many splendours. Of the ancient theatre at Taormina Richard wrote in his diary:

> We climbed to the theatre just before the sun set. Some are more perfect; none has a setting nearly as beautiful. Through the arches behind the stage are cypresses with the sea behind and the little port of Giardini where Garibaldi embarked for Calabria. Over all broods Etna. In spite of a constant plume of smoke the great conical mountain seemed peaceful enough, and Taormina, with its immense backing of rock, looks ready to withstand any act of God or man.

Myrtie and Flash had been to the temple at Segesta in the north-west of the island in the 1930s. I told her we were planning to go and asked her about it. But she never could bear to recall the things that she and Flash had done together, always saying, 'I can't remember.' In fact it was magnificent. No one was around and we spent most of a day there. Richard's diary again:

> Garibaldi's soldiers, after the battle at Calatafimi, had climbed to

the theatre and temple at Segesta. Diana and I followed in their footsteps. Mainly because of the situation of both theatre and temple, we thought them the noblest of all the Greek remains on the island. The theatre was built a century before the Parthenon and is infinitely more peaceful.

The mosaics at the town of Piazza Armerina were another highlight, among several. At Mass in Syracuse the congregation was minute. We found far more life outside the churches on a Sunday morning than within. All in all, we had seen marvellous things and we were impressed by the intense pride that Sicilians take in their island, but somehow we did not find ourselves longing to go back there. It seemed a sad place, and it was hard to resist a sense of relief when we returned to the mainland.

CHAPTER 14

'Monsieur Will Beat Me as It's All My Fault'

The North African desert still exerted an irresistible pull on both Richard and me, and we had always planned to travel the full length of it from Egypt to Morocco. Having reached Tunisia from Egypt a few years before, we decided in 1968 to start from the other end, from Morocco, and travel across Algeria to Tunisia.

Meanwhile earlier in the year, in May, Richard had been asked to attend the annual Anglo-German conference at Königswinter, on the Rhine near Bonn. Long-winded discussion-group conferences were not to Richard's taste at all and this one only served to reinforce the lesson he had taken away from the Bermuda conference of the previous year: to avoid such gatherings whenever possible. Because we enjoyed doing things together, I asked if I might go and I was told that, if he *really* needed me to look after him, of course I could. I was furious and refused instantly.

Taking Ed with us, we set off in the motor-caravan in mid-August for Morocco via France and Spain. We camped every night, with occasional exceptions. One of those was the night we spent at Château Latour, thanks to the generosity of the Cowdrays who then owned this world-famous wine estate. In fact, John never drank wine; he had bought it as an investment. Elizabeth, with the help of John Fowler, had transformed the décor of the chateau and we were given a sumptuous dinner and comfortable rooms.

The next day we were taken around the vineyard by Monsieur Martin, a legendary figure in the Bordeaux wine trade. We were warned that he spoke no English, but I was glad to find that my

French was equal to understanding the various secrets he told us about the making and storing of this wonderful wine. When tasting the wine we of course had to spit it out, which I thought a terrible waste. We were also shown the new houses on the estate that John, with characteristic thoughtfulness, had built for his workers.

Another exception to camping was the night spent in Luis Bolin's flat in Madrid. Bolin had married a great American friend of ours and the Halifaxes, Cecilia Parker, after her banker husband died. Luis was the man responsible for bringing Franco back to Spain in 1936. When caravanning we always took a set of smart clothes, which was useful for occasions like this. The Bolins thought it a great joke with Richard and Ed in blue suits and collars and ties, and me in a smart white dress. It was, of course, but we always did it. We spent two wonderful hours at the Prado but none of us greatly liked Madrid. In Granada, the caravan chugged up the steep hill to the Alhambra. The Christian architecture in this city was no match for the exquisite decoration of the Moors. The Spanish seemed to us if not actively unfriendly certainly unwelcoming, and we felt some relief at crossing the Strait of Gibraltar and arriving at Ceuta.

Our feelings of relief were seriously upset on our first morning in Morocco by the discovery of the theft of Ed's new camera and telephoto lens from under his camp bed in the middle of the night. Ed's enthusiasm for photography, which was then at its height, went back some way. The Revd Philip Hopkinson lived on Dartmoor and used to hunt there with Richard's brother Peter, who was MFH. Philip couldn't drive and kept a horse to ride to his church services and visit parishioners. When Ed was born, Philip sent Richard £100 towards his first pony. When Ed was older, he got Philip's permission to spend the money on a camera instead. Philip became a great friend.

In Morocco we were dogged by youthful observers, in the evening and again in the morning, though they usually kept their distance. After visiting Rabat, Meknes and Fez we were soon into Algeria. The country had only become independent from France a few years before, in 1962, but the French influence seemed to have faded more quickly than in neighbouring Morocco. The signposts were still in French but nearer the towns the names had been changed to Arabic.

In Oran we searched unsuccessfully for a good map of the country. One shopkeeper told Richard, with some satisfaction, that there were no longer any maps of Algeria: 'All that has gone.' It seemed a strange way to measure progress. In Algiers we collected a mass of letters from the Embassy, and the Consul produced an old Michelin map of Algeria which we promised to return to him when we reached Tunis. He confirmed that no other map was likely to be available. This one was marked, like a soldier's map, with the scenes of skirmishes or of French casualties noted with distinctive signs. He said if we were caught with it in our possession we could be in trouble.

In Algiers we put Ed on a flight home and set off towards Tunisia. A strong *khamsin* – the hot dry wind from the south – began to blow, full of sand, and stayed with us for several days as we tried to inspect various Roman ruins. Our thermometer registered temperatures of over 100. We felt as if every last bit of energy had been drained out of us. I had always heard about these winds from Myrtie and Flash as well as those who had fought in the desert and from Minta MacMichael (later Aldington), but had never believed what they told me. It did have one great advantage in that it drove everyone away, so we were totally alone. The largest and most impressive Roman ruins were at Timgad in the Aurès Mountains. Long paved streets stretched out towards stubble fields in every direction. But it was a shame to have seen them with the sun struggling behind a haze of dust.

As we drove through the hills near the border with Tunisia we looked for a place to camp, but all the level ground was inhabited by goats. So we decided to cross the frontier and spend the night in Tunisia. This was not so easy. We tried to make our accounts conform with the financial declaration we had made when we entered the country. But the Algerian customs official decided otherwise. I was taken into a filthy back room with bars on the windows and dirty sheets on a bed. Richard recorded the next developments in his diary:

> Again and again it was impressed on us that we had made a false declaration. 'Were we aware of the very heavy penalties?' Diana wisely judged that this argument was getting us nowhere. She quickly decided on new tactics. She produced a performance which put all her triumphs on Christmas nights at Garrowby into the shade. I tactfully withdrew from the customs hut, but I heard a snivelling from outside. I peeped in. Diana was in tears. The heart of stone was at last touched. I heard her say: 'Monsieur will beat me as it is all my fault.' Then I heard: 'Ne pleurez pas, Madame,' after which she came out smirking, with all won except for the demand to inspect the cupboards in the caravan. This was a small price to pay and soon over. As soon as he left us in peace I congratulated her on her performance.

We then had to drive two or three miles down a narrow track hemmed in by barbed wire on both sides, which after what had happened was rather scary. But we got out safely at the other end.

On our way to Tunis we saw more Roman ruins, notably at Dougga, which has one of the finest positions in the whole of North Africa. In Tunis we collected letters from John Creighton, Shell's manager in Tunisia, before visiting the Bardo Museum. This was a museum full of magnificent treasures. Perhaps the most exciting was a large collection recovered from the sea off the Tunisian coast. They were being carried to Italy in a Greek ship which sank in a storm in 81 BC and had first been noticed by sponge-divers in 1907, who reported seeing large objects on the seabed. Sadly the Museum was the site of a horrific attack by three Tunisian terrorists in March 2015 in which twenty-one people were killed.

For the next ten days we travelled about, down the coast from Tunis and inland, to some of our old haunts. We were regularly bothered by inquisitive onlookers and visitors, who would either follow us on foot or hover about the caravan. At times we started to feel that we were never going to be left alone for very long. We began to long for twenty-four hours when we saw no one at all. Some would politely withdraw when asked to do so; others were harder to move. A number wanted to be helpful. One man simply wanted us to admire a very ugly squid he had recently caught, which he laid on the table that Richard had just finished cleaning.

We visited the war cemetery at Enfidaville, where Donny Player is buried. Donny was Flash's great friend and had taken over command of the Sherwood Rangers after Flash was promoted to a full colonel. He had bad asthma and should not have fought but had insisted on doing so. Myles was with him when he had been hit by a shell and had tried to revive him but couldn't – which sent Myrtie back to bed for several days. Biddy, the cook, said that if any more of her friends were killed she thought she'd have no interest in living.

The mosaics at Sousse, which had been reorganised since our 1965 visit, seemed finer even than we remembered. The vast amphitheatre at El Djem struck us once again as one of the great marvels of North Africa. And we revisited the apparently unexciting island of Djerba, just off the coast, which held a mysterious charm for us both. Anne Balfour Fraser, Saharan explorer and my great friend, reported just the same feeling about it.

At the Sfax war cemetery, when Richard went to visit the Indian graves, the cemetery-keeper turned to me and referred to Richard as my father – his beard made him look years older. When I politely explained who my father was and that he was actually buried in the cemetery, the man answered immediately, with a delightful smile: 'Yes, I know him.'

We left Africa at the beginning of October, taking a boat from Tunis to Palermo. Richard had grown a beard in order to avoid shaving and therefore save scarce water. I persuaded him on the boat to shave it off, which he did. The fierce cabin steward whom we referred to as a 'wardress' came in with our breakfast, took one look at Richard and said she would not serve me with a 'new man' in my bed.

Lady Halifax was holidaying at Assisi, with Polly Percy and Molly Baring – referred to by her as Polly, Molly and Dolly. We collected her and took her with us to Milan, after seeing the St Francis things at Assisi for the second time. Richard wanted to pay for our meals, but Lady H disagreed and divided up every last thing meticulously, driving us potty. (Remembering this, I always divide bills equally no matter who had what.) We dropped her at the airport.

At the French border with Italy the man inspecting Richard's passport remarked tersely, 'Better without the beard', before looking at me and adding, 'Better for you too.' On our last evening in France we had a memorable meal at Arras's best restaurant, dressed in our best clothes, as we had done for the Bolins, before camping in the dunes near Calais. When Lord Halifax had returned from France in untidy trousers and an old jacket I ticked him off and said he ought to dress properly to return to London. To my surprise, he obeyed this the next time he came back to England.

★   ★   ★

This desert journey had hardly ended before we began planning to go there again. This time we wanted to go inland, into the deep desert, down to Chad.

But that would have to wait until later in 1969. Before that we used the Whitsun parliamentary recess to take Lady H and

Catherine Peake with us to the Dordogne. We had exchanged our Commer motor-caravan for a more powerful Ford one of the same size. It could seat at least four comfortably, but while Richard and I camped each night as usual, we searched daily for hotel rooms for my mother-in-law and Catherine.

It rained incessantly. The highpoint for Richard and me was a visit to the Gouffre de Padirac, a vast cavern with an underground river system and flat-bottomed boats to get you around. Part of the cave looked more like the vaulted roof of a vast cathedral. Lady H was distinctly cool when we returned. When we had mentioned it the day before she said in no way could Richard go there, which was why we went before we collected them. For most of the rest of the day she would not speak to us – and me in particular.

The plan for late summer was for an expedition deep into the Libyan desert. Richard's godson John Hills, the son of his Eton housemaster, was commanding a squadron based at El Adem near Tobruk. We planned to meet them there with Ed – and originally with Emma, but she told us she had accepted an invitation to stay with Freya Stark – and drive south with John and his soldiers to the oasis at Kufra in south-eastern Libya and then on into Chad if we could. We would be travelling in an Army vehicle and John warned us that we would be lucky if in some places we covered five or six miles a day in deep sand. Ed was at that time planning a short service commission in the Army and the junior Labour minister at the War Office, surprisingly, was willing to get him out to Tripoli or Benghazi on a military plane.

Richard and I left England in mid-August and made our way through France and Italy to Sicily. There we camped one night, almost certainly unlawfully, at Segesta. An Italian family were picking little white snails off the thistles at the top of the theatre, but when they left we had this spectacular place entirely to ourselves. As darkness came we could see in the middle distance the lights of

Calatafimi, the hill where Garibaldi had won his famous victory over the Bourbons in 1860.

We sailed from Palermo. When we reached Tunis we received news of the coup which replaced King Idris with Colonel Gaddafi. We called on the Ambassador, who was very old-fashioned and most surprisingly wearing spats. For a few days we still expected to get into Libya, but then the borders were shut, and there was no aeroplane for Ed. Revising our plans, we sent a telegram to Ed asking him to meet us in France instead of North Africa. We decided to spend another week in Tunisia and see more of the country before putting the motor-caravan on the boat to Marseille. We then headed south from Tunis.

Recent heavy rain meant that the motor-caravan was often in danger of sliding off the road. The rescue of travellers like us had rapidly become a national occupation. Teams of boys waited at every damp and flooded wadi crossing. My patience was more tried by the little girls. In desperation I said in French to the leader of one gang of girls, 'If you don't improve your manners, you'll never get married.' This produced gales of laughter, probably because the tiresome little teenager had long since been betrothed. On one occasion we needed help from the Travaux Publiques to pull our heavy vehicle out of the soft sand.

Before long we found ourselves on the edge of the Chott el Djerid, a large salt lake in southern Tunisia. It is the largest salt pan in the Sahara Desert and was later used as a location for the *Star Wars* films. In winter there is enough water to make it impassable. In summer it is a vast expanse of sandy earth covered by a thick crust of salt. The danger, for a car, is that the salt crust is not always firm. We started across it with some trepidation. There was a notice saying that it was impassable. The silence was absolute and the mirages were spectacular. Sometimes we thought we could see impossibly tall camels in the distance. We managed several miles before turning back, determined one day to cross it.

We had no money for the boat to get us and the caravan back to Europe, but the Ambassador very trustingly lent us the fare. The caravan was so high that the only way we could get it into the boat was by letting all the air out of the tyres and somehow pushing it on. Back in France after a very rough crossing we collected Ed from Nimes airport and had a celebratory dinner at La Baumanière. The legendary Raymond Thulier, creator of this Michelin-acclaimed restaurant, made his rounds as we dined. With perfect manners, he pretended to recognise Richard and me and said he was 'enchanted' to meet Ed. Instead of thinking a motor-caravan infra dig, he insisted on coming out to see it and admire it. A thunderstorm broke as we left.

At the Pont du Gard Ed and I climbed into the aqueduct itself while Richard waited phlegmatically below. In the steps of our journey earlier in the year we crossed the Lot and the Dordogne and again descended into the Gouffre de Padirac, safe from the disapproving eyes of my mother-in-law.

The remaining days of this trip were spent in Brittany and Normandy. Richard somehow got to the top of Mont Saint-Michel with some pulling, pushing and shoving from Ed and me. Our last two nights in France were spent on the vast beach at Omaha, warm but pleasantly empty in early October. This beach with its high cliffs had seen the heaviest Allied casualties of all the landings on D-Day. Richard reflected on this in his diary:

As the sun sank behind the great American cemetery above us, we all had sombre thoughts about the vast loss of life on this very beach. I tried to be cheerful by suggesting that the thousands of Americans had died in order that we could do just this; but I am not sure that this did not make us even more miserable. The contrast between the present tranquillity and the horror of past days compares with what one felt at Gallipoli three years ago. At the very least it is days like this which give meaning to all the things one says, with no great sincerity, on Remembrance Day and other occasions, about sacrifice.

Back in London a recent letter from John Hills told us that the Libyan frontier was still closed and his squadron still confined to its narrow camp area.

CHAPTER 15

Journeying through East Africa

Ed, having left Eton, planned an epic drive to Australia by Land Rover with two friends: David Ker, the grandson of James Howard who gave me away, and Tim Collins. They duly set off in a snow-storm just after Christmas 1969 from 14 Eaton Place, accompanied to Dover by Emma and David's sister, Caroline.

Regular letters arrived from parts of Europe, Afghanistan, India and Australia, carefully omitting any causes for anxiety. These were only divulged when he returned almost a year later, totally unexpectedly and unannounced as he was determined to be at Emma's marriage in Westminster Abbey to Nicholas Brooksbank, the son of our old friends and neighbours, Billy and Ann Brooksbank. Ann's father, Tom Clitheroe, had been a great friend of my step-grandfather, Alby Cator. Richard had just overlapped by one half at Eton with Billy, who was five years older. We saw them a great deal in Yorkshire and they used to come to Garrowby almost every Christmas, where Billy and I – later with Nicholas, and Ian Watson separately – laid on very elaborate charades.

Early in 1970 – instead of a dance, which she didn't want – we planned a twenty-first-birthday journey for Emma to join us, along with her great friend Cindy Fletcher, on a trip to Africa, starting in Kenya, going on to Ethiopia and ending in Egypt, from where Richard and I would continue to Libya and Tunisia.

We began with a busy week in Kenya before Emma and Cindy arrived. Richard's status as a Shadow Minister was a blessing, except for endless social entertainment and, for me, the terror of flying.

We benefitted greatly from High Commission accommodation and help with travel, and saw some fascinating things we otherwise would not have done. But there were lots of hands to shake, lengthy meals to put up with, and so on. An early expedition, for example, was to the western wall of the Rift Valley to see tea production. Both the big tea producers, James Finlay and Brooke Bond, wanted us to see their estates. We also visited their tea factories and training centres and even the Brooke Bond hospital!

The next day we were at Lake Nakura to see, alongside the massed ranks of flamingos, the pelicans, sacred ibis, Egyptian geese, spoonbills, cormorants and herons. Brooding over them all, standing five foot high, were the sinister Marabou Storks.

The surprising highlight of the week was a visit to the Starehe Boys' School in Nairobi, with its energetic headmaster Geoffrey Griffin and its enthusiastic boys, who showed us around with a perfect mixture of politeness and self-confidence. This very impressive part-boarding school was started in the late 1950s to cope with the overflow onto the streets of poor and destitute Mau Mau orphans. At the school we were amused to see a notice, 'Special visitors today – please avoid careless talk.'

We met Emma and Cindy at Nairobi airport and we all flew on to Tanzania, where we made for the Ngurdoto Crater, a depression about a mile wide in the Arusha National Park. Richard described that afternoon in his diary:

> We climbed a grassy slope at a vantage point called the Rock, from where there is a bird's eye view of the whole crater. It is more or less circular, with a diameter of something over a mile. The eastern half looks marshy, with tall reedy undergrowth and a few small trees. Much of the other half is thick jungle; but between the two, and among the big trees, is a very considerable area of short grass which from our great height almost looked as if it were mown. It was

crowded with animals, chiefly buffalo and warthog, but I saw five rhino and a baby; a few giraffe; bushbuck and baboons. We all dozed in the shade after our picnic... We looked down on the tall trees from a point above the Crater forest on the way to our final vantage-point, a place called Loitong on the western side of the crater. I find it hard to think one could ever see a more beautiful view. Below us lay the thick forest of the crater, with the green sward and the marsh beyond. Out of the marsh, almost unbelievably, suddenly appeared no less than fourteen elephants. Beyond the crater, the great mass of Kilimanjaro slowly cleared itself of cloud, and its flat peak was very plainly visible before we began our descent. Behind us was Mount Meru, 15,000 feet high but dwarfed by Kilimanjaro.

The next day we were at the much bigger Ngorongoro Crater and gazed down into Olduvai Gorge, made famous by the Leakeys. Easter Day at the Ngorongoro Old Lodge was incongruously celebrated with Christmas carols. A couple of days later Emma and Cindy took the bus to Nairobi – their 170-mile journey on a bus crowded with Masai costing just twelve shillings and sixpence – while Richard and I were driven 400 miles to Dar-es-Salaam.

Richard was taken to meet the Speaker of the National Assembly (his room had 'Spika' on the door) before the High Commissioner, Horace Phillips (for whom we later published Turkish books), accompanied us on a brief visit to Zanzibar, then under the dictatorial rule of Abeid Karume, who had violently deposed the last Sultan of Zanzibar just a few years earlier. A lunch had been arranged and, as I was there, they brought in women to make equal numbers. But they all sat together wearing niqabs and none of them communicated in any way. With the Union Jack flying on Horace Phillips's car, I was surprised by the locals' hasty dive for the ditch wherever we drove. Perhaps it was not easy to tell Phillips from Karume as the car sped by.

Soon we were flying on to Zambia, and the next day to Livingstone by the Zambesi. When we got to our hotel room Richard said rather crossly, 'I will *not* have air conditioning in here. Honestly, you can't come to a place like this and have air conditioning. The *din* of it!' 'Don't be silly,' I replied, 'that's the noise of the Victoria Falls!' I enjoyed that.

I enjoyed much less the tiny aeroplane, a four-seater, that flew us a couple of days later to a copper mine. We had to climb over a wing to get into the plane, and a black official maddened me by loving it all while I was simply terrified. But I got my own back when we descended two thousand feet in a cage down the mine. I absolutely loved it, and now this same man was petrified. Richard said I was being horrid, trying to score off him, but I said that he had scored off me first.

In Lusaka, Oliver Green-Wilkinson apologised for not having us to stay at Bishop's Lodge. He was apprehensive of Kaunda's anger if he entertained a once-and-future Conservative Minister. We both thought it very feeble of Oliver and very unlike him too. And Richard's reception by Kaunda a few days later suggested that Oliver needn't have worried. Kaunda gave a party for us where everyone was given a can of beer to drink from. Richard thanked Kaunda for the programme that his office had arranged for him and they had a long talk. On Rhodesia Richard was impressed with the moderation with which the Zambian president argued his case.

At the High Commission we much enjoyed the company of Laurie and Jean Pumphrey (Jean's father was Richard's godfather). We would see more of them later in Pakistan. I was delighted to find that Laurie enjoyed teasing as much as I did. Sadly we had news, through the Pumphreys, which put paid to our hopes of getting to Egypt by train and then a boat journey to Aswan. We flew back to Nairobi to collect Emma and Cindy and then we all flew on to Addis Ababa.

On Sunday in Addis Richard decided to attend a Coptic Christian service. He was solemnly led to a chair while the rest of the congregation had to crouch throughout the service, only sitting during the sermon. The next day we were shopping, and Cindy had bought an extremely smelly rug clearly made from uncured skins, when we met the cavalcade of the Emperor, Haile Selaisse, returning from a tour of the Ethiopian coast. We all got out of the embassy car and lay flat on the ground, Cindy wrapped in the rug, with our faces down, as no one was allowed to see the Emperor as he swept past.

★   ★   ★

In Cairo we met our Ambassador, Richard Beaumont, who seemed relieved that Richard was in the country as a tourist and had no wish for an interview with Nasser. In the magnificent Cairo Museum we saw some of the treasures of Tutankhamun's tomb, which we saw again later in the British Museum when we went there with Lady Evelyn Beauchamp, who had been the first person to enter the tomb when her father and Howard Carter had discovered it. Fears of trouble with Israel meant that we had the museum almost to ourselves. There were sandbags everywhere and protective tape on the windows and glass cabinets. The guides were sadly ignorant and unable to answer any questions.

In the evening a train took us up the Nile. Looking out of the train window, Richard thought of India:

> The flat valley in the early morning reminded me of the walks outside Delhi – little patches of barley being cut by sickle and winnowed in the wind; the buffaloes and the oxen; bright green patches of alfalfa; the houses of brown mud brick, with the bricks for more baking in the sun. The railway runs for miles beside a wide canal and a good tarmac road, with the Nile some way off to our right.

We had breakfast at Luxor and were soon at Aswan, where we stayed in the New Cataract Hotel, right by the Nile. Richard and I took a felucca to Kitchener's Island and revelled in the peace and the heat, as Richard recorded:

> Felucca travel is utterly peaceful. Usually there is just enough wind to drive the boat along at the gentlest pace. In the lea of one of the many islands one of the boys had to make use of the giant oars, but their regular splash subtracted nothing from the earlier unhurried tranquillity. I greatly admired the skilful handling of the boat through the narrow channel between the islands.

We visited the High Dam, which was still being built. Lake Nasser, behind it, stretched over 300 miles down into the Sudan. At that time it still had over a hundred feet to rise and was not expected to be full for seven years. Our next expedition was a five-hour journey in a hydrofoil to the great temple of Abu Simbel, perched high above the rising lake. When the train had taken us back to Luxor, we saw as much as stamina permitted of the vast and imposing temple complex at Karnack. (Here the guide told us that we should remember Queen Hatshepsut as 'Hat, cheap suit'.) The next day we crossed the Nile to visit the Valley of the Kings. The smallness of Tutankhamun's tomb confirmed the shortness of his life and it was hard to believe that it could contain all the treasures we had seen in the Cairo Museum.

The tempo of life in Luxor, with its horse-drawn carriages and few cars, was delightfully and therapeutically slow, and we left very reluctantly to catch the sleeper back to Cairo. There we stayed at the rebuilt Shepheard's Hotel (the original was burnt down in an anti-British riot in the early 1950s). A taxi took us out to the Pyramids at Giza. Emma and Cindy were brave enough to mount camels while Richard and I followed more sedately in a light cart.

It had been quite a holiday, but now it was time to part. Emma and

Cindy flew home, while Richard and I flew to Tripoli. Alcohol was completely forbidden in Gaddafi's Libya with the exception of foreign Embassies, so we bought surgical-spirit bottles which we emptied and filled with vodka. We then wrapped them carefully and put them in the bottom of Richard's tin legs. During the flight Richard went to the flight deck and, while he was there, my seat collapsed totally onto the floor. I thought he must have been messing with the controls! We were helped through Customs by Paul and Pat Gore-Booth's likeable son David, who had been serving in Zambia when we were staying with Laurie and Jean Pumphrey. The ambassador, Donald Maitland, no doubt living under great strain since Gaddafi's coup the previous year, briefed Richard on the situation.

We were lucky enough to be taken for a whole day to see Leptis Magna once again. There was a marked increase in cars since 1965 but the place itself was as superb and appeared virtually as deserted as ever. It was agony to have to leave it in the late afternoon for a cocktail party planned by the Maitlands, where the guests stayed for ever because the Embassy was the only place in Tripoli where alcohol was allowed. It was followed by a dinner-party for twenty-four.

Before we left, Richard was taken to meet various members of Colonel Gaddafi's Revolutionary Command Council, most of whom were startlingly young. David Gore-Booth, who had parted from his wife, drove us to Tunisia, along with a pretty girl whom he had successfully concealed from the disapproving Mailtands. We spent a night on our beloved island of Djerba, then went on to Tunis without David and his girlfriend. Floods had destroyed a number of roads, but we reached Tunis safely.

★   ★   ★

Ted Heath unexpectedly won the election in June 1970 and Richard accepted the job of Minister of Overseas Development. I was appalled. The prospect of all the flying that would be involved was horrific. Yet I knew that I ought, and wanted, to go with Richard on these trips if I could. In practice I did hate the flying but the places we went to were – mostly – fascinating.

Our first trip that summer was actually a holiday and it took us to a part of the world I'd never been to: the Baltic. We had been asked by our great friends Bob and Hilaré Ryder (a sister of Oliver Green-Wilkinson) to join them on their small yacht, then in the Baltic. Bob had won the VC for his part in the raid in 1942 which destroyed the German naval base at St Nazaire on the Brittany coast. After the war he was briefly an MP, but he hated it. He went on to a grand job in John Lewis, which he hated even more, and he then ended up buying and running small newsagents. He should never have refused promotion to admiral and should have stayed in the Navy after the war.

In August we drove our motor-caravan through northern Europe and met them on the Norwegian coast at Kristiansand. For ten days we sailed happily among the islands. I definitely prefer the desert to the sea, but I have to admit that at sea bystanders don't appear out of nowhere.

The holiday ended dramatically and very sadly. When we got back to Kristiansand and collected letters there was a telegram telling us that Oliver had been killed in a road accident in Zambia, so we dashed back to the boat to break the news to Hilaré. Our journey home through Holland took us past Kaiser's Wilhelm's final retreat at Doorn. We avoided a guided tour of the house but walking in the garden we inspected the graves of his dogs. The door of the little mausoleum where the Kaiser is buried was locked. Richard told the guide that his cousin was married to the Kaiser's grandson, hoping we would be allowed in, but to no avail.

Our next trip abroad was very different. In November 1970 a very powerful tropical cyclone struck the Ganges Delta of East Pakistan (which became Bangladesh the following year after a civil war), one of the worst natural disasters in this very disaster-prone part of the world. Clearly Richard had to visit, and be seen to visit, the stricken region. I went with him despite being in the middle of completing plans for Emma's wedding in Westminster Abbey a few days before Christmas.

Meanwhile messages arrived from Baba Metcalfe – not only Lord Curzon's daughter but a leading light of the Save the Children Fund – who was convinced that any good Richard could do in Pakistan must depend on the experienced help she could offer him while he was there. Baba rang me to say that she wanted to join us. Richard said I must say No. He never liked her – she had had an affair with both Lord H and Sim Feversham – and my parents had also disliked her. So there was no love lost between her and Richard. But she ignored this and somehow got herself out to stay at the front of the Governor's Palace in Dacca while we were at the back. We both had an Indian servant guarding our doors.

We flew first to Islamabad, the new capital, in mid November. We spent some time there because Richard's arrival in East Pakistan was delayed by several days to coincide with that of HMS *Intrepid*, sent from Singapore to help with relief work. At the High Commission in Islamabad, Cyril Pickard and his wife entertained a mixture of soldiers and politicians. One evening the seating plan had to be hurriedly altered when the protocol expert told Lady Pickard that soldiers were of much greater importance than politicians.

In East Pakistan we were taken to a camp where there were people who had been flooded out and had nowhere to go. They were mostly lying or sitting on black plastic bags, and I was taken around with oranges in a basket. I was asked to give an orange to each person and told 'they will then love you'. I found it acutely embarrassing.

From Dacca Richard and I were flown by helicopter out to HMS *Intrepid*, anchored with other British ships some miles off the coast. Baba rang on the house telephone to say she wanted to come too. But there was only room for three and Richard refused to leave his secretary behind. On the flight we could see below us the massive Ganges and, beside it, serpentine waterways twisting in every direction. The British were helping to move supplies to where they were needed. On the deck of the *Intrepid* the spotless white uniforms of the naval officers were almost incongruous beside the destruction and squalor we had seen. We might have spent the night on the ship but in those days women were not allowed to do so. After a few days in Dacca we flew back for a brief stay in Karachi before returning to England.

CHAPTER 16

I'm Afraid the Cook's Been Murdered

Richard's constituents had been very patient with our long absences during the summers of the late 1960s but some were not at all pleased to discover that his new job as Minister of Overseas Development would necessitate a lot of journeys abroad. They had always made it clear that they much preferred having a backbencher as an MP. Their mood was not improved when Richard's constituency agent at that time, Tony Butler, told the organisers of a coffee morning that 'Richard would try to look in' when he knew we were on the other side of the world that day, in Indonesia.

The first ministerial journey, to cyclone-devastated Pakistan, had been accepted. Less popular was the next one, in February and March 1971, beginning with a Commonwealth Education Conference in Australia, followed by visits to some South East Asian and Middle Eastern countries. Richard attended the conference in Canberra reluctantly, feeling himself to be an amateur among educational professionals. But we then escaped on an expedition of our own, to see for ourselves the wilds of northern Australia where Ed had worked the year before.

We flew up to Darwin in the far north and then hired a car to drive the 500 miles to Kununurra. Darwin was hot and damp but that indispensable item of Australian travel, an Esky – a water-cooler and ice-box – came with the car. We passed groups of brown ant-hills, looking like a forest of stumpy trees. On Ed's advice we gave the occasional but terrifying road-trains – a truck hauling three gigantic trailers – a wide berth.

I was driving because the car was not adapted for Richard to drive. It was so hot that my right arm got sunburnt even through my shirt, as the sun was on our right for the entire journey. Before long we found ourselves driving on a dirt road, where cars were very few and far between. We had lunch in the shade of a baobab tree, disturbed only by the flies, which we had been warned were a plague in Australia however remote the place. Neither Muscatol or cigar smoke deterred them.

Finally we reached the town of Kununurra, close to the Ord River Dam project, where Ed had been working the year before. The plan was to build a huge artificial lake to prevent seasonal flooding and irrigate large areas subject to drought. The scale of the operation was unbelievable. The volume of water was informally measured in 'sydarbs' – the amount of water contained in Sydney Harbour – and this lake was due to hold 9½ sydarbs!

We met various people connected with the Ord River Dam and they all spoke well of Ed – he had clearly been popular. As for the project itself, the Australian Foreign Minister McMahon had talked very enthusiastically to Richard about it in Canberra. But in the following years it struggled, and most people see it as a costly failure. One afternoon an Australian banged on our door while we were reading and said why hadn't he been told there was a British Minister staying and he would expect us at six for a drink in the hall. There was clearly no refusing. When we arrived we discovered it was teetotal and the other people were very dreary. All in all I thought it was a most God-awful place, but I was glad to have been to this remote part of Australia.

From Darwin we flew to Hong Kong, where we met Peggy Lewthwaite. She had been kind to Richard in hospital in Cairo and invited him to be godfather to her son, who was later killed in an earthquake near San Francisco. They took us out into the harbour in the Governor's launch from which we got a splendid view of the whole city. Two days later we flew to the Philippines. This was back to work. In Manila security seemed to dominate the conversation. Our ambassador, John Curle, insisted that the violence in Al Capone's Chicago had been far worse, but everyone had a gruesome story. One woman, dangling her hand out of the car window, had her finger slashed off for the sake of the ring on it.

We attended a reception given by President Marcos and his wife Imelda, the 'Iron Butterfly', and indeed we were stuck with them for over half an hour. They were then just at the beginning of their corrupt and dictatorial rule, and their son, known as Bong-Bong, was at school in England. Before the Pope's visit the year before, it was thought expedient to ship the President's current mistress back to the United States. She did not leave without a struggle, giving a press conference before her departure at which she played a tape-recording of the latest bedroom encounter between the President and herself.

On Ash Wednesday the Ambassador came with us to church, as Richard recorded in his diary: 'The church is Protestant and Episcopal, à l'Americaine, and I felt at home. The vicar is a Belgian ex-Roman Catholic who saw the intellectual difficulty of Papal infallibility and the charms of a Filipino girl at about the same time.'

We were soon on to Singapore and then Indonesia, where we stayed with our Ambassador, Willis Combs and his wife Grace. The reception party included the Sultan of Jogjakarta, whose palace we were able to visit, as Richard recorded:

I received a note which told me that the Sultan's palace – the Kraton – was closed today because of the national holiday, but arrangements would be made to show it to us if we could arrive punctually at 11. We were there soon after and were received by Prince Prabuningrat, a relation of the Sultan, with a *kris* (dagger) tucked into the fold of his garment in the small of his back. I thought it must be inaccessible unless he were double-jointed, but he produced it on demand and explained that it was cleaned in lemon juice, salt and oil once a year, after which it is dipped in arsenic to increase its effectiveness in the coming months. He looked such a kind man!

While Richard was occupied with the Ambassador I went to the British library, which was run by a nice middle-aged spinster. I spent a lot of time there. The next morning the Coombs gave a cocktail party and I noticed the spinster on her own, so I went up to her and said, 'I so much enjoyed my visit yesterday.' She burst into tears and ran from the room. Later Grace apologised and said the lady had said I was the first person who had been kind to her.

A couple of days later the Combs had asked about eighty people to dinner. Richard didn't want to stand for more than an hour, so I asked what time to come down and was told 7.30. We went down; 8.30 and 9.30 came and went, and finally Grace Combs apologised to me and said, 'I'm so sorry about the delay. I'm afraid the cook's been murdered.' The production of dinner after this was something of a miracle, but I don't think anyone but us was told. Richard whispered to me after dinner, 'I do hope we haven't been eating the cook.'

The next day we were asked to inspect the British submarine *Orpheus*, which was paying a goodwill visit to a number of capitals including Djarkarta. We were astonished that the crew of sixty-three could fit into roughly the same area as the back hall at Flat Top. I was full of questions, all of which were skilfully turned aside (or stubbornly refused) by the sailors. Richard, having only his arms to help him, had some difficulty mounting back up the pole to get out of the submarine. Luckily I was wearing a silk trouser suit, so I had no problem getting down or up again. But Grace Combs was unwisely wearing a ball dress, which climbed up over her head as she descended.

One very strange thing happened in Indonesia. For several years I had had a horrible nightmare. I was in an awful room with khaki-coloured walls, with the only vent high up on one wall with bars over it. There was an arched gap low down on one wall and I knew there was something dreadful on the other side. In my dream I never went through that gap, but I'd wake up screaming. Well, in Jakarta, when Richard had gone to see the Foreign Secretary, I was asked to go to a hospital to be shown why they needed help from Britain. I was first shown a circulating platform with many corpses stretched out on it, and told that people could have free burials if the hospital was allowed to work on their corpses when they died. The dean of the hospital then took me to a room almost exactly like that in my dreams. There was a gap in one wall and we went through it. On the other side were several lepers lying on black plastic bags, missing a nose or an arm or something else. Clearly the dean was simply doing his best to shock me, to underline the case for aid. I hate hospitals anyway, and this was utterly pitiable. But from that day onwards, I never had that horrible dream again.

We said goodbye to the Combs with regret and flew to Beirut. In those more tranquil days, that city seemed delightfully peaceful. Richard jotted in his diary: 'From the window of our sitting room there is a superb view of the great wall of snow on the mountains above Beirut. To see snow; to hear the lapping of the Mediterranean below; and to be staying in a French hotel – all this brings home very near, and Diana is blissfully contented by the sights and smells which she misses east of Suez.'

Richard had plenty of official meetings and it was a real joy to have lunches with sophisticated people who spoke French, but we still had time to see something of the country. I remember a picnic near the great Roman ruins at Baalbek, where the Ambassador's enormous black Austin Princess, with the Union Jack flying, looked incongruous in the barren desert.

It took us less than an hour to fly to Amman. On our way to the Ambassador's house we were taken on a short detour to avoid disturbing the Queen Mother. She was said to hate noise. Certainly the heart of Amman, long before the middle of the night, was deadly quiet. Richard had a number of meetings with the Prime Minister (who was later assassinated) and others, and he became convinced that Jordan was a country that needed and deserved our help.

A couple of days later we set off towards Petra by helicopter. Richard hoped on the way to pass over the castle at Kerak, which he achieved later when King Hussein took him in his helicopter:

> My wish to circle above the old Crusader castle at Kerak was refused for reasons of security, but later allowed by King Hussein. He said that the Kerakians had often shot at him in vain, so it was probably all right for me to follow him! Kerak had always thrilled me – the scene of the chivalry between the crusaders and Saladin, who had begun his attack on the castle during the wedding feast of Humphrey of Toron and Isabel, sister of Baldwin. When the bride's mother sent out a delicacy from the feast, Saladin asked in which part of the castle the feast was being held, so that he could avoid bombarding it.

And then we were at Petra:

> We drove into Petra through the Siq in Army Land Rovers. It is just wide enough for them to get through. We were face to face, for the first and most memorable time, with the magnificent façade of the Treasury. The capitals of the Corinthian columns look as though they might have been chiselled yesterday. More remarkable than any of the carving are the colours of the ceilings of the large caves, which served the Nabateans both as places to live and to be buried. The ceiling of the Urn tomb is a vivid mixture of reds and blues, created by no painter but by the action of the weather on the sandstone. Time was all too short before we had to turn back through the Siq in order to get to Aqaba before darkness.

At Aqaba we were driven straight to the King's palace, the modest bungalow in which Hussein lived on the edge of the Red Sea. Richard and I swam. We were told the King expected us to dine with him at 8.30, suitably 'undressed', no jackets or ties. Clearly we were expected to leave as soon as dinner was over. The King personally gave us all drinks, being quite unbothered by our consumption of alcohol. (Richard's Socialist Press Secretary was with us and asked for a gin and tonic. The King gave him gin and soda. Instead of drinking it, he insisted that he had asked for tonic and the King had only given him water. The King tipped out the drink and went to get some tonic water. Richard and I kept our tempers with difficulty.) The next day we were taken to see the runway that was being built at Aqaba which Britain was paying for – the main reason for our visit was to consider if it should be extended to take their Boeing 707s.

We had first seen King Hussein when he brought his first wife, Dina, to the Royal Box for a ballet in the mid Fifties. (We had taken Emma and in the interval we bought a postcard for her to send to Ed. She couldn't think what to say, so we suggested: 'The King and Queen of Jordan are in the Royal Box.' To which Emma answered: 'Wouldn't that be a bit above Ed's head?') The King was married to her for just over two years. He then wanted to marry an English girl whose father was working in Jordan, but great pressure was put on him by the British Government not to marry anyone English. He did marry her but he respected the British concern that she should not be Queen, and she was known as Princess Muna. She is the mother of the present king, Abdullah.

Our final port of call was Istanbul. The first great suspension bridge over the Bosphorus (there are now three) connecting Europe and Asia was then nearing completion. Richard's department had contributed substantially to it, and Richard hoped to be the UK's representative at the opening. To his disappointment, when it opened in 1973 a more senior politician, Geoffrey Rippon, went instead. It was snowing hard in Istanbul when we flew home.

★   ★   ★

It was a blessed relief to me that our next trip, to North Africa, involved no flying. This time we combined a short official trip to Tunisia with an exploration, in our own time, of some less familiar parts of the country.

It was the last day of August 1971 by the time we had driven through France and loaded the motor-caravan onto a ship in Marseille bound for Tunis. We had hardly got under way when, walking past the ship's swimming pool and with Richard steadying himself with his hand on my shoulder, a sudden lurch toppled us both into the empty pool. Luckily it was covered with a stout net. I had to crawl out, my knees getting bruised by the thick cords, and Richard somehow managed to roll to the edge. The spectators were vastly amused. The French Captain had asked us to dinner that evening, although clearly embarrassed about the swimming pool incident. At dinner the ship again lurched violently. Chairs and tables shot across the floor, and the Captain observed that he had had a message that 'the Minister had fallen into the pool'. This broke any tension and we had a jolly dinner.

From Tunis we made our way to the island of Djerba, revisiting other familiar places – Enfidaville (renamed Enfidha), El Djem, Sfax. Richard's diaries record some of the almost constant visits from strangers:

> A young man approached across the salt-lake from the direction of Zarzis while I was shaving outside. He presented me with a large loaf of bread. I tried various presentations in return – a cheroot and a can of syrup. He was a little choosy, but a biro pen was acceptable. Having been greeted by Diana on arrival from behind the curtains of the caravan, he seemed unwilling to leave without the pleasure of

another glimpse of her. So she was prevailed upon to lean out of the window and wish him a gracious farewell, after which he departed on his motor-cycle completely satisfied.

I had asked Anne Balfour Fraser what we should take as presents. I was thinking of all sorts of nice things, but she said that simple things like small gilt safety pins and biros were always highly valued by nomads and others.

We made our way to the extreme south of the country where the borders of Tunisia, Algeria and Libya meet. With the help of old battlefield maps which had been lent to us by Patrick McCraith, we were confident that we identified the place where Flash had been killed – a lonely, rather beautiful place almost surrounded by hills. How much I longed for him to have remained buried there. Patrick McCraith had revisted these old battlefields along with Mickey Gold, who had been a great regimental friend of Flash's, and two German officers who had also fought there.

Our next objective was the great salt-lake of Chott el Djerid. It was very hot indeed, 120 degrees on the caravan's thermometer, but we managed to cross it this time and even spent two nights on it. Richard asked me if the caravan got stuck, I thought I could walk twenty miles in the cool of the night to get across the Chott. The answer was yes to the walk, but no to finding the way. Luckily I never had to try.

We made our way back towards the sea, as Richard recorded in his diary:

The sea here is very shallow and not particularly attractive, but we both plunged in after finding a place for the night from which we could easily reach the sea. After the heat and dust of the day, this bathe in two feet of weedy water, on black, sour sand, was immensely satisfying. D brought food, cooker and lantern to the beach, where we ate our dinner in the company of many of the insects of

North Africa – moths and crickets and beetles, but mercifully no mosquitoes. Three small boys walked along the beach just before I began cooking. They were going fishing when the moon rose, and suggested bringing us their catch about 4 a.m. Diana was for more gentlemanly hours and suggested 9 o'clock. We never saw them again.

Afterwards we began to make our way northwards for the official part of the trip. Richard was in the caravan, not far from the city of Gafsa, and was in the process of changing into his smart clothes when a car stopped nearby. A white-robed figure climbed out and asked if Richard was Monsieur Wood. The man was the Governor of Gafsa, and we were suddenly transformed into VIPs. In Tunis Richard met a number of Ministers including Bourguiba, the country's long-serving President, a small, slight figure with a gentleness that belied the vigour of his struggle against the French. Richard was charmed by Bourguiba's courtesy and his apparently sincere affection for the British.

Back in France, enjoying the comforts of the Baumanière at Les Baux, Monsieur Thulier looked older. But his manners were as perfect as ever. He clearly had no idea who we were but you would never have guessed it.

★   ★   ★

Richard had long looked forward to going back to India, the country he had left forty-one years ago when his father was still Viceroy. My mother-in-law, not far off ninety, said she would have given all she had to be coming with us. She had been at her happiest in India and looked back on those years with great nostalgia. For myself, I had heard much about the country both from Richard and Lady H, and also from Myrtie who had been there with Ruth and Anne staying with the Linlithgows in the war when it had been impossible to get directly back to England from Palestine. But I had never been there.

The terrace at the Villa Cimbrone, the Grimthorpes' spectacular house on the Amalfi coast.

Pam Baring.

Ursula Bethell on the beach below
Cimbrone.

Senior ministers in Harold Macmillan's government at Chequers in April 1963. *Back row, from the left:* Michael Noble, Julian Amery, John Hobson, Jack Profumo, Timothy Bligh, Martin Redmayne, Michael Fraser, Knox Cunningham, Frederick Erroll, Geoffrey Ripon, Keith Joseph, Richard Wood. *Middle row:* Peter Carrington, Christopher Soames, Edward Heath, Niall Macpherson, Edward Boyle (with eyes shut), Peter Thorneycroft, Hugh Fraser, Reginald Bevins, John Boyd-Carpenter, William Deedes. *Standing alongside the Prime Minister:* Henry Brooke, R.A. Butler, Reginald Maudling. *Standing in front:* Enoch Powell, Ernest Marples, Iain Macleod and, on the right, Oliver

Archie and Susie's Kidston's daughters, Janie and Cath, at Redenham.

Launching *British Dragoon* on the Tyne when Richard was Minister of Power. Peter Irwin is behind Ed and me.

Going down a coal mine with Richard when he was Minister of Power.

Anthony Eden in Privy Council uniform.

Grouse shooting at Bolton Abbey in Yorkshire. I was Richard's loader.

Our trip across North Africa in 1965. Richard is standing among old petrol cans at Bir Zidan in the Libyan Desert, where he had lost both his legs in late 1942. Our motor caravan is in the background.

Richard writing his diary in the desert.

A melon-seller in Afghanistan, who we passed on our way to the Khyber Pass.

Henrietta Scott.

On the House of Commons terrace with Sir Paul Bryan before taking Hilda Slater and Eleanor Mounsey to a garden party at Buckingham Palace.

Charlie Allsopp and Fiona McGowan at the Grosvenor Chapel, 1967.

Emma's marriage to Nicholas Brooksbank in Westminster Abbey, December 1970. Behind them are Brigid's daughter, Victoria von Preussen and, on the right, Cindy Fletcher.

King Hussein of Jordan, one of my heroes.

(above) Looking out to sea at Aqaba from King Hussein's house.

Hilaré and Bob Ryder VC, on their boat off the coast of Norway.

Building the pool at Les Collines de Guerrevielle.

Richard and Timothy Tufnell in France.

Richard with his cousin, Brigid Ness.

Richard being introduced to the House of Lords by Nat Saye and Sele and Peter Carrington in 1979.

(above) Julian Holland-Hibbert.

(left) With Margaret and Denis Thatcher at a regimental dinner for the 4th Battalion Royal Green Jackets in 1989.

Myles Hildyard in his garden at Flintham.

Joh Seb Peake.

(above) Richard with the legendary racehorse Desert Orchid at Richard Burridge's house.

(right) Richard on duty as Honorary Colonel of the 4th Battalion Royal Green Jackets, with Nick Eden, on the left, the commanding officer. Davies Street, London.

The wilderness at Les Collines de Guerrevielle which we made into a garden.

A sketch by Graham Rust of our house in France at Les Collines de Guerrevielle.

Richard in Port Grimaud.

Ed and Katha after their wedding.

With John Major in the drawing-room at
Downing Street.

Graham Rust at our golden wedding
dinner.

Georgina Howorth on the lawn in front of Plantation House on St Helena, where Sir Hudson Lowe, the Governor, had lived when Napoleon was a prisoner on the island. The giant tortoise Georgina is talking to is Jonathan, said to be the world's oldest living animal (184 years old in 2016).

Looking down a huge flight of steps onto Jamestown, the capital of St Helena, 1994.

Patrick McCraith reaching the top of the steps.

(above) Richard on his quad bike, after the fire around our house in France.

(left) On the quad bike at Flat Top. The view looks out over the Vale of York.

(below) Hugh Trenchard and Ed.

Crystal Tweedie in France.

Sir Edward Ford.

Toby and Araminta Aldington.

Myles Hildyard (on the left) and Michael
Parish reminiscing about their dramatic
escape from the Germans in Crete in 1941.

With Mary Sheepshanks in St Petersburg.

Edward in Libya with a poster of Gaddafi, 2010.

At Leptis Magna, 2010. At the back: Liz Scarbrough, Ed, Janie Kidston (sitting). Middle row: Phillipa Weatherly, me, Margaret North, Patrick and Sally Lort-Phillips. In front: Leo Wood and David North.

(above) Frances and Michael Howorth.

(right) Mark and Mary Buttle.

(below) Ed's family. From the left: Ella Wood holding Evie Scott (Leo's daughter), Leo holding Frankie, her younger daughter, Ed, Georgie, Jemima and Katha Wood.

We arrived at a very nervous time in India. Relations with Pakistan were at breaking point, and a short but intense war broke out two days after we left. On our first night in the country, at the Taj Mahal hotel in Bombay in mid-November, there was an air-raid practice before dinner. And later, at Chandigarh in the Punjab, an air-raid siren sounded during dinner, to the surprise of the rattled-looking politicians present. Candles were lit and the lights switched off.

In Delhi we stayed with the High Commissioner, Terence Garvey, and his wife Rosemary. Rosemary was very intelligent and very left-wing. She disapproved of Richard being the son of a Viceroy and would not join us when we went to see the Rasthrapati Bhavan (Lutyens' palace for the viceroys). But in spite of sharing few of her opinions – she was an unmoveable admirer of China, for example – Richard and I grew fond of her and kept in touch with her, arguing constantly about things like the poll tax on which we took totally opposite sides. Terence was her second husband. When she married her first husband, Sir Con O'Neill, he told her that if the girl he'd always wanted to marry was ever widowed, he would leave Rosemary and marry her. Which he did.

One morning we were given privileged access to the Taj Mahal, which we had to ourselves for half an hour. The delicacy of the tomb, inside and out, is exquisite. No reproduction or picture that I have seen captures a fraction of its glory.

The next day Richard insisted that we visit the former Viceregal Lodge, a bungalow in Old Delhi, where Richard and his family had lived for three years until the new Lutyens palace was finally ready for the Viceroy, the staff meanwhile (generals, ladies-in-waiting, etc. and their accompanying husbands or wives) all having to live in marquees surrounding the Lodge. It was now part of Delhi University. In what had been Richard's night nursery in the late 1920s there was a plaque with a message from Mountbatten, which told us that it was in this room in 1923 that he had asked 'my dear Edwina' to be his wife. When I later told Rosemary Garvey, she naturally asked: 'What could Dicky and Edwina be doing in the night nursery?'

Richard found the rooms hard to recognise:

The dining-room and the drawing-room, with most of the windows blocked, were unrecognisable. But the ballroom, where I remembered the glittering investitures, sitting humbly on the steps of the throne with the Maharajah of Rajpipla, was much the worst of all. It is now washed a bilious yellow; desks and vast tin files lie in complete confusion; the windows are all blocked; and the pigeons are in obvious possession... I almost wished I had not gone, but I should have missed it if I had not. I doubt whether reliving the past is a good idea in India, or anywhere else. Almost everywhere else I am ready to welcome the new India and thoroughly enjoy it, but the new Indian transformation of the old Viceregal Lodge almost made me weep.

Our visit in the afternoon to Richard's last Indian home was more cheerful. This was the former Viceroy's House, the vast palace designed by Lutyens, the final decoration of which my mother-in-law largely oversaw, exchanging numerous letters about it with Queen Mary. It is now the Presidential Residence. An ADC showed us Richard's old suite of rooms and through the windows we could see the Mughal Gardens whose waterways had been perfect for Richard's little battery-powered boat.

Our Indian trip ended in Calcutta, where we stayed at the very imposing former Government House. It is now called Raj Bhavan and is the official residence of the Governor of West Bengal. But in the days of the Raj it was the Viceroy's residence until Curzon moved the capital to Delhi. Previous occupants of our vast bedroom included both Edward VII and Edward VIII when they were Prince of Wales and more recently the Queen. I wrote a note to Baba Metcalfe on Raj Bhavan writing paper to tell her that we had seen her old room.

In Calcutta the High Commission's street address had changed from Harrington Street to Ho Chi Minh Serani. This was too much for the Americans, who had moved out when the name was altered. Calcutta was a city that fascinated us both. With its squalor and poverty and all its problems, this is a city which many would particularly want to avoid. But its vitality was so remarkable and delightful that we wanted to return. It never felt poor to us, the cows reminded us of Jersey and Guernsey ones and seeing them being washed under hosepipes in the street somehow removed all idea of hardship.

We stopped briefly in Cairo on the way home. We stayed in Shepheard's Hotel. That night, in the Sheraton Hotel just across the river, the Prime Minister of Jordan, whom Richard had met just months before, was assassinated by some Palestinians. The Egyptians were very calm about it. They just smiled and said how lucky it was we were not staying at the Sheraton.

CHAPTER 17

A Well-Armed King

We began 1972 with yet another journey. To be in the Caribbean in January would be most people's idea of bliss. But this was work. Seven islands to be visited, each with their own combination of High Commissioner, Governor, Premier, Cabinet and so on. And all desperate for development aid from Britain. And for me, flying from island to island in a tiny aeroplane, a six-seater Beechcraft, was no fun at all.

We landed first in Barbados. The next day we had lunch at Ronnie Tree's famous house, Heron Bay, on the western shore of the island. Edwina d'Erlanger was there, Antony Head and Derek and Anne Parker Bowles. Marietta was not there. Ronnie was happy to let Derek and me look round Marietta's cupboards and we enjoyed trying on her hats. We lunched in the dining room with windows wide open to the garden and the sea, and afterwards Ronnie gave us a tour of the garden with all its exotic plants. One snag was that the public had the right to walk everywhere, so we kept finding locals in the garden. Jeremy Tree was a great friend and I saw him a lot with Little Porchy and later when he often came to shoot at Garrowby. I knew Michael also and their mother Nancy, who gave me a beautiful side table as a wedding present, and Ronnie was one of those people always nice to the young. They were fun.

In the evening Richard was taken to see a cricket match, Barbados against Trinidad, in the capital, Bridgetown. It was, he reported, rather a violent affair. One of the batsmen retired hurt with a fractured forearm, another had to have four stitches in his jaw. The Barbadian crowd yelled with delight at every injury, urging on their bowlers.

We were soon on to St Lucia. One of the reception party in the island's capital, Castries, who was now the Housing Minister, remembered waving a Union Jack exactly fifty years ago when Richard's father, then Major Edward Wood, had visited the island. We watched bananas being packed for England. Learning about all the problems of growing bananas and all the opportunities for bruising between the tree and the final destination, I was astonished, if not ashamed, at the low price that we pay for them.

The next two islands were St Vincent and Antigua. In Antigua we drove past an almost derelict sugar factory and through acres of precious Sea Island cotton, beginning to blow. It was a depressing sight and we felt very critical of the islanders' laziness. We were told it was impossible to get the labour to pick the cotton and machine-picked cotton was substandard. For all these islands, tourism – rather than crops, industry or other opportunities – was the great nirvana, so they were all bent on having a bigger harbour, an extra runway.

Flying into Montserrat was interesting. The pilot had to come in with his starboard wingtip almost touching a low hill. And because the runway was very short, the brakes were applied almost as soon as we touched the ground. The Governor and Chief Minister met us. The latter, who pleaded eloquently for an extended jetty, was an enthusiastic Seventh Day Adventist. The back window of his car was plastered with slogans and messages. One read, 'Jesus Speaks'. Another announced, possibly appropriately, 'Eternity Ahead'.

We were always asked to state our interests when we made these journeys and one of mine was visiting prisons. There was a tiny one in Montserrat with just six male prisoners, one of whom was going to be executed the next day. The others were teasing him and saying how lucky he was to be able to choose exactly what he wanted to eat for his last meal. Shaking hands with him to say goodbye was never going to be easy. I said something inane like 'Good luck' to which he said 'Thank you' with a big smile.

The enormous yellow and black Rolls-Royce of Robert Llewellyn Bradshaw, the flamboyant Premier of St Kitts, was evident on the tarmac as we arrived at St Kitts' airport. The 1933 Rolls, bought by Bradshaw a few years before, had been brought out for our benefit. He liked to drive it himself, a police corporal by his side and Richard and me sitting behind. Born a slave from Ashanti on the old Gold Coast, Bradshaw had had a remarkable life and was now the undisputed 'king' of St Kitts and Nevis.

Bradshaw came with us to see the imposing fortress of Brimstone Hill, designed by British military engineers and built and maintained by African slaves, and now a World Heritage site. Because of its height and the steepness of the hill it was known in its heyday as 'the Gibraltar of the West Indies'. Afterwards Bradshaw came with us on the short ferry ride to the next-door island of Nevis.

We had seen many delightful things on these islands. But it had been a whistle-stop tour and a tiring itinerary, especially for Richard as there was a lot of walking, often quite steep too. I was not too sorry to fly home from Antigua and be back in London on a cold February day.

★   ★   ★

Three months later we were flying to Jordan to mark the opening of the new runway at Aqaba. Richard had persuaded Alec Home that this was a good use of development money – after all, the Israelis had an airport at Eilat and, as far as Richard and I were concerned, nothing was too good for King Hussein.

The King met us in Amman, having arrived in a helicopter which he had piloted himself, dressed very casually. We then climbed into a vast Boeing 707 with all his Ministers and flew to Aqaba, the King once again being the pilot. He enjoyed bringing the aeroplane down very low and then immediately climbing back up. With my fear of flying this should have terrified me, but when Richard sympathised I said I knew we would be alright as it would be impossible for the King and all his Ministers to be killed. The vast aeroplane landed safely amid everyone's joy at having the new runway.

We sat on old leather sofas at the airport for the ceremony and speeches, and then Hussein asked us to get into his car, which he was driving himself. Richard kept hitting metal when he tried to get his legs in. King Hussein apologised that his (loaded) automatic rifle was in the way. He picked it up and threw it onto the back seat beside me. He drove us to his palace by the sea. The King could not swim but we watched him water-skiing beautifully (wearing a stout life-jacket).

At lunch King Hussein and most of his guests ate the *mansaf* – the traditional Arabian meal of lamb, rice and dried yoghurt – scooping up little balls of food with the right hand while keeping the left hand behind the back. The King spoilt my day when he produced an air-hostess (Alia, whom he later married) and paid her a lot more attention than the rest of us. This was one of the half-dozen occasions in my life when I really felt jealous.

After lunch the King took Richard in his helicopter to see the new road being built to the Saudi Arabian border, as Richard recorded in his diary:

I was driven to the helicopter in the King's car, still with the automatic rifle which had been at my feet on the way from the airport. I hoped I should not be called upon to use it. We were in the air for about half an hour, eastwards over Aqaba and from there down the foundations of the road. We followed its every bend at a height of less than twenty feet. I found it alarming, but did my best to smile bravely to His Majesty, who was clearly enjoying himself. At the Beau Geste fort on the frontier we turned sharply and flew back on the edge of the coast, again only a few feet above the sea.

I thought we might decapitate some bathers off one of the Aqaba hotels, and the King skimmed his palace within a hundred yards of the Israeli border before we were safely down again and I was travelling back in the Mercedes with the automatic at my feet.

We left King Hussein in Aqaba, while we were driven on the Desert Highway to Petra, arriving in the very last of the light. The next day was an epic one, for we were due to climb to the very top of the Petra site, to the Monastery, with Richard riding a donkey. He described the ascent:

Breakfast was brought to us at 7, and we left in two Army land-rovers at 7.30. The Treasury, at the end of the narrow Siq, was lit magnificently by the sun when we reached it a quarter of an hour later. It was already warm when we reached the Theatre. I chatted with a burly corporal of the Tourist Police. He pointed out to me the ruins of the Roman triumphal arch; the Museum in the rock behind it; the old crusaders' castle far above; and the very pinnacle of the Monastery, which we were about to climb to see.

What a climb it was. We selected a powerful donkey (with another in reserve) to carry me to the Monastery. The police corporal took his duties very seriously and, for the next two hours, never left my side or relaxed his iron grip of my waist. If the donkey was essential for my ascent to the Monastery, he was almost equally so. The path is narrow, often with an alarming drop on the right or left; much of it is very rough; at a number of points I had to dismount; and there are well over a thousand steps. It was not comfortable, and I thought that the police corporal, no longer young, might well die in the ascent. Once or twice my right leg looked like parting company from the rest of me.

The reserve donkey, taking its turn half-way up, broke its 'girth' of very primitive string; but the corporal's devotion to duty eventually triumphed, and we emerged onto an acre of flatness in front of the façade of the Monastery, similar to, but much less delicate than the façade of the Treasury far below. It is perhaps a century later, possibly soon after 100 AD and very near the end of the Nabatean Kingdom. Although less splendid than the Treasury, it has the magnificence of remoteness. Whoever rediscovered it in the last century – whether Burckhardt or someone later – must have been even more amazed than the rediscoverer of the Treasury. Civilisation has now caught up again and we drank Pepsi-Cola in the shadow of an enormous rock, while the donkeys wandered among the thistles. Before our descent I rode another quarter of a mile to the very edge of the steep wadis which run down to the Wadi Arabah. The whole of this south-western corner of Jordan has become for me the most exciting place on earth.

Petra was an astonishing place. Since I was a child I had always wanted to see it. As you approached this massive cluster of rocks, no hint of its magnificence was apparent unless you were in a helicopter. Myrtie and Flash had spent several days there in the 1930s on their journey to Afghanistan and had commented on its remoteness and the total absence of people.

Of course this element of its great appeal, its timeless peace and remoteness in the desert, is very vulnerable. I have realised since how very lucky we were to see it before the crowds and package tours arrived. After Emma and Nicholas married, Richard offered to pay for them to go there but sadly they didn't want to.

A few years ago Patrick Lort-Phillips, Patrick McCraith's son-in-law, who had just been with me and Ed and other friends to Libya, told me he was going to Jordan for the Army and what did I recommend him to see. Of course I said Petra was a must. On his return he telephoned and thanked me, but said nowhere had he ever seen so many plastic bags blowing in the wind, thirteen grand hotels looking down from above, nor so many crowds anywhere as at the Treasury.

Back in Amman, and before flying home, we had dinner with Crown Prince (as he then was) Hassan, King Hussein's younger brother. Hassan was much less charming than the King but he was very intelligent and has always kept himself ferociously well-informed. He has an Indian wife, Princess Tharwat, who was expecting to be Queen. We still exchange Christmas cards but I haven't seen him for a long time. It must have been a great shock when, just before Hussein died, the succession passed not to him but to Hussein's son Abdullah, Princess Muna's son.

Three years later we were back in Jordan. The Conservatives were no longer in power but the Jordanian Government was still grateful to Richard for what he had done for them and they were keen to show off their progress.

After a series of meetings in Amman we flew by helicopter to Petra, directly over the castle at Kerak, much to Richard's delight. At Petra we managed to see some things we had missed before and we had a warm reunion with the owner of the donkey which had carried Richard up to the Monastery on our last visit and the police corporal who had kept Richard firmly on the animal all the way up.

The only fly in the ointment was that we were entertained to lunch in a cave. All that was on offer was a *mansaf* and no one was allowed to drink until they had swallowed sheep's eyes and washed their hands. They told me this, but not Richard. I managed to swallow the eyes, and hoped Richard would be quick and wash so we could have a glass of water. He never moved until in despair I said, 'Richard, will you please wash your hands.' He answered, 'Don't be so bossy, I'll do it when I want.' So I asked someone if I could please have a drink and they emptied some of the juice from the *mansaf* into a plastic glass for me to drink. I don't know how I swallowed it.

The helicopter took us on to Aqaba, where the director of the port showed us the various projects that are planned – a refinery, a fertiliser plant, hotels, chalets, nightclubs. It is such a beautiful place that I found it impossible not to regret these developments that the Jordanians are so keen on.

We were driven back to Amman and had dinner with Crown Prince Hassan at the Basman Palace. Although he is very anglicised and had been to Harrow, no alcohol was offered despite the fact that when we'd dined with him in his club in Amman there was plenty. The next day we had an audience with King Hussein. Queen Alia, who was expecting a baby, was said rather improbably to have sent messages to us. Richard impressed me by boldly asking for the King's photograph. When it arrived it said, 'To my good friend Mr Richard Wood'. I wanted people to think it had been given to me, so as soon as we had brought it back I stuck a bit of paper over those words and hung it in my bedroom.

I was a huge fan of the King, I thought he was terrific. He was one of those people who was quite incredibly brave, had perfect manners and a huge sense of humour. When he died I went to his memorial service at St Paul's with Ursula and David Westbury. Prince Charles gave the address and it was clear that he also had a very high opinion of Hussein.

$$\star \quad \star \quad \star$$

On the longer flights during these years it seemed to be necessary to touch down en route, sometimes in several places, before we got to the final destination. If Richard was on an official visit, such 'stops' would usually involve a fleeting visit from the local Ambassador or High Commissioner, and small talk at some appalling hour on the tarmac or in the airport's VIP lounge (or the *Salon d'honneur*, as the French more elegantly called it). This was a trial for us and a damn nuisance for the diplomats too. It also occasionally involved going through security, so Ron Deare, Richard's very nice and long-suffering Private Secretary, used to go ahead and explain that Richard had metal legs, which could set off the alarm.

When I complained about these unwanted visits, Ron explained, 'We have to let them know – it's in the regulations.' Iona Carrington told me that at the end of a very long flight the Ambassador had come into the aeroplane to greet them. She and Peter were then taken to the VIP lounge where, exhausted from lack of sleep, she felt she must do something and seeing someone whom she recognised, she went up to greet the Ambassador, only to be told they had just met in the aeroplane.

In August 1972 it was Anthony Duff, our High Commissioner in Kenya, of whom we saw a great deal the following year (and who later accompanied Christopher Soames to Rhodesia for the handover for Zimbabwe), who came to chat to us as we waited briefly in Nairobi on our way to South Africa. In Johannesburg we were met by our Ambassador, Sir Arthur Snelling. He had told his staff that he wanted them to have social consciences, but they must be prepared to take them off like an overcoat. 'To have one in summer', he added, 'is damned uncomfortable!'

After Richard's meetings in Pretoria we were on our way, travelling in comfort in the Ambassador's Rolls, to Gaborone, capital of Botswana. There were lovely views of rolling hills and as the sun went down, animals and birds seemed to converge on the road. We had been warned about the extreme religiosity of David Anderson, our High Commissioner in Botswana, and his wife. At their house their servants were drawn up in two ranks to meet us and on a nearby stand a Bible was open at the 23rd Psalm (each day it was replaced by another Biblical quotation). I boldly met Mrs Anderson's offer of tea with a request for alcohol.

A couple of days later we were entertained at the dinner that Sir Seretse Khama, Botswana's freedom-fighter-turned-president, was putting on for King Moshoeshoe (pronounced Mo-sheshway). Seretse's controversial but popular wife Ruth, who was white, indeed almost albino – their marriage had caused a great furore twenty years before – was there; also their outspoken and rather attractive daughter Jackie. I had arrived at the dinner wearing long white gloves – the Foreign Office sent you instructions and I had been advised to wear them. Jackie Khama took one look at them and said, 'What *are* you wearing those for?' I took them off as swiftly as I could manage to unbutton them, not an easy thing to do in a hurry.

I was much amused the next day when, having introduced Jackie Khama to a tiresome South African woman, she said to me later, 'Thanks *awfully* for introducing me to that bitch!' Later it was Richard's turn to be on the receiving end of this rather engaging African bluntness. He had said to a Botswanian that he would like to return to see the country's progress 'when I am an old man'. The reply was immediate: 'I should call you an old man already!'

Our affection for the Ambassador was not increased when he denied us an expedition to the Kalahari Desert, saying he could not possibly put a British Minister in danger there. He replaced it with visits to diamond and copper mines and a dam, and tedious socialising with the staff at lunch by a pool. As Richard was not prepared to show himself without legs, he simply had to make boring and long drawn-out conversation. I did at least get into the pool.

But we were soon off to our next port of call. We drove across the Orange Free State to the little mountain kingdom of Lesotho, where Richard had meetings with Chief Jonathan, the Prime Minister and the young king, Moshoeshoe. Richard felt rather sorry for the King, an intelligent young man with not enough to do. I had meanwhile gone to see Queen Mamohato at their country house outside the capital, where she was giving a ladies' lunch. We each had little pink paper napkins with pictures of Snow White on them – she sweetly told me she had got them to make me feel at home.

When Queen Mamohato came to stay with us at Flat Top the following June, we gave a party for her, courtesy of Anne, in the Ionic Temple at Rievaulx – one of two Palladian temples built by Sim's ancestors in the eighteenth century on a site overlooking the ruins of Rievaulx Abbey. Meanwhile the Queen's son Mohato (the king of the country today), who was then at the preparatory school for Ampleforth, had also arrived to stay, looked after by the Queen's lady-in-waiting. He had been sent without luggage of any kind and went to bed in the suit he had spent the day in. The Queen thought his hair was too long, and the schoolroom was taken over for the lady-in-waiting who cut it so short it was almost shaven.

The next few days in Lesotho were a blizzard of visits to local industries and projects, schools and missions. Richard went up in a Cessna to see Lesotho from the air and landed at a primitive airstrip to look at a future game park, on the edge of the glorious Drakensberg Mountains. At the time it had only two animals. At Bushmen's Pass, 7,000 feet above sea-level, we ate a picnic in the sun, warm enough to counteract the cold wind that was blowing.

Our final stop was Swaziland. Richard left a bag behind with his Teddy, which had been given to Ed by Sykes, his first constituency agent, and passed on to Richard when Ed went to Eton. He was much loved and came everywhere with us. I still have him on my bed. Ron Deare volunteered to get him back. He made a mass of telephone calls and organised a car to bring Teddy back to us.

Richard had an audience with King Sobuza, a fine-looking man in his seventies who had more power than his regal counterpart in Lesotho. He made no secret of his strong disapproval of Idi Amin, who had just replaced President Obote in Uganda and was expelling all the Asians from his country. During the audience a private secretary approached the King crouching as low as possible, like a soldier advancing across bare ground in the face of enemy fire.

The King was nominally a Christian but had a host of wives. I discovered via Ron that his eldest son, and even his second son, cannot be his heir. They simply prove the King's virility, after which he gets down to the serious business of producing an heir. At the final dinner, with the Prime Minister and others, I enjoyed teasing them about their polygamous habits, which they took in good part.

We flew home from Johannesburg. Anthony Duff had mercifully heeded Ron's command to keep away when we touched down in Nairobi at some unearthly hour.

CHAPTER 18

Afghanistan, Pakistan and India

In April 1972 we celebrated our silver wedding anniversary. We took the River Room at the Savoy with dinner for ninety people. The delicious dinner was only £4 a head, unbelievably, and even with flowers and music the bill (which I still have) was only £940.92. At the last minute my mother-in-law said she was too deaf to come, although she had much wanted to sit next Harold Macmillan. She was waiting up to hear all about it when we got back. Alec and Elizabeth Douglas-Home and Jeremy Thorpe had to pull out as they were dining with Queen Juliana.

In October Richard's work took us first to Afghanistan and then on to Pakistan and India. On our way to Kabul we spent a night in Teheran, where Peter Ramsbotham was in the middle of his term as Ambassador. Peter was an old friend. Only a year older than Richard, they had been in the same house at Eton. Peter had fought in the war when he needn't have done, as he'd had polio. Moreover he wanted to be a diplomat but he wasn't prepared to take the Foreign Office exam and avoid the war that way. When in 1976 he was suddenly replaced by Peter Jay as Ambassador in Washington – because Jim Callaghan wanted to get his daughter away from David Owen – he accepted it all with good grace. When he died, a few years ago, I found that I missed him terribly.

Peter's father, Lord Soulbury, had been a great friend of Lady H and of ours too. He was unlucky with his wives. His first wife had diabetes and was unable to go with him when he was Governor of Ceylon, and she was then run over and killed in Sloane Street.

Some years later he took his second wife to New York for their honeymoon. In the New York hotel she had a sudden heart attack in the night and died. Ram (as we called him) rang down and asked the hotel if they would deal with his wife's body. They said they couldn't do anything about a dead body except in the middle of the night. They would bring a piano up the next night with its insides removed and take her out that way! Which they did.

Kabul was like a garden city, with the trees turning yellow, few tall buildings and ringed by mountains including the mighty Hindu Kush, already covered with snow. We were straightaway taken on a trip to the north of the country, through the Hindu Kush mountains, to the city of Konduz. The next day we went up to the border, formed by the Oxus river, and gazed across at this far-flung outpost of the Soviet Union.

In Konduz we were in a bungalow hotel and our room had been done up for Princess Alexandra a short time before. It had two tin 'servants' beds and a very grand candelabra between them which tinkled each time either of us turned over. Richard had been told to bring a black tie. He went to have the first bath, with hot water heated by a fire in the bathroom and took his clothes, putting them beside the bath. I heard a sudden call for help. When he let the bathwater out it just ran all over the floor and his clothes, as there was no waste plumbing. He had to wear a very damp dinner jacket. It was Ramadan and later that night our sleep was disturbed by a siren at 3.30 a.m. to warn the faithful to eat quickly before dawn.

After inspecting a sugar factory, to which Richard's department was considering giving help, we were back in Kabul after stopping for half an hour or more when it grew dark for the drivers to end Ramadan by eating. The next day, a Sunday, Richard insisted on going to church. It turned out to be a clandestine service taken by a retired priest (as the incumbent had been expelled for proselytising). The acting Ambassador thought it very unwise of us to go and would not risk sending his car. A taxi dropped us some way away and we had to walk across a sewage farm to get to the house where the service was being held. Its windows were blacked out, and we whispered our names through the door and were let in. There were about six people there. We felt a little like Early Christians in the catacombs. The priest embarrassed us by saying in the middle of the Communion Service: 'We are very honoured to have Her Majesty's Minister of Overseas Development and the Honourable Mrs Richard Wood with us.' At the end of the service we weren't allowed to go back the same way, but climbed over different sewers and somehow we found a taxi waiting for us.

Richard had a number of meetings with Afghan politicians, and after talking to the Deputy Prime Minister he reflected in his diary: 'At each of these talks we cover almost exactly the same ground. In any other country it would be utterly pointless, but here things move so slowly that there may be merit in the constant repetition of a point of view.' I was supposed to be meeting the King's daughter, but she lost her nerve and put me off, so I went instead to a fascinating open-air market.

On a hill above the city a cannon is still fired daily at noon. The gunner claimed that he set his watch by the main clock in Kabul, and the clock-keeper is sure his clock is right because he sets it by the midday gun. Ron Deare had meanwhile been collecting horrifying drug stories. He reported that there was no more room to bury dead hippies, who are left outside the city to be eaten by dogs.

★   ★   ★

At the end of October we were fetched in the Daimler belonging to Laurie Pumphrey for a glorious drive up the Khyber Pass to the Pakistani border. Laurie had been High Commissioner but was now Ambassador following Pakistan's recent exit from the Commonwealth (they later rejoined). Laurie met us at the border, where Richard inspected a guard of honour mounted by the Khyber Rifles and was charmed by an old bearded soldier who took both of Richard's hands in his while his eyes filled with tears. At the border Ron announced that he had a headache so I unpacked a large pigskin dressing-case which Myrtie used to take on their desert journeys, and produced aspirins from the very bottom of it while everyone looked on. I didn't think travelling with a dressing-case in the least odd.

Life with the Pumphreys was the greatest fun, despite the tendency of Jean (who was the daughter of Lord H's best man, Walter Riddell) to agree with everything one says before it was said. Being with Laurie was so enjoyable and he was a great tease. We toured the bazaar at Peshawar with a police escort and bought a vast copper ladle, which we thought would be useful for shooting parties. At the Embassy in Islamabad James Pumphrey, then eight, greeted us in the uniform of the Scots Guards. Laurie reported that he had a proper view of things and announced one morning: 'Get the flag ready. Excellency's just coming.'

Richard had long talks with the immigration controllers at our Embassy, where some fifty civil servants were struggling to check the credentials of Pakistanis wanting to emigrate to Britain. In the evening we had dinner with President Bhutto, who was occupying the house of the former British Commander-in-Chief at Rawalpindi, where as a child Richard had greatly enjoyed watching the Army's drill. Richard found Bhutto 'an entertaining companion with no obviously discernible principles'.

Laurie came with us on the night train to Lahore and the short drive afterwards to the Indian border. He was allowed to cross the no-man's-land up to the Indian side of the border, where we said a sad farewell. Then heavy garlands were hung around Richard's neck and he was led away to inspect a Sikh guard of honour.

We were welcomed with only moderate enthusiasm at the

Embassy in Delhi by Rosemary Garvey, although she talked less tragically about India that she had the year before. An early visit was to the former Durbar ground to inspect a statue of Lord H. It was lying on the ground under tarpaulins, together with the statues of three other viceroys – Lords Chelmsford, Reading and Willingdon. It was cast in concrete rather than marble and had suffered from the weather – the nose and an ear were missing. I had had an idea of getting it back to England and re-erecting it at Flat Top. But it was clearly not worth it. Respecting and loving Lord H as I had done, I was greatly depressed at the treatment of that statue.

The final leg of this trip was a visit to Madras. While we were briefly away from Delhi a telegram purporting to come from Terence Garvey offered us the use of the President's coach on the train to Madras. We were surprised but happily agreed. When we got back to Delhi, Rosemary rang my room and I was summoned down to see her. How dare Richard get this special treatment just because he had been the Viceroy's son! I explained that her husband had arranged it. She rang Terence in the Chancery and told him to come over straight away. She then lectured us both. Poor Terence confessed that one of his staff had sent the telegram in his name.

To her credit, she was then all smiles. She allowed us to take one of their bearers with us and she even came to see us off at the station and admired the comfort of the coach. The coach included a double bedroom, a dressing room, a drawing room and two bathrooms. There was also a room for Ron. This luxury was the more appreciated when students in the state of Hyderabad lay down on the line in protest at some grievance – and then climbed on top of the stationary train and banged on the windows – making a long journey even longer. Ron told Richard he was in danger sitting in the window where the students could see him, but he refused to budge.

Richard and I both had connections with Madras. At St Mary's

Church in the city – the oldest Anglican church east of Suez and the oldest British building in India – we were shown the record of the burial of Richard's eighteenth-century ancestor, Captain Charles Wood. My connection was more recent. My mother's boyfriend, Sir Arthur Hope, had been Governor of Madras throughout the war (after the war Sim was asked if he'd like to be Governor, but Anne put paid to that). In Madras I asked people about the Hopes. We liked *her* very much, they said. But he was dreadful. He picked up all the women!

⋆   ⋆   ⋆

Before this trip to Afghanistan and the Indian subcontinent we had spent a month in France and Spain. I had long had a passion for a particular area of the south coast of France, between Ste Maxime and St Raphael, ever since I had been taken there by my parents as a child. So Richard, Ed and I set off for France in the motor-caravan in early September with house-hunting very much in mind.

We were soon in Provence and began our searches with the help of a property agent. Near the village of Crestet in the Vaucluse, Richard and Ed became very enthusiastic about an old stone house with some outbuildings and a few acres, being offered for sale at a remarkably low price. They discussed its possibilities with growing excitement. I was much less keen. It was nowhere near the sea, for a start. Besides, I attached great importance to returning to where I'd been with my father.

We camped overnight nearby and met the agent and the owner again the next morning. I feared the worst. But as the price of the property was once again discussed I could sense a sudden change of heart in Richard. The reason was simple. The day before he had believed they said *mille* when they had actually said *million*. The owner wanted 16 *million* old francs, which meant 160,000 new ones (the French franc had been revalued in 1960 at one new franc for 100 old ones). Richard thought the price was 16 *mille* francs

(16,000 francs, then about £1300). What had seemed a bargain was now far from one. We made a rather embarrassing getaway, Richard muttering about the need to consult trustees.

In Ste Maxime we saw a notice about properties for sale and went to look at one of a number of modern houses on the side of a hill looking towards the sea, part of a new development. Ed and I immediately liked the design and layout of the house, Richard rather less so. He was never attracted to modern buildings and in particular to living beside other people. The next day we returned and were shown no.144, higher up the hill. This had a marvellous view of the whole of the Gulf of St-Tropez and even Richard was enthusiastic. The house had a steep bank below it, but we could see the possibilities of terracing it. The house was not at all what we thought we were looking for, but we liked it very much.

Having taken Ed to Marseilles to catch a plane home, we returned to the property office responsible for 144 Collines de Guerreville and completed the initial stages of the purchase. We began to look for basic furniture – the house was new and had none. After an all-important meeting, further north, with the Notaire, we began our journey to Brigid and Patrick Ness's house in Spain. A couple of days' driving along the coast of France and down the east coast of Spain took us to Casa Brigida, on the coast south of Valencia.

Brigid had married Patrick after she had left her first husband Fritzi, the Kaiser's grandson. I listened to Patrick talk about his earlier life while Richard chattered away to Brigid, his cousin and the great friend of his childhood. She had gone out to Rome to be with him when he was so unhappy in the Embassy and I think he always hoped to marry her – but she had other ideas.

We felt greatly refreshed by five days of complete peace. We slept downstairs beneath their bedroom but, finding twin beds with a table in-between, we moved the table and put the beds together, making a great noise on the stone floor in the process. Brigid apologised in the morning and said she'd heard it and couldn't think how she could have expected us to sleep in different beds as they wouldn't have. We went out in a small boat and swam in the sea and bought fish from the little fishing village of Calpe. The early October sun was still very hot and the siesta was an important part of the day. We left to drive across Spain to the port of Santurce near Bilbao, where we put the motor-caravan on a boat. We arrived in Southampton thirty-six hours later.

★ ★ ★

A week later we were in Paris for the annual UNESCO conference that Richard was obliged to attend. This year it came at a very helpful time, enabling us to take the next steps in the complicated process of buying a house in France.

We were given a splendid suite at the Crillon and Richard managed to get away from the conference for lunch *à quatre* with Christopher and Mary Soames at the Embassy. Christopher was in ebullient form: 'Of course, I should like to have been Foreign Secretary, but Teddo no doubt thinks I'm the best person for this job in Brussels. And he's obviously right.' (He went to Brussels in January 1973 as European Commissioner for Trade.) He was thrilled by the prospect of the next two months in England, with twenty-eight days' shooting. 'All the big houses, you name them, I'll be there.' Mary was much looking forward to living more in England.

My relationship with Christopher had greatly improved from a low point not very long before. He and Mary lived in Eaton Place a few doors down from us. Christopher had a large chauffeur-driven car. When he came out and I was washing our minute, bright-yellow Renault (given to Richard because he had lost his legs in the war) and I said hello, he cut me dead – and again when we met in the street. When, later, we were in Paris for his fiftieth birthday he came and sat on the arm of my chair after dinner and said, 'Why is it dear girl that I never see you?' I told about him cutting me, whereupon he stroked my back and we became friends thereafter, so much so that when he was dying in the Cromwell Hospital I rang to know how he was and they said he would like to talk, so we chatted a little and he died the next day.

That evening Richard had to fly back to London for a strongly whipped vote on the Common Market. He returned to Paris the next morning. Meanwhile I had been given invaluable help over the French property by Mary's very able secretary, Jane Morton, and had had useful meetings with the lawyer she had recommended. By the time we returned to England the legal documents were more or less in order. All that remained was for us to find – somehow, in that era of exchange control – the French currency needed to complete the deal.

CHAPTER 19

Coming Home to France

'I felt I was coming home and wondered why we ever went anywhere else. Only Bransdale and the desert hold the same magnetism ... The Côte d'Azur is as beautiful in winter as when I first came – aged seven and eleven-twelfths – to Val d'Esquières with Daddy [and Myrtie and Beakey] or with R in 1950 & cooked on the beach. How lovely that something is not spoilt, when one had thought it would be.'

This is what I wrote in a little diary that I kept on my first journey to the new house in France.

It was mid-December 1972 and I drove there on my own. Richard was due to fly to Nice a few days later. I set off in our Volvo in the dark early on Friday and arrived on the Saturday while it was still daylight. I had driven through frost and freezing fog, but after Vienne south of Lyon there was marvellous sunshine. I wasn't expected by Monsieur Fischer, the *Régisseur* or manager of the properties, for another two days, but he rigged up a light in the house, contrived to make the loo work and I moved in. My mother-in-law had said that I must send a telegram to say I'd arrived. Sending it took an interminable time – at first they refused because they said Bishop Wilton wasn't an exchange, although it was and still is – and it cost a great deal of money. In fact she never received it.

By the time Richard appeared with the unexpected and welcome addition of Ed who had been able to leave earlier than planned, a great deal had been done to make the place habitable. The terrace outside our bedrooms had even been completed. We worked hard, as did the local plumber. Richard used an electric drill with growing confidence, overcoming his fear of drilling through cables. The sun shone and we had our lunches outside, admiring the glorious view.

On Christmas Day we went to Matins in the Anglican church at St Raphael. The congregation was tiny. Lunch was woodcock from Garrowby. A huge treat rather than turkey, which I've never enjoyed.

Lady Halifax arrived at Nice airport to stay for a few days, quite proud of being able to get to us in the south of France in her eighty-eighth year. Somehow she managed to clamber down the steep garden without breaking a leg. Ed reported that one day his grandmother had four baths! A few days later we drove her to stay with a friend of hers, the widow of the brother of Lord Carnarvon (whose death in 1923 had been attributed to 'the curse of the pharaohs'). Catherine Peake joined them. We dropped Ed at Nice airport before we ourselves took the road home a couple of days later. It had been a memorable Christmas. Such fun to be alone, in the sunshine, with that heavenly view and the ever-changing sea; able to eat out and to have no feeling that we should entertain neighbours or call on people. Total luxury.

★   ★   ★

We were back at Les Collines for a couple of weeks at the end of May. We had paid a deposit on it but we still hadn't paid the bulk of the money that we owed. There were strict exchange controls and restrictions on the amount of sterling that could be freely converted into francs for export. The French owners had accepted the necessity of a delayed final payment, but time was running out.

John Astor, who had married my bridesmaid and Emma's god-mother Diana Drummond and was PPS to Richard, came to our rescue. His father, Lord Astor of Hever, had gone to live in France some years earlier because the Socialist Government had made his tax position in England impossible. In a clandestine operation, with no receipts asked for or given, John organised for a Swiss man to come to our flat and I handed him a carrier bag full of £s.

Then in France, at the Mandelieu service station on the motorway near Cannes, leaving Richard reading in our car, I got into another car and a man handed over a fat packet of French francs. Again, no receipt of any sort, all totally on trust. With these francs, and with great relief, we paid for the property.

Between January and May several people had been to stay, including my half-sister Fiona and her husband Charlie Allsopp, Joe Craddock (the very skilled joiner who did all the work for us at Flat Top over many years) and his wife and daughter, and Myrtie and Billy. The rosemary and cypress we had bought at Christmas had been planted and were growing well. We had brought out with us thirty iron stanchions to hold up the terraces.

Peter Smithson and his wife and four sons stayed in the house just before we returned. Peter was a senior government driver who drove Richard on official business and also on many private occasions. Peter's memoir, *Driven to Downing Street*, includes an anecdote about Richard:

During the time I was driving Richard Wood, one of the main things I had to do was make sure I always had a spare pair of his artificial legs in the boot of the car. I remember one amusing incident when he arrived from his Yorkshire home by train. He would always make his way down the corridors to the front of the train until he was close to the engine, so that when the train came to a standstill, I would be opposite his carriage door. On this particular occasion, the train stopped and he stepped out of the carriage, but unfortunately there was a small patch of oil on the platform and as soon as his foot went on it, his legs slid from underneath him and snapped his artificial leg at the knee. He landed on the platform, with one leg over his shoulder. I knew I had a spare pair of his artificial legs in the car, so I grabbed a porter's trolley and helped Richard onto it and then proceeded to take him to our car. As I wheeled him towards the station entrance where the car was parked, we got some very funny looks from passengers when they saw this immaculately dressed man sitting on a porter's trolley with one leg over his shoulder and with a big smile on his face!

Peter had been Michael Foot's driver. When Richard was interviewing him, he said that Michael Foot would not let him wear a chauffeur's cap; he thought it was demeaning. Richard would have preferred Peter to wear a cap but he was not brave enough to insist.

Richard's first regular driver had been a man called Fred Wilson. He had left to start a business and asked Richard if he would be prepared to lend him £2,000 if he really needed it; he would pay it back of course. Before Richard went abroad he told his mother to give Wilson the money if necessary. She did give him the money, reluctantly. He then went bankrupt. Later, Richard saw him in the street outside Cadogan Place, looking very down and out. The only job he could get was cleaning the streets. At that time Charlie Halifax had just been made Lord Lieutenant and wanted a chauffeur. Richard suggested Fred Wilson. He got the job and the use of a house and Mrs Wilson worked in the house at Garrowby. A happy ending, even if Wilson never offered to pay back any of the £2,000!

If I was alone I had always sat in the back of a government car. But then Elizabeth Home told me that she always sat in the front with the driver if Alec wasn't there. The unspoken implication, I felt, was that it was rather pompous to do otherwise. So I followed suit.

Elizabeth always had the nicest manners and was responsible for a 'Ritz and the ditch' moment when Alec was Foreign Secretary. I was in Yorkshire and I happened to have been scrubbing a floor when I got an urgent call from her. Someone had fallen out, so could I come, that evening, to the grand dinner in the Painted Hall in Greenwich for ambassadors that the Foreign Secretary gives to celebrate the Queen's birthday. I rushed down to London and arrived at Greenwich in tiara and ball dress, just in time. The Painted Hall is probably the grandest room in London. Elizabeth walked down the entire length of it, past the array of diplomats, to take me up to my place on the top table.

★   ★   ★

Early in the new year Richard's job took us back to Africa – to Zambia and Kenya – and then on to Mauritius. The Mauritian High Commissioner came to see us off at Heathrow – it was hard to escape such people who were only doing their job, however unwelcome such attention was to us.

Lusaka was a sadder place for us without Oliver Green-Wilkinson, and Richard found Kaunda himself less friendly than he had been before. A number of Zambians had recently been killed by Rhodesian land-mines and the problem of Rhodesia was poisoning relations between Britain and Zambia.

Tony Duff met us at Nairobi. He was highly competent, work-obsessed and single-minded – and rather exhausting. Perhaps he was determined to show up the idleness of his Ministerial visitors! We set off with him the next day on a long drive to Lake Rudolf in the north of the country. We could have flown, but we had said that we preferred to drive. We got considerable credit for this. It was put down to our supposed desire to meet as many Africans as possible, although the real reason was my dislike of flying. It was a glorious drive. Richard wrote in his diary:

We were delayed by District Commissioners' welcomes and police

changeovers – the police are determined to accompany us the whole
way to Lake Rudolf – but we made good progress on a very adequate
track, down the escarpment from the highlands to drier hill country
and so down to the hot plains. I loved it, and so did Diana, saying
pointedly in Duff's hearing, 'This really washes away all the cocktail
parties and the aeroplanes.' We stopped several times for a cold drink
and had a splendid lunch under the trees on the dry sandy bed of a
river … Duff and Diana [sounds like the Duff Coopers!] paused to
climb a low hill to inspect an apparent water-tower in the middle of
nowhere. The whole contents of a police Landrover shadowed them
up the hill, with rifles at the ready.

We reached the lake, its shore lined with multitudes of birds, as light
was fading. The inexhaustible Duff made us join a cocktail party the
moment we arrived, not even allowing us to wash and tidy up. No
wonder his wife Polly had refused to come with us. The next day
we inspected a fishery project in its infancy, going out in a research
boat and making a short trawl of the lake. The tiger fish were the
only beautiful ones and a large Nile perch at the bottom of the
net.

On our way back to Nairobi we inspected various enterprises –
cattle, sugar, tea. We found that a constant stream of un-jolly parties
and the eternal obligation to politeness was slowly draining the
energy out of us. My parents had adored Kenya before the war.
They had been in the country when Josslyn Erroll was there and
had enormous parties day after day, including Jock Broughton, Bert
and Mary Marlborough and Porchy Carnarvon (who had given
Myrtie a silver Cartier cigarette box with a map of their African
journeys engraved on the lid, a tiny jewel or gemstone marking
each pivot of the journey). But I didn't feel the same. Somehow
it felt sham. It seemed that the English who were there, with the
exception of Pam Scott, a Buccleuch granddaughter who had lived
in Kenya all her grown-up life, no longer really belonged there.

Waiting in the official car while Richard was calling on a Minister, the driver told me quite unashamedly that he had never bothered to take a driving test. He then asked me which tribe ran the shops in London. Thinking quickly I said, 'The Scots'. With which he seemed entirely satisfied.

Mauritius was humid and wet, but it was something of a relief to have left Kenya. The island nation was lovelier than I had imagined and we stayed in a little white chalet on the edge of the sea. It was newly independent, but still a member of the Commonwealth. The French had been gone for over 150 years, yet the French influence was tenacious. Most people spoke French more readily than English. The Prime Minister, Sir Seewoosagur Ramgoolam, a cheerful old Hindu from Bihar in India, gave me a bracelet of Indian gold and Richard a large and beautiful model of a sailing ship, which we carefully brought home.

We left the island with regret, I think because the connection with Britain was strong and everyone had seemed so pleased to see us.

⋆ ⋆ ⋆

It was heaven to get back to Les Collines at the end of August. We had let it for a month, so there was some tidying up to do. But both house and garden were beginning to seem more established. Our Swiss neighbours next door, George Durst and his wife Heidi, were pleasantly agreeable and helpful. It was hot. Anne came to stay for a week and we showed her some of the surrounding country. She knew the bit beyond Cannes well, as she and Sim had stayed there several times in the house of Sim's friend, Lady Price.

We continued planting, including over two hundred camomile plants which we had brought out from England for a lawn, as the grass grew so badly there. And we made some expeditions into the hills to dig up plants. We had acquired a gardener called Monsieur Perichou, who took some care to inform us that his great-great-great-grandfather had been a Marquis before the Revolution. He organised two Moroccans to build three small flights of steps in the garden, very necessary given the steep slopes. Unlike us, the French allowed Moroccans and Algerians to come to France if they had a job to come to, but they had to return when they had no work. They could not bring their families.

Towards the end of September Richard began an official visit to West Africa. I was due to go too, but I backed out entirely because of my fear of flying. What a coward I was. As well as Mali, the itinerary included the Ivory Coast, the Gambia, Sierra Leone and the Canary Islands, which I decided I couldn't face. I missed seeing Timbucktoo. Richard was eagerly looking forward to setting eyes on this legendary place, to which he had insisted taking Teddy. He reported that the reality was very disappointing, but perhaps he was there too briefly. In Sierra Leone, looking down from a helicopter on a bay near Freetown, he reflected that he had been in that bay thirty-two years before, on board the troop-ship *Franconia* on his way to the Western Desert.

★　　★　　★

The year ended with a far-flung trip right around the world, eight countries in three weeks, from South America to New Zealand and Australia via Fiji. We began with Peru. In Quito in Ecuador I visited a women's prison. Among the prisoners was a young American wife in tears, waiting indefinitely to be tried for not uprooting the marijuana in the garden which she and her husband had recently taken over in Quito. I was impressed by the reasonably smart appearance of most of the prisoners, many of whom were serving up to twelve years for abortions. (In Egypt, where I had visited a women's prison where many of the inmates were also serving sentences for having had abortions, all the female prisoners had been given new white clothes for my visit – so I had perhaps helped them in a small way.) In Bogota the Ambassador took us for a drive, as Richard noted in his diary:

We drove north out of Bogota in a Daimler so large that all the Colombian drivers – and the traffic was very heavy – turned their heads in amazement. The windows were sealed and the doors locked. Two policemen in plain clothes drove close behind us. We were in constant touch, by radio telephone, with the outside world, and the Ambassador carried a small spray in his breast pocket which would immediately paralyse any attacker. Alarms were fitted in his house to alert the police immediately if any windows were opened. I was the more glad not to be staying there!

In Bogota's Gold Museum we gazed at the exquisite artistry of the El Dorado Raft, made of pre-Columbian gold and turning under a spotlight on a lake of glass. In Fiji Richard was presented, by a tall Fijian, with a black ebony stick inlaid with mother of pearl, the only stick ever given to him which he found long enough to use.

Then it was on to New Zealand. We moved from the South to the North Island, and Richard insisted on driving the train, just as he later did when, as a member of the Committee investigating the viability of the Channel Tunnel, he drove a TGV at nearly 200 mph. Lady Halifax's father had been Governor of New Zealand at the end of the nineteenth century and Richard made a note of places that his mother might remember from her childhood years, including the seaside where she and her sister were banished because there was an outbreak of typhoid. Her sister Gwenny had had to do her lessons on the telephone, with the result that she would barely use one for the rest of her life. Her younger brother, who was born in 1890 and christened Victor because Queen Victoria was his sponsor, was always known by his Maori name of Huia and was given a Maori house which is still at Clandon where they lived.

After a brief visit to Australia and an even briefer one to Singapore – where I did some shopping and Richard ordered two suits – we turned, thankfully, for home.

CHAPTER 20

Producing China and Books

Only a few months later, in February 1974, after the trauma of the three-day week, there was a General Election. It was very narrowly lost by the Conservatives. Even so there was something like a four-day wait before Ted Heath gave up the possibility of a coalition with the Liberals. Jeremy Thorpe pondered but refused. He wrote to Richard and said he would have liked to be working with him but did not think he would join Ted. We prayed hard that Jeremy would come up trumps, but it was not to be. So we had a Labour Government. Later in the year at the next election the Socialists substantially increased their majority and it looked likely that they would be in for several years.

With the election of Margaret Thatcher to replace Ted as Conservative leader the following year, Richard's political career was effectively at an end. Margaret did not get in touch with Richard. John Peyton, who had been Richard's Parliamentary Secretary at the Ministry of Power but who was not in Ted's Government, decided to see Margaret and ask for a job in her Shadow Cabinet. She appointed him Shadow Minister of Agriculture, so John told Richard to do likewise. Her answer to him was very different: 'There is no going back.' He minded very much not being in the Government but realised he would not have been happy in any government of hers. They had little in common; unlike him she was a very political being. He also minded that she had no sense of humour, though he admired her as a politician.

An incident a few years earlier had suggested that times were changing. In the early 1970s we had gone to a lunch given by Alec and Elizabeth in the Foreign Secretary's house in Carlton Gardens. Richard had to answer Parliamentary Questions that afternoon and left early. I was sitting next to Norman Tebbit, a new MP, who had arrived in a zip-up leather jacket, very odd for those days. When Richard left, Tebbit said to me: 'Who is he, anyway?' I never liked him after that.

Richard didn't, however, give up all Parliamentary interests. He was recruited onto the Hansard Commission on Electoral Reform, to try and come up with a fairer voting system than first-past-the-post. (In the end he decided that its unfairness was preferable to the pitfalls of the other systems.) Sunday trading was another much-debated topic, one on which we felt the same. We wanted Sundays without racing, football, etc., and thought seven-day shopping unnecessary.

It was clear however that we now had more time for other interests. One stood ready to hand. We had had a connection for a long time with Queen Elizabeth's Foundation for the Disabled. It had been started in the 1930s by my mother's cousin, Dame Georgiana Buller (the daughter of General Sir Redvers Buller), and the Queen Mother had become its patron when she was Duchess of York. After the war Dame Georgiana wanted to involve disabled ex-servicemen, so she drafted in Richard and Julian Holland-Hibbert, who had been paralysed at Enfidaville, as governors.

Richard had become a governor in 1947, and in 1954 I too became a governor and I sat on committees. Years later Diana Holland-Hibbert joined us. In those days new people were not imposed on us from outside, but instead everyone who was a governor was a friend of someone else who was. We all felt that worked much better than what happens now – but there is no putting the clock back. Charles and Catherine Peake's son, Joh Seb, having had a house at Eton and then become headmaster of a school in South

Africa, came home and needed a job. Richard and I asked Malcolm Clark, who was then running the Foundation, if he would consider appointing Joh Seb to run the Training College and he would live there free. Malcolm generously agreed.

In 1965 Myrtie and I, along with Jocelyn Crean whose husband was Treasurer of the Foundation, had started Guinness and Oyster Luncheons in aid of the Foundation. We got Richard's Guinness cousins to give us the Guinness for free. The first year the tickets were £3 for everything, increased to £5 a year later, and we moved from one livery hall to another, only inviting people we knew. We had taken Margaret Thatcher to a lunch in aid of the Foundation when she was Richard's Parliamentary Secretary at the Ministry of Pensions and National Insurance in 1964. I tried to sit on the bridesmaid's seat in the official car, but Peter Smithson said that Margaret should sit there and me beside Richard on the back seat.

Myrtie was firm that we must never hold these lunches on a day there was racing, as her friends would always put that first. Her other insistence was that she and I must cut the brown bread and butter because no livery hall cut it thin enough. It was hard work. Now, fifty-two years since the first Oyster Lunch, many more people come and invitations are sent to anyone. It is always held in the Mansion House and the tickets have increased from £5 to £75, the Lord Mayor no longer wears morning dress and most guests often no tie.

The Foundation ran a Training College at Leatherhead and had a workshop for the disabled at nearby Dorincourt, where some rather ordinary tiles and other products were produced. We thought there were considerable possibilities if only they could produce something more attractive. We enlisted the help of John Cowdray, whose Pearson business had bought Royal Doulton. He agreed to supply us with fine bone-china plates at cost and an expert to come down and teach the disabled workers the necessary skills.

We then got the painter and muralist Graham Rust, who had done a mural for us at Flat Top – his first mural had been a huge one for his friend Hugh Hertford at Ragley – to produce some beautiful plate designs for a number of country houses. One commission was for plates and mugs for Purdeys, then owned by Richard Beaumont who had been a childhood friend; another was for Jubilee plates for King Hussein of Jordan. We also got the workshop to do some decorations on glass. We ran the marketing at the Foundation between 1978 and 1989, helped at Dorincourt by two superb secretaries, Nancy Hand and Sylvia Lawes, with both of whom I'm still in touch. (A list of our more important commissions is in an appendix at the end of the book.)

Before she was famous – she was living and working in one room off the King's Road at the time – Emma Bridgewater approached me and asked if the QEFD would make her pottery. She came down to Leatherhead and was marvellous with the workers and explained to them what they would need to do. Richard and I were mad keen. Sadly, the powers that be felt it would put too much strain on the disabled workers, and they said no to her. What an opportunity wasted.

Another person that I came across before she was famous was Jo Malone. In the late Seventies I used to go once a month – as did Princess Alexandra – to Jo's mother to have my face done in a dreary basement off Kensington High Street, where Jo, in her mid-teens, used to fetch and carry for her mother. One day when her mother wasn't well, she asked if Jo could do my face if I paid half price.

★   ★   ★

We were back at Les Collines just before the second 1974 election, pleased with improvements inside and delighted that what we had planted was growing well – plumbago, bougainvillea, wisteria, rosemary and buddleia, cypresses and a lemon tree. One day we made a little expedition along the coast to St-Tropez in a tiny fibreglass tub hired at Les Collines' private beach and powered by a small outboard motor which we had brought out. All went well until we reached St-Tropez harbour at what appeared to be the rush hour. The wash from a large boat swamped our outboard motor and we nearly capsized. But eventually we refuelled and restarted the motor and got back safely.

The pleasure at this little success was spoilt the next morning when we discovered there had been a thief in the night, who had got in through an open window. Some money and Richard's tape-recorder (which was huge, had belonged to Lord H and cost £75 in 1958) had been stolen, along with a lead peeing-boy fountain (a small replica of the one in Brussels) from the garden. Once the police had taken some details about my parents and Richard's mother's maiden name, they seemed to lose interest.

We began to wonder if there might be other houses in the development which might suit us better, as 144 was very small. On our next visit in the following May we found exactly that, further down the hill: 65 Collines de Guerrevielle. It had an extra floor, which was badly needed. Best of all, it had a larger and flatter garden. And beyond the garden was an area of wilderness stretching towards the sea. The possibilities of developing it were too exciting to be missed. So we bought it.

At the end of August we were back again, in a Citroen piled high with beds and mattresses, to move into number 65. We set about digging and planting without delay. The wilderness beyond our garden was neglected by everyone so, without asking anyone, we decided to look after it ourselves. Ed came out to stay, as did Anne. Bizarrely, there was another thief in the night, a year to the day after the burglary at the last house. Ed's Gucci case and a watch from his bedside table were taken. He had gone to sleep with the light on and the thief had thoughtfully turned it off.

In the early 1970s Ed had gone out with a rather pretty girl whose parents were a bit strange. He had taken her to Cambridge for the weekend. The next thing we knew was that her stern and humourless father had gone to Richard's office and demanded to see him. The Private Secretary said that was impossible, so he was soon outside our front door at Eaton Place. 'I need to see you,' he said. 'Something very serious has happened. Do you realise that your son took my daughter to Cambridge for the weekend? Well, he's got to marry her now.' I tried to calm him down. The next moment he was on the phone, summoning his wife from Hertfordshire and telling her: 'When you arrive I will go and walk in the street outside.' I had a truly ghastly couple of hours with him before she arrived. She was rather feeble and simply said, 'What will we do if our daughter doesn't marry him?' Eventually they left. Later her father wrote to Richard, declaring it was all perfectly awful and Richard was responsible. It had felt like a scene from a nineteenth-century novel!

★   ★   ★

In the mid-1970s the Provost of Eton, Harold Caccia, was close to retirement and Richard was approached to succeed him. Elizabeth Home was on the school's Governing Board and wanted Richard to be the next one. Both Richard and I longed for him to do it, but in the end the job went to Martin Charteris, the Queen's Private Secretary. I am told he did it very well, but I would have loved it for Richard.

Another possibility was running the Royal Ballet School. While this was being considered, we had a thorough look at the junior ballet school at White Lodge in Richmond Park and the senior one, then in Talgarth Road. But in the end the powers that be decided that Richard would find it difficult to stand up to Ninette de Valois, the formidable founder of the School and still a dominant force in its affairs.

Being on the Friends of Covent Garden committee, Richard was allowed to ask for things that the Opera House was going to get rid of. That's how we got the scenery from a production of *Tosca*, which we used to decorate the walls of the enormous barn at the bottom of our drive at Flat Top. The scenery provided a dramatic and elegant background to the parties, dances and shooting lunches we had there.

I had had a strange evening at the Opera House while Ted was still Prime Minster. The Emperor Haile Selassie was in London and had expressed an interest in seeing the ballet. Knowing Richard's connection with Covent Garden, Ted asked him if he could borrow me to sit in the Royal Box with the Emperor and his daughter. After we had watched the first scene, I got up and suggested to the Emperor that we move into the dining room for dinner. I was answered with 'No'. I then tried his daughter, who said, 'The Emperor says no.' Ted looked in but got the same answer. At the end of the second scene I tried again and had no luck. So I never got to see the Royal Box's dining room, which I was curious to see, and I'm sure we would have had a good dinner! It was very odd having only three people in the Royal Box which can hold about sixteen, and Richard sitting by himself in the stalls.

★ ★ ★

Myrtie flew out to stay with us in France for a week in January 1976. She had never come on her own before, but Fiona promised to look after Billy in case he got drunk. It was fun for a few days and then one morning she woke up and was very slow and sometimes confused. But she flatly refused to say anything was wrong. We had never been allowed to know that she had had cancer, since the year after we married, though Anne who always told one everything had done so, which was awkward knowing but not being supposed to know. When we took her to Nice Airport she could hardly walk, but she declined a wheelchair.

We went to see her the day we got back from France, as we always did, and although she was still finding walking difficult she went out gambling with Monica Sheriffe. She then collapsed in the street and was taken to St Mary's Paddington, where an inoperable brain tumour was diagnosed. As there was nothing that anyone could do, we were allowed to take her home, where Billy and their housekeeper looked after her.

At the hospital Myrtie had been put into a public ward, as the nurses were on strike and wouldn't admit private patients. Richard went round and he was told that Roger Bannister was coming to see her the next morning. So I went and hung around, and when I saw Roger Bannister I said, 'I hear you are very kindly coming to see my mother, Mrs McGowan.' He answered very coolly, 'I'll see who the staff tell me to see.' When I saw him some years later at Leeds Castle, where he was on the board, I said 'Good evening' to him but nothing more. I was still furious with him.

My mother-in-law died on 2nd February. Then Billy's sister, Nan Sheffield, was murdered on 11th March by a young house painter. He had tried to steal her car and she had attempted to stop him. Carmen (Billy's brother's wife), not having any idea Myrtie was ill, came to tell them the news about Nan. Five days later, on 16th March, Myrtie died. Her funeral was held in the Guards Chapel and Antony Head read the lesson. The service was taken by the same man, George Hales, who had been Flash's chaplain in the desert and had buried him thirty-three years earlier to the day. We took Myrtie down to Shipton Moyne in Gloucestershire, where she was buried with her sister Iso.

Three days after Myrtie's funeral, Nan's was held in Oxfordshire. Her children only discovered that morning that they were not allowed to have the body because of the murder, so they just processed up the aisle as if with a coffin. Richard and I then had to rush back to Yorkshire, where Ted Heath – never the easiest person to entertain – was coming that evening to stay and address Richard's constituents. I wasn't surprised when one constituent said to me, 'You look a bit tired, dear.' 'Yes, I am,' I replied. 'It's been quite a week.'

My cousin Susie and her husband Archie Kidston stayed with us happily in France in May 1977 but less than a year later he had died too. He had a brain tumour, and Richard and I stayed with them for six weeks while he was dying. She refused to tell her children how ill he was. After his funeral we returned to London and I went with Susie to the bank, expecting to find a tiara and her engagement ring and her pearls. But in the bank vaults there was only tissue paper. Archie, who had once had so much money, had spent it all – on a cook and a butler, for whom he bought a house, on fishing rights, a grouse moor and race horses. Susie couldn't understand what had happened to all the money. But she never blamed him, even for selling her engagement ring.

Their daughter Cath, who went on to become such a successful entrepreneur, developing shops all around the world, is my god-daughter and Richard and I were for a time guardians of all the Kidston children after Archie died. When Cath had been born I had gone to see Susie at the London Clinic. When I got there, I was told she wasn't there. I said that I knew she was, as Archie had rung me up. They then said that Matron would like to see me. By now I was convinced that she'd died. Matron arrived and asked me to go through to the back. Susie had either mumps or measles and you weren't allowed an infectious disease in the hospital. So they had hidden mother and daughter in one of the nurses' rooms.

*   *   *

Life at Flat Top was now rather quieter. Beakey had left at the end of the 1960s, long after her usefulness as a nursery governess was over. When in Morocco with Ed we had discussed with him the question of her leaving, but he had vetoed it, so she stayed on for two or three more years. We bought her a flat in York and later she moved into an old people's home. Then in the mid-1970s Hilda left us, having been offered a brand-new council flat in the local town. We were very fond of her, and she had been with us since before Ed was born. We missed all she did for us, but also seeing her. We still had a part-time gardener and we employed, part-time, Eleanor Mounsey who lived in Bishop Wilton, for help in the house. But getting back from London every weekend to an empty house was not at all easy.

Eleanor Mounsey's employment had ended abruptly. She had become a friend and I was lazy about buying her National Insurance stamps, so I gave her my share of it and asked her to get the stamps from the post office. After about ten years she came to me in tears and confessed that she hadn't bought the stamps. Instead she had helped herself to the money and now the Pensions Department were after her and had told her she had to get me to send all the money, including her share, for all the missing years. It was a financial blow, but I felt guilty and, worse, she was so embarrassed that she couldn't go on working for us. She was, however, still willing to come with us and Hilda to a Garden Party at Buckingham Palace!

A visit from Princess Margaret to Flat Top took us by surprise. Her marriage with Snowdon was in meltdown and she had asked herself to stay with my brother-in-law Charlie Halifax when he was Lord Lieutenant. Charlie then persuaded us to lay on a barbecue in our farm buildings below the house. I'd never done one before, but Richard's niece, Sue, and I did our best. We curtsied to Princess Margaret in our gumboots and said we hoped the barbecue was alright. 'Much too hot' was the answer.

Later I asked her if she would be kind enough to meet Hilda, who was in the kitchen next door to the Barn, only to be told that she was on holiday, so she wouldn't. Then she asked for coffee, which we'd forgotten. While Ursula Westbury and I went up to the house to get it, she started playing the old out-of-tune cottage piano. When she was given the coffee, Tatton Sykes took over the piano. As his playing was so much better than hers, she was thoroughly put out and said, 'Charles, I think we'll go home now.' Not a successful evening.

Richard retired as an MP at the 1979 election and was given a life peerage. He chose the title of Lord Holderness – he suggested Flamborough, but Fiona Allsopp said that would sound as if he was in flames. Holderness was obvious. I was descended from the last Earl of Holdernesse (as incidentally was Myles Hildyard, which made us twelfth cousins), my uncle had been MFH of the Holderness Hunt, we had always worn Holderness Hunt gloves as children and Holderness was about a third of the Bridlington constituency. But Richard had to ask permission of Lady D'Arcy de Knayth, who (although she didn't know it) was the direct descendant of the last Lord Holderness.

We gave a lunch for fifty or sixty people in a private dining room in the House of Lords that November before Richard was introduced to the Lords by Peter, the 6th Lord Carrington, and Nathaniel, the 21st Lord Saye and Sele. Peter told us that the first Lord Carrington had been booed because he was 'in trade'. We would very much have liked to have had Jeremy and Marion Thorpe at the lunch, but feelings against him were still running strongly among some. He said, Look, if people aren't going to come because of me, I won't come.

The following February Richard made his maiden speech from exactly the same red-leather seat that he'd used for his maiden speech in the Commons thirty years before (when the Commons was being rebuilt after the war and had made use of the Lords' debating chamber). Richard had few regrets at leaving the Commons and I had even fewer. It was true that the late-night sittings in the Commons did mean that people could have another job in the day and thus have a better idea how most people lived. But I remember an occasion when Richard had said he'd be back at about eleven in the evening. At 2 a.m. he wasn't back. I rang the Commons to ask, 'Could you tell me, are they still sitting?' 'They are,' was the answer, 'and you're the fourteenth wife who has rung to ask.'

CHAPTER 21

St Helena

'No, not individual cottage pies. We've got an Indian princess, a Field Marshal and the Foreign Secretary. You've *got* to do better than that.' A distraught Ed was on the telephone to a local take-away shop. It was the early 1980s, and Richard and I had borrowed Ed's large flat for a grand dinner party. But the best-laid plans had gone awry. Ed had organised a butler and a cook for the evening but neither had turned up.

The guests were Ayesha Jaipur, Roly Gibbs (the Field Marshal) and his wife Davina, Valerie and Francis Pym, then Foreign Secretary, and Johnny Cornell and his wife Caroline, who was Bill Adams's granddaughter. Johnny was commanding the 4th Battalion Royal Green Jackets and Richard was their Honorary Colonel. I reported Ed's telephone conversation to them. I'm glad to say that no one minded – except Ed, who was furious. Instead they thought it very funny. I still laugh about it when I see Davina Gibbs.

Toby and Minta Aldington were old friends – Minta's father, Sir Harold MacMichael, had expelled Myrtie, Anne and Ruth from Palestine in 1940 as 'illegal wives', but we didn't hold that against her! She used to go and see Richard when he was in hospital in Cairo and her first husband was Paul Bowman, whose sister Pam wanted to marry Richard, so there was always a joke that Richard and she might have been brother- and sister-in-law.

When Toby was accused of war crimes by Count Nikolai Tolstoy and Toby sued Tolstoy for libel, we attended a number of the court hearings. Richard managed to avoid Nigel Nicolson, who he thought had behaved very badly towards Toby by supporting Tolstoy, who lost the case but declared himself bankrupt, so Toby never got the £1,500,000 he was awarded. Years before, in the 1950s, we had met Nigel's parents Harold and Vita at a rather terrifying private dinner party with the Queen and Prince Philip at Buckingham Palace. Nigel was then married to Philippa Tennyson d'Eyncourt, who was an old school friend of mine.

Around this time Toby and Minta had us to stay at Leeds Castle, where Toby was the chairman of the trust that ran the castle. On the Friday night there was a dinner for the Crown Prince of Luxembourg. Ted Heath was expected to come for dinner but at the last minute he never turned up, so all the seating had to be changed. The next morning I ran into him as I came in from the garden. He was in dirty white clothes and shoes, so I said, 'Hello, Ted. Have you been playing tennis?' He answered very brusquely, 'No, why should you think I have?' On the Saturday evening there was grand concert where we sang 'Land of Hope and Glory'. Ted said he strongly disapproved of it. He was not easy to please!

*   *   *

In the 1980s, with Richard in the Lords rather than an MP, we had fewer ties than we'd had before and we continued the printing and publishing which we had begun at Queen Elizabeth's Foundation, using the name 'Wilton 65' (Wilton from Bishop Wilton in Yorkshire and 65 from Les Collines in France). We were greatly helped by Michael and Frances Howorth, who had started a stationery shop in Sloane Street. I had met them going in to buy a biro, but they had a photocopier and we began to take things in to be copied. Soon they were helping us with the printing. They became great friends, as is their daughter who was only two when we first met. Michael had been a sailor and we gave him the lovely model of a sailing ship that had been presented to us in Indonesia on Richard's official visit there.

In 1984 I bought a cheap electric typewriter in order to typeset Patrick Ness's autobiography, *Also Ran* – but at Les Collines Catherine Peake tripped over the typewriter cord and everything I'd done was lost. I had to start again. (We published *Also Ran* in 1986 and later several more of his books.)

I realised I needed a computer. In Peter Jones a very helpful young man called Mark Buttle tried to explain about using a mouse and so on. It all made no sense to me. But we arranged for him to come and give private computer lessons to us at home, and this made all the difference. He helped us set the first book we published about St Helena, dealing with all the artwork including photographs taken by Frances Howorth. In turn Richard helped him to get an operation which he badly needed. He and his wife Mary have remained friends ever since.

In 1989 our working association with Queen Elizabeth's Foundation ended when a fire destroyed their headquarters at Leatherhead. Our office and all our files and records were destroyed. But Richard remained its President until 1996 when I succeeded him and then in 2007 Corinna Hamilton took over from me.

As well as books we printed other things, notably Orders of Service and Christmas cards. December became an anxious month, often dealing with orders in a hurry, especially for Paul and Ingrid Channon, who always had 800 cards but never came to a firm decision about what photograph to use until mid-December or later.

I had never met David Montgomery, Monty's son, until we found ourselves on the same table at Peter and Iona Carrington's golden wedding party in the Banqueting Hall. Paul Channon had begun to be forgetful and didn't turn up, so we were only nine at our table. I found myself next a woman absolutely covered in emeralds and diamonds, who was foreign and who had had a stroke. The other side of her was David Montgomery. *Faute de mieux* we started trying to talk as three, but David and I ended up, very rudely, just talking to each other – particularly about Boy Browning, who was his father-in-law. Eventually the poor woman asked us if we would like her to move next to her friend on the other side of the table. Shamefully we agreed. Fiona, having seen this, came running down the room and told me I had behaved disgracefully. She was right as of course I had. But it was fun. I saw David again later that year, together with Rommel's son, at the El Alamein service in Westminster Abbey and at lunch afterwards – the fiftieth anniversary of the battle.

Emma's son Tom was born on 9th August 1982, and he was christened at Kirby Underdale where Richard and his parents and Charlie and Ruth are all buried. Emma and Nicholas held a christening party in our barn afterwards. In April 1983 they brought Tom out to stay with us in France. It was a very happy time, and Nicholas and I often used to carry Tom for walks around places we knew so well. Emma speaks French fluently and, though Nicholas never much liked the French, on this occasion I think he much enjoyed himself. We looked after Tom while they went out to dine and we missed them when they left.

Ed had married Joanna Pinches in Westminster Abbey in 1977 and their daughter Leo was born on 11th August 1982, just two days after her cousin Tom. Ed and Hugh Trenchard had been best friends since the day they arrived at Eton. They were in Australia together for part of their gap year and they were best man for each other, as well as each being godfather to the other's eldest child.

*　　*　　*

Trips to Les Collines had by now become a major part of our lives. We usually made three a year. I calculated that, by the time we finally left, if you added up the months we had spent there, we had actually lived in France for more than six years.

We always drove there and back. On early journeys we visited the battlefields of the First World War. And quite by chance, near

Arras, I found the grave of Flash's brother. Discovering he had died of wounds I burst into tears. (How lucky Flash was to have had his head blown off, and die immediately, as Lord Freyberg had told me he had, at lunch when I was twenty-three.) One year it was Ypres and Passchendaele; another time it was Verdun, a fine old town with steep narrow streets and a grim but fascinating museum where there had once been a village. We saw the railway carriage (or, strictly speaking, a replica of it) where Foch had accepted the German surrender in the Forest of Compiègne. Most dramatic was the Lochnager Crater at La Boiselle on the Somme. We crept nervously to the edge of the crater and peered into it, 90 feet deep and 300 feet across, the result of 60,000 lbs of explosives from a British mine underneath it.

At Les Collines there was always plenty to do. Lots of people came to stay. They included my cousin Susie, Myles, Catherine, Mothy, Brigid and Patrick, Anne, Fiona and Charlie, Graham Rust and David Cossart, Bob and Hilaré Ryder, John and Pip Green-Wilkinson, Crystal Tweedie (Billy Brooksbank's younger sister), Mary Sheepshanks and many more. The garden, and especially the huge wilderness beyond, always needed work.

Moreover we were often typing or working on books. For a while we even did personalised children's books on request. You wrote a fairly simple story and put in the child's name as the main character, as well as the rest of the family and the name of their house. Sometimes we put in photographs too. These were commissioned by Eximious, that rather smart luggage shop, and John Hayter, a very old friend from the 4th Battalion Royal Green Jackets, used to take them back to London as he had a house near Nice and went there and back a lot. But they took ages to do and we never made any money with them.

We had built a small swimming pool after we first moved in, digging out the hole and bringing a liner for it from England. We built a well-head over the old well, we made new paths and banks, and we put in countless plants as well as some shrubs and trees. We sawed up old cork trees for firewood. My weapon of choice was a strimmer, a very good one. Once, having worked with it for something like eight hours, I strimmed the head off a snake by mistake and it landed on Richard who was working nearby.

On one occasion Richard went by himself to a very smart and well-attended funeral for the chairman of Les Collines. Lady H had told us that Roman Catholics all over Europe considered white and not black to be the correct mourning colour. So, not having a white suit, he put on a white shirt with a starched collar and wore my father's old (but very stylish) 1930s white buckskin shoes (I couldn't bring myself to get rid of them). Richard was following the coffin when the laces of one of the shoes broke and the shoe then flew off, hitting the coffin with a thump. Of course no one had a spare shoelace, so Richard couldn't walk any further. Humiliating, but funny too.

Richard's pride and joy, and a real godsend, was a three-wheeled quad bike, later replaced by a four-wheeled one when they became available. We brought it out from England and then it stayed in France (he had another one at Flat Top). This took him around the garden and our larger 'domain'. It also took us both on glorious day-long expeditions into the mountains, from which we would often return with plants we had dug up for the garden. It was great fun. You could go almost anywhere and, unlike a car, you could push it if it got stuck.

We had planted a camomile lawn at the first property because we thought a conventional grass lawn would dry out and die between our visits. But it was expensive and not a great success. The new bigger garden had ordinary grass. One morning we found the whole lawn had been grubbed up, including the flagstones. The culprit was obvious: a wild boar. Richard worked all day putting everything back as best he could. He decided that he would borrow a shotgun from the guardian at the Club. Then we'd sit up all night in the garden and he'd shoot the boar when it returned. And he told me to have a pickaxe ready in case I needed to have a go at it too! We sat there and it was very difficult to keep still, I remember. And of course it never came back. (I was rather glad, I've always liked wild boar.)

A drama of a different sort happened when our old friend Diana Holland-Hibbert, Julian's sister, was staying with us in September 1990. There was a rat-tat-tat on the door one night. Get out of your house immediately and get down to the beach, we were told. A forest fire was raging, and getting closer. Close your windows and shutters, and take your cars and passports. Richard insisted on driving his beloved quad bike down to the beach, even going right past a gas storage tank with flames close by. All the residents assembled on the foreshore. At about five o'clock in the morning we were allowed back up the hill. The trees in the garden were burnt, although they grew back surprisingly quickly. The fire had got very close and the inside of the house was absolutely filthy.

Ed and Katha were married in October 1993 and Donald Coggan took a Service of Blessing for them in Bransdale Church, followed by dinner in the Lodge where Anne lived. While Archbishop of Canterbury he had taken the marriage service in Westminster Abbey for Nicholas and Emma and also, in the same place, Ed's first marriage. In retirement he moved to Winchester, where we used to see him and his wife Jean.

*　　*　　*

From childhood onwards I had wanted to go to St Helena. My father was mad about Napoleon and I had inherited his obsession. I so wanted to see the remote island where he had spent his last years.

You could only get to St Helena by a five-day journey from

Cape Town, or an even longer one direct from England, on the mail ship RMS *St Helena*. Richard had said he'd go if I agreed to fly to Cape Town, but in the end we decided to fly to Johannesburg and take the train to Cape Town. So in February 1994 we boarded the famous Blue Train in Johannesburg. It was certainly comfortable, but sadly various delays prevented our stopping in Kimberley, where we wanted to see the Diamond Museum and where, I hoped, we might even buy some diamonds.

Our old friends Patrick and Pip McCraith were making this trip with us and we met up with them once we had boarded the *St Helena*. Some crocodiles from Namibia were also being loaded on board, for release in Tenerife. We saw them being sprayed with water and not looking very happy.

St Helena is a rugged island with dramatic cliffs. Landing at the capital, Jamestown, involved the 'active' passengers being landed at some steep harbour steps. Meanwhile the old and infirm, which included Richard, were first put into a cage which was winched onto a barge and then lifted and swung by a crane onto the island. I was glad that Richard had arranged for his quad bike to be shipped out from the UK for our stay here. He had made a point of meeting the St Helena representative in London and getting his agreement to this.

Richard collected the quad bike – which seemed to be the envy of all Jamestown – and drove it up to the hotel where we were staying the first couple of nights with the McCraiths. No one locked anything on St Helena, and Richard was kindly reprimanded by a local when he tried to take the key out of the bike. There were no keys for hotel rooms. We were then bidden to stay in Plantation House, the Governor's home and the residence in Napoleon's time of Sir Hudson Lowe who had treated his prisoner so shamefully.

We were made very welcome by the then Governor, Alan Hoole, and his wife Delia. (They later came to live in York. Alan got cancer, but thought he was better and was walking near Whitby when he stumbled and fell straight down a hill, killing himself.) Plantation House is a lovely and gloriously peaceful house, surrounded at the back by tall trees, with a perfect view of the vast expanse of sea. The only problem was that our bedroom had very thin curtains and floodlights shining up at the windows. I can't sleep without total blackout. So Richard asked Alan if the lights could be switched off. Alan said that would be a problem because in total darkness Delia always fainted.

A number of giant tortoises wandered about in the grounds of the house. Visitors are allowed to talk to them (but not sit on them). The most famous was Jonathan, who had been brought to St Helena from the Seychelles in 1882, aged fifty. Not surprisingly, much fuss was made of him. (In 2016 at the age of 184 he was said to be the world's oldest living animal.)

I told Richard I had to go and see Napoleon's grave. Leave me alone, I said, I'll go by myself. Don't be silly, he said, he's not there, he's buried in Paris. I knew that his remains had later been taken to Les Invalides but I wanted to see the place where his body had first been buried. The empty grave was covered in concrete and surrounded by iron railings. Nearby was a box for a sentry.

I had been to Les Invalides once with Sammy, Myrtie and Flash when I was ten, but I insisted on going again with Mary Sheepshanks, having won the visit in a competition in *The Times* and Richard deciding he couldn't walk round the streets of Paris. Mary couldn't understand the fascination I felt for Napoleon.

Longwood House, where Napoleon was imprisoned, and the land around it is French territory, owned by the French Government. The French Honorary Consul lived there, although not in the few rooms that Napoleon had occupied. Napoleon's rooms were a museum, but visited by appointment only, so not many people went. Alan Hoole told us that he had not been invited as he was not welcome there, but Richard and I had been asked, privately, to visit. So we did, and much enjoyed the champagne and smoked salmon that we were given, as well as the modest but well-presented museum.

Ruth Halifax's grandfather, Lord Rosebery, had collected many of Napoleon's things, including the shutters from Longwood, which had survived well, being made of very hard wood. Napoleon had wanted the shutters so that no one could look in on him. They had been left to Ruth, but Charlie and Ruth thought them of no interest and gave them to their gardener, who was planning to make a garden shed out of them. Richard and I discovered what they were and, when we were at Malmaison, the Empress Josephine's chateau outside Paris, we asked the curator if he would like us to take them to St Helena when we went there. He was thrilled. But by then Charlie had died, and Peter Halifax had sent them to Ruth's cousin, the present Lord Rosebery, who collected Napoleonic things. So they never returned to Longwood, as we had hoped.

We had an early tour of the island in a 1929 Chevrolet bus, still going strong. The cost of getting vehicles to the island is such that they are kept going for far longer than would happen elsewhere. Traffic coming up the steep roads always had priority.

Alan Hoole took us to several places on the island in his car. He showed us where several thousand Boer soldiers had been held as prisoners of war in a tented camp – they had their own separate cemetery for those who died on the island. We also explored the island on Richard's quad bike. On one day, a Wednesday, we needed petrol, but on St Helena you cannot buy petrol on a Wednesday. We had to bribe a local to give us some from his shed. The hills were brown and rather forbidding, but we were astonished by the lush vegetation in some of the valleys. Trees grew quickly here.

On the quad bike we found we had reached the preferred site for the island's airport. At the time of our visit the Governor's Executive

Council had yet to decide if the islanders really wanted an airport. The Governor's own preference seemed to be for a dedicated ferry service between St Helena and Ascension Island and then to use Ascension Island's air links to Britain.

Richard's cousin's grandson, Ned Iveagh, had succeeded to the title and had nothing to do in the House of Lords, so Richard suggested he interest himself in St Helena. He became President of the Association and fought tooth and nail to get them an airport – much against what Richard and I wanted. (The airport has now been built, at a cost of £285 million. It was due to open in early 2016 and Pip McCraith and I had been planning a visit, but the opening was delayed due to the discovery of severe 'wind shear'. Someone did not do their research properly.) It finally opened in October 2017, but at the moment you can only fly to it from South Africa.

We had a number of people on the island to see, including Sammy's cook's daughter. We were asked to tea parties, of the sort children used to have before the war – it was clearly the meal of the day. The time sped by. I loved every minute. All too soon it was time to get back on the boat. The sea voyage home was much longer than the journey out from Cape Town because we were headed for Cardiff, more than 4,500 miles away, stopping only in the Canary Islands on the way. It passed pleasantly enough, with all the usual sea-voyage distractions. I danced on deck under the night sky with Patrick McCraith. He danced beautifully and it was heavenly. (When I told Sammy the fun I had dancing on deck in the night in mid-Atlantic, all she said was: 'What an incredibly strange thing to do, to dance in the Atlantic. I've never heard of anyone doing that.')

I knew from experience that dancing for me was dangerous if I had any remotely romantic feelings for my dancing partner. Luckily I had none at all for Patrick, great friend though he was, nor he for me. He had been in the Sherwood Rangers with Flash, and Pip told me that he had always blamed himself for Flash's death. Patrick had been in the Long Range Desert Group and had joined the battlefield and made a disturbance at a time when Flash most unwisely insisted on standing up in his tank to shave. Patrick believed that he had somehow caused the Germans to notice Flash.

We stopped briefly at Tenerife and the crocodiles were unloaded. Soon we had reached the coast of South Wales and a pilot arrived to take us into Cardiff docks where we unloaded ourselves and caught a train to Paddington. So ended five fascinating weeks.

CHAPTER 22

Without Richard

We killed Mothy. Not on purpose of course, but we did. We went down to see him at Hernes Keep near Windsor, as we did every week in late 1997. He had pancreatic cancer and hadn't moved for many weeks. As we were leaving, Richard told him we would stop for some pub food on the way back. Mothy said he didn't like pub grub, so we would all go to a Chinese restaurant together. Amazed that he was up to coming, we followed his car, driven by the man who was looking after him. In the restaurant he ordered a bottle of white wine. Knowing that Mothy had drunk no alcohol for ages, Richard protested, saying he was driving and had to be awake in the House of Lords, but Mothy said he wanted it. He clearly did, as he drank most of the bottle. He died later that night. We were appalled, but his friends said it was the kindest thing we'd ever done. To die from drinking with your friends is not the worst way to die.

That same year Fiona and Charlie held a party at their London house to celebrate our golden wedding anniversary. It was such fun seeing Edward Ford again after so long.

The year before, Richard was finding the very long steps and two flights of spiral stairs in the house at 65 Collines de Guerrevielle too much, so we bought a small house near the village of Grimaud. Mary Sheepshanks came to help us move (while throwing unwanted things into the tip she managed to throw herself in as well, cracking some ribs, about which none of us took much notice). La Cheneraie was a bit further from the sea, sadly, but we had a lovely view of Grimaud and the house was more practical. It came with a tiny vineyard, which we paid the local Co-operative to come and harvest and they repaid us with a few bottles of wine.

The garden had a very big cabin up in the trees where Leo and her friends would sleep. It had a good swimming pool just outside the house and lots of open-air places to eat. We had a bedroom (we were in bed when we heard the news on the radio of Diana Princess of Wales's death), dressing room and bathroom, and a study where we used to print and bind the children's books for Eximious. There were two spare bedrooms and another bathroom, and a big drawing/dining room with an open fireplace, off the kitchen.

Crystal Tweedie came and stayed a lot and we used to take her on the back of the quad bike the three or more miles to the private beach at Guerrevieille, which we had kept the right to use. Most evenings Richard and I when alone would go a few miles towards the hills to a lovely wild place with cork trees and lush grass where we drank our whisky and stayed till almost dark. It was fun, but I knew I would never be happy there without Richard.

Our social life in Yorkshire was diminishing. Charlie had died in 1980 and Anne in 1995, Billy Brooksbank in 1983 and Ann later, Tony Bethell in 1996 and Jane later – she was in a nursing home having had a bad stroke. But we continued to spend most weekends at Flat Top and then back to London on Monday, where Richard would go to the House of Lords. We regularly had lunch at Flintham with Myles and quite often spent the night; though I was glad to be let off taking a boat across to the island to bury the ashes of Myles's friend Jimmy.

We also continued to produce a wide-ranging list of the memoirs and reminiscences of friends and others who approached us. (There is a list of these books in an appendix at the end of this book.) In 1998 we produced Richard's own book, *I Like My Choice: The Story of Garrowby*, which Peter Halifax and his wife Milla had asked him to write for the twenty-first birthday of their son James

Irwin. Richard's book combined Wood family history from the late eighteenth century onwards with plenty of detail about the development of the estate and those who have worked there. When David and Ursula Westbury asked us to lunch with the Queen Mother, Richard presented her with a copy of the book and got a charming, handwritten thank-you letter back from her. Also at the lunch was Jack Profumo, to whom the Queen Mother was very loyal. It was the last time we saw him.

Richard began to be aware, as the 1990s wore on, that there were lots of things he was no longer able to do. At some point he was told it was dangerous to be tall – he might break a hip or have a bad fall. I tried to fight the medical establishment on this. I suspected it was health and safety gone mad. But I lost. He was given legs two inches shorter and then, for the last two years of his life, very short ones, like those he had had at the end of the war. In the autumn of 2001 we went to the memorial service for Martyn Beckett (Sim's half-brother and a well-known architect who had built us the wing at Flat Top) at the Guards Chapel, and Debo Devonshire, seeing Richard with his very short legs, said, 'I'm so sorry. What's happened?' It was awful. I wanted the earth to swallow me up!

It was time to sell Flat Top. So many of our old friends and neighbours had died, and the house was expensive to run. Over the years we had done a lot to develop and improve it, and more recently there was no more which needed doing. Ed's help was invaluable in smartening it up and getting it ready for sale, aided greatly by Michael and Frances Howorth and their daughter Georgina who spent a week helping us clear everything in the barn and cottage as well as the house. We were sorry that it was sold to someone who, it turned out, had bought it in order to sell it all off separately – the house, then the cottage and finally the barn, which was turned into several homes. Peter Halifax took back the park in front and the big field behind which we had only rented.

We bought Mothy's old house, Hernes Keep. It had a spiral staircase out of a big hall with a double bedroom and bathroom upstairs. Richard said he would never have lived in a bungalow, though that is what La Cheneraie in fact was – maybe he felt it was different in the south of France – and he insisted on climbing the stairs to check it out when we first arrived. It had been sold very cheaply by Mothy's executors and in order to get it in 2002 we had to pay a lot more.

★   ★   ★

Richard died very suddenly in August 2002, just a couple of months after we had moved into Hernes Keep. Ed and his family were at La Cheneraie but Ed had come back to stay with us for a few days. Crystal Tweedie, who had become a great friend, had come to lunch. She and Ed were sitting in the drawing room after church with Richard, and I was cooking lunch when Richard suddenly rolled his eyes, let out a cry and slid off the small chair he was sitting on. Crystal said, 'I think he's had a stroke' (it was actually an aneurysm), and Ed immediately rushed to help.

Crystal dialled 999 and the emergency services sent a helicopter to the field at the bottom of the garden. Things happened fast. The room filled with paramedics wearing fluorescent jump suits. The dogs tried to bite them. They got Richard onto the floor and tried to resuscitate him, but he died before they could get him into the helicopter.

'First a police doctor came to do a death certification,' Ed recalls. 'Then a bit later, a Sikh doctor followed suit. It was hard to find time with Pa on my own. I wanted to be alone with him to say goodbye. I eventually found my moment. I kissed him on the forehead. He would have liked that.' Ed then rang all the family, and went and tidied Richard clothes. He threw out medicines, toothbrushes, etc., so that I wouldn't have to find them. He had to return to France the next day, so Kirstie Allsopp (Fiona's daughter and my god-daughter) very kindly came and stayed at Hernes Keep and then my granddaughter Leo.

Richard's funeral was at Kirby Underdale in Yorkshire, where all his family are buried. Richard wanted no address. Apart from at Ruth's funeral, there had been no address at the weddings or funerals in our generation. Richard had wanted the candles around the coffin to be kept alight throughout the night before the day of his funeral, as they had always been for other family members. But the parson wouldn't allow that, despite the fact that the candles were special Roman Catholic ones which were perfectly safe. There was a Requiem Mass first thing in the morning. I had long ago agreed with Richard that I wouldn't go, because without me it could be as High Church as he wanted, which I would have hated. My cousin Bidger Ker and Sammy didn't go either.

Nor was there an address either then or at the later memorial service. Ed said that people would think that no one loved him, but I explained that Richard didn't want one and no one on either side of the family has ever had one that I knew of, so he accepted it. After the service the surgeon who had been responsible for his short legs stopped me outside the Guards Chapel and asked if I recognised him. I said that I certainly did. I told him in no uncertain terms that he had ruined the last few years for me! He looked very surprised and said that he would have been liable if Richard had had an accident.

Marion Thorpe brought Jeremy, by then seriously ill with Parkinson's disease, to the service. She made a point of making sure I talked to him, which I was very happy to do – he was an old friend – though I remember people looked surprised at me for doing so. I had a nice letter from John Major saying how sorry he was not able to come but at that moment the press were hounding him – Edwina Currie had just published her book with the revelation of their affair – and he feared the whole service could be wrecked by attention on him.

★ ★ ★

If you have done almost everything together – as Richard and I had – you pay a heavy price when that person is gone. I had been his secretary in London, I had done all his constituency things and surgeries, we had travelled together all over the world. I'd always loaded for him shooting; we'd almost always gone to the ballet and opera together and had made friends with each other's great friends – for example, Myles Hildyard (my friend) and Nat Saye and Sele (his). We'd certainly done most things together – even church, though we disagreed about it! Being on my own was not going to be easy. It still isn't. I'm surprised when friends whose husbands have died tell me that they enjoy being able to do what they want without a husband wanting something different!

Old friends were a great help. My sister Fiona in particular was a huge comfort. I hadn't liked her much when she was a child, but in later years we became great friends and I missed her terribly when she died, much too young, in January 2014. I often went down to see Peter Ramsbotham in Ovington, near Alresford, and he'd take me to lunch at a nice pub which he owned together with the fishing. On other occasions he would come up to Hernes Keep. His second wife, a psychiatrist called Zaida, never came too. I telephoned her a lot when Peter was dying and when he died she wrote to thank me, saying that I had made more difference to her life than anyone. We had never been friends, so I felt awful.

I saw a lot of Myles of course. At his ninetieth birthday party in 2004 he gave me the little volume on Napoleon that my father used to carry around with him. Myles had dived into Flash's tank and rescued the smoke-blackened book, as well as Flash's dispatch case which had belonged first to Alby Cator and has his name, then Flash's and finally my name on it.

After Myles died in 2005, I continued for a while to go to Flintham, once or twice a year, with Tatton Sykes. With the permission of Myles's nephew, we'd bring a picnic and sit in the garden and then wander around the house and the superb conservatory. But then this seemed odd, and a long journey for both of us – Tatton from Yorkshire and me from Hernes Keep – and we stopped going.

I used to see my cousin Sammy a lot, until she died in June 2015. She was exactly like a sister, so even without Sim and Anne and Charlie and Ruth I still had someone who had been so very much part of my life. Mary Sheepshanks has been a widow for a long time – her husband Charlie was twenty years older than her – and we did many things together, including foreign journeys. Patricia Beauchamp lived not far away at Sunningdale towards the end of her life, so I saw her a lot and I published her autobiography, *The Short Story of a Long Life*. Before she died in 2012 I saw a great deal of Minta Aldington.

Robie Uniacke was another old friend we had first met years before, staying and shooting with the Cowdrays. He always smoked cigars and still does, and I encourage him to do so when he comes to see me. But he now lives in France. There were younger friends too, such as Cindy and Houston Shaw-Stewart (after Houston died, Cindy married Christopher Chetwode) and John Hayter, who had been in Richard's regiment. Although he is in Africa from October to April, we keep in touch and always go to the Regimental lunch together.

After Richard died, Emma very kindly took me to stay with Cindy and Houston at Ardgowan. When we arrived I found that Cindy had made us martinis in hand-me-down glasses of Lady H's in the drawing room, and Houston struggled to his feet to greet me. By this time he was on kidney dialysis and moving was difficult for him. As he got up to kiss me he lost his balance and fell over, pulling me down too. We both landed up on the floor, covered in martini. We roared with laughter.

I decided to keep on with the typesetting and printing work, and in the years after Richard's death I produced a stream of memoirs and other books for a variety of people. We had always employed a secretary to help us running Wilton 65 from home. At Flat Top, John and Penelope Patrick had filled that role. Tania Ward followed them at Flat Top – where, like the Patricks and the Sergeants before her, she lived in the cottage at the bottom of the drive and then, when we moved to Hernes Keep, in a flat over the garage – but she left after a year to work with horses in Yorkshire for Sue Watson. Frank Dobson was great fun and helped me with a lot of complicated leaflets and handouts as well as the publishing and printing. He stayed until he had to return to his (second) wife. He was a staunch Roman Catholic despite having been divorced.

Celia Summers came next. She had been secretary to John Cowdray's eldest daughter, Teresa, and she stayed for four years. She was followed by a woman who was always buying cashmere jerseys and other luxuries. She disappeared from the flat in the middle of the night in January 2011. She hadn't stolen anything from me but she owed thousands of pounds to various firms. They tried to track her down through me, but I had no address for her. Celia then returned for a bit, before Wendy French took over and bought Wilton 65 off me at the end of 2013. I still do a small amount of typesetting work from time to time myself: mainly for memorial services, funerals and weddings. It gives me something to do and I enjoy it.

★   ★   ★

I had always loved travelling with Richard and now I felt I mustn't give up completely. I went to the Collines with Ed and Katha in 2003 and to St Petersburg with Mary Sheepshanks in 2005. Tanya Tolstoy took a group of us around the great palaces and galleries. It seemed almost unbelievable that all these original paintings were still there, given all the revolutions and catastrophes they have had. Despite the cold, we walked almost everywhere. We went to the Opera House to see *Aida* and to the small theatre in the Palace to see *Swan Lake* by the Bolshoi Ballet. The guides, the women dressed in full-length mink coats, were terribly underpaid and were embarrassingly grateful for our tips. When I gave a miniature bottle of whisky to one guide it was as if it was a magnum of champagne. We came back with fur hats and caviar.

Pip Weatherly (Patrick McCraith's widow) generously paid for me to go and see her in Australia in 2005, where she had been widowed for a second time. Her son Michael, who was my godson, died in 2008 and another godson, Richard Astor, died in 2016. I went with Crystal Tweedie to Corsica, wanting to see Napoleon's birthplace. A few years earlier Crystal had been enormously efficient and had organised us all when we went to Crete with Myles. She was fine when we went to bed, but getting up at 5 a.m. for the flight to Corsica she suddenly seemed muddled. She was unable to deal with her luggage at the airport and was not allowed to sit near the emergency exit. She could do virtually nothing when we got to the house we had rented, and just sat by the door as I shopped. I was so worried I rang her elder daughter in France, who clearly thought me mad. I think she must have had a stroke in the night before we left, and sadly she was never the same again. She died in 2006.

In July 2006 Ed, Emma and I went to Clonacody, the Kelletts' family home in Tipperary which Flash had sold in the 1930s. I much enjoyed seeing the room which was to have been mine, and the church and all the family tombstones.

That year I went to Spain with Ed and Katha, to Rome with Clarissa in 2007, and in the same year stayed in Provence with Caroline Ker and enjoyed working in her garden. In France I went on a barge, something I'd never done before, with Frances and Michael Howorth and her mother. I spent Christmas 2008 at El Noque, the Spanish house Ed and Katha owned, and her mother, Frances Ormerod, came too. I went again in 2009, followed by Rome with Mary Sheepshanks. Apart from Libya in 2010 my last foreign journey was to Madeira with Pip Weatherly in February 2016, where I was ill almost all the time and very unhappy.

In 2010 I went with others for what must clearly be a final visit to Libya. John Green-Wilkinson (Oliver's younger brother) – who died in 2015 – had told me about a little-known provision of John Major's Lottery which would pay for veterans with their wives, or their widows and a companion, to revisit the place where they had fought. The scheme was barely advertised, in case too many people took it up – or so it seemed. I took Ed, and Leo (Ed and Jo's daughter) and Susie's daughter, Janie Kidston, came with us. We made up a group. Pip brought her daughter and son-in-law, Sally and Patrick Lort-Phillips. Liz Scarbrough, Dickon's widow, came, and Margaret North and her son David.

People expected me to know my way around, but it had been quite different with Richard years ago. There were many more people at Leptis Magna, but it's a big site and in some places there was no one but us. At one point we lost Janie – she was quietly (and illegally) digging up some lilies.

I had sold La Cheneraie in 2003 with Ed and John Atkins's help. I didn't want to go there without Richard. I find that if I'm reading something and I come across houses for sale in France I turn the page over quickly. I can't bear to look at them.

Nicholas had inherited Menethorpe Hall when Ann died, but in 2015 they decided to sell it and move almost next door into two cottages which their son Tom, who is an architect, completely revamped for them. It was built exactly as they wanted it, starting virtually from scratch, and they have made the old walled kitchen garden into a lovely garden with a stream they have created near the house. In the same year Tom married Tiffany Lawson and his sister Mary married Daniel Abbott. Tom and Tiffany now have two sons, Oliver and Nick. The house, Cunelands, has been a great success and Tom has worked incredibly hard to achieve this. In 2017 he received a RIBA award for Engineering Architect in the Yorkshire Region and a RIBA Regional Award for Cunelands. My granddaughter Leo married Rupert Scott in 2012 and they now have two daughters, Evie and Frankie.

★　★　★

In 2013 I decided that if I found myself unable to drive I would be completely stuck at Hernes Keep, and Wendy French had her own home, so there was no one in the garage flat. I thought that if I was in London I could see more people and go to exhibitions, etc., and also get to stations if I wanted to stay with people. I had always wanted to return to Eaton Place where I had lived as a child and where Richard and I had bought a flat, but prices made that impossible. We had often dined with friends in Rivermead Court, next to the Hurlingham Club, and always wondered why on earth they wanted to live so far out of London and in a mansion block. I only came and looked at it when Michael Chetwode, Cindy's stepson, who was helping me to find a flat, suggested it. I had begun to get a bit desperate, so I decided that as I could park a car, there was a Tube and bus nearby, 24-hour porters, heating and hot water provided, and a garden down by the river, I'd better go for it.

In the few weeks before she died Fiona found me carpet people, curtain-makers and just about everything. She said she wasn't going to die till I'd got a flat and her son Henry a house – and she achieved both. I and her cousin Laura Sheffield (the elder daughter of Nan, who had been murdered) were with her in the few days before she died. We buried her in the garden.

I'd had an operation for a twisted gut and the surgeon said I shouldn't move till the end of January. But just before Christmas the man buying Hernes Keep threatened to pull out if I didn't give him possession in December. So I agreed, and Ursula Westbury kindly had me to stay for five or six weeks until I could rent an upstairs flat in Rivermead.

I stayed with Emma and Nicholas for Christmas 2015 and the next year I spent Christmas with Sue Watson, whose elder sister Caroline had died in 2014. Caroline had been in the London Clinic and I used to go and see her most days and take up to ten paperbacks from the Hurlingham Bookshop, a marvellous shop in Fulham which sells second-hand books. The owner generously allowed me to bring back the last ones and borrow replacements without paying any more. Sue was able to take Caroline home and was with her until she died. She missed her dreadfully.

The England of my childhood and youth has gone for ever. It is hard to look back and not regret some of the changes. To look back to a time, for example, when respect for, and friendship with, servants was a part of daily life. To a time when the incomparable words of the King James Bible and the 1662 Book of Common Prayer had not so often been replaced by more banal and inferior phrases. Religion is a precious thing. I realise I was brought up with too much of it, but there is nowadays probably too little. At the same time, something intangible but valuable has also been lost in today's wholescale disdain, even contempt, for formality, etiquette and ceremony. After all, contrast is so often the spice of life – 'the Ritz and the ditch'.

At the same time so many super things have appeared year after year which have made life easier and more enjoyable. Automatic cars, mobile telephones, email, microwaves, small-scale scanners, printers and copiers are just some of these things. Air fares are much cheaper, buses and Tubes are better. Shopping online is much less effort than shopping on your feet. Cash can be withdrawn at any hour day or night, instead of having to go to a bank during limited opening hours.

I have been incredibly lucky in having a father I loved so much and a husband equally. Such a strange thing happened. After I married, Charlie Halifax said to me that he could no longer 'hear' Flash's voice, despite the fact that they had all lived together in Palestine, and to my astonishment I realised that also applied to me. But after seventy-four years I can still in my head smell him as if he was in the room, as Charlie told me he could also, and this despite the fact that I lost my superb sense of smell in an accident years ago.

I still think of Flash and Richard every day of my life. I also had much-loved cousins who, with my mother and half-sister, born after I was married, were a huge joy to me, as are my children, especially in old age. I was very lucky with my in-laws; many are not so fortunate. I have stayed in many lovely houses, been to many different parts of the world and lived for long periods in a beautiful part of France.

One can't have everything in life at the same time, even if it would be fun if one could. But living as long as I have, I find I greatly enjoyed both the things of my childhood and right through my life. Mary Soames and I once discussed how lucky we were as children to have been on terms with our parents, and they with us, as equals, always able to say what we wanted. Many people now say that the generations are more equal and easy with each other than in the past, but both she and I had this blessing all our lives. What more can anyone want? It is hard to describe how grateful I feel, just as I am sure she did too.

Appendices

APPENDIX I

The Prince of Wales Sells his Horses

Concerned about injury to the Prince of Wales, King George V ordered him to stop hunting and to sell all his hunters. The Prince sent a note to my mother, along with the sale catalogue, marking the horses that he thought might interest her.

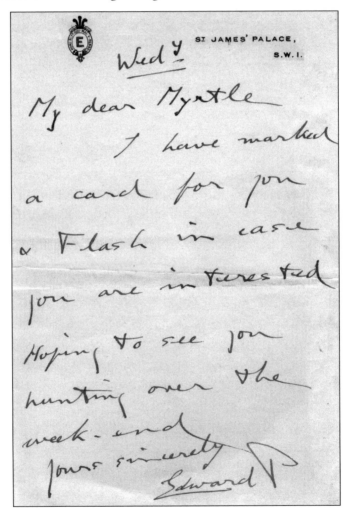

LEICESTER.

Warner, Sheppard & Wade, Ltd.

Are favoured with instructions

TO SELL BY AUCTION,

At the Repository, Leicester,

ON

SATURDAY, FEB. 23rd, 1929,

THE FOLLOWING

HORSES

The ENTIRE STUD (with the exception of one old horse),

THE PROPERTY OF

H.R.H. the Prince of Wales,

who is not hunting any more, or riding in any Point-to-Point races this season.

They will stand in the Star Boxes and be sold at about 1 o'clock.

Books that we Published

Abrahams, Peter. (2009) *All is Well with the Child.*

Arnold, Constantia. (1994 & 2003) *Happy as Kings: The Story of the Fenwicks of Abbotswood, 1905-45.*

Astor, Bridget. (1996) *A Feather from Heaven.*

Astor, Bridget. (2003) *Dearest Donkeys.*

Astor, Bridget. (2006) *A Butterfly Blessing.*

Astor, Bridget. (2009) *Smile with Love.*

Bain, Kenneth. (1993) *St. Helena: The Island, Her People and their Ship.*

Baker, Ian. (2004) *St Helena: One Man's Island.*

Baring, Sarah. (2004) *The Road to Station X.*

Barclay, Jean. *Verity: The True Story of a Shetland Pony.*

Barr, John. *Journey to the Gambia.*

Barton, David. (1996) *The United Nations Comes of Age.*

Bates, Martin. (2006) *To Ypres for a Haircut.*

Birch Reynardson, William. (2008) *Letters to Lorna.*

Bird, Lindy. (1991) *The Art of Drying Flowers.*

Birkenhead, Margaret. (2005) *Angelo the Rabbit.*

Boles, Elizabeth. (1992) *Never Make a Fuss.*

Bryan, Gerald. (2008) *Be of Good Cheer.*

Butler, Mollie. *A Rabanthology.*

Charlton, Mamie. (1997) *Nothing Venture, Nothing Win.*

Charlton, Mamie. (2005) *Memoirs of North Tyndale.* (Facsimile reprint.)

Clegg, Richard. (2009) *Forged by Fire: A memoir.*

Cotes, Peter. *Joannie's Jottings.*

Coubrough, C.R.L. (1999) *Memories of a Perpetual Second Lieutenant.*

Cozens-Cugat, Rosamund. (1995) *The Pushkins.*

Cromer, Ruby. (1994) Edited by Margaret Walker, *Indian Journal 1905-1906.*

Cromer, Ruby. (1995) Edited by Margaret Walker, *Letters and 2nd Indian Journal, 1886-1961.*

Cunliffe-Lister, Susan. (1999) *Days of Yore.*

Davies-Scourfield, Gris. (1991 & 1992) *In Presence of My Foes. Travels & Travails of a P.O.W. A Memoir of Calais, Colditz and Wartime Escape Adventures.*

Dawe, Oliver. (1993) *Hector Innes.*

Delany, K.W. (2002) *A Journey of Memories.*

Dogramaci, Ihsan. (2001) *History of the International Paediatric Association 1910-2000.*

Edgedale, Mercy. *Five Million Africans Say No.*

Ellis T. E., ed. Thomas Seymour. (2006) *The Byzantine Plays.*

Ewing, Ken, and Ernie Lepard. (1999) *Breakthrough at Tebaga Gap.*

Feversham, Anne. (1993) *A Small Anthology of Poems and Prose.*

Feversham, Anne. (2005) *Strange Stories of the Chase: Stories of Foxhunting & the Supernatural.*

Feversham, Anne. (2005) *The Fox from Boden's Thorns.*

Fiennes, Martin. *By Bicycle to Istanbul.*

Fiennes, William. (2007) *Travels in the Cevennes Without a Donkey.*

Ford, Barry. *Reminiscences.*

Forder, Kenneth. (2011) *Fifty True Stories from Life: Never Before Told.*

Foster, Philip. (1994) *A Trooper's Desert War.*

Fox, Phyllis. *Christmas Crackers.*

Fox, Phyllis. *Poems and Christmas Crackers.*

Fox, The Revd Colin (ed.). *The Wartime Diary of Revd George Fox : June 16th 1944 - June 6th 1945.*

George, Basil. (1994) *The Pepper Tree.*

Gerhold, Dorian. (1994) *Courts of Equity.*

Gerhold, Dorian. *A Few Friends and Neighbours.*

Glazebrook, Peter. *At the Recital.*

Goodhart, Charles. (2007) *John Flemming 1941-2003: a Biography.*

Goodhart, Sir Philip. (1993, revised 2013) *Colonel George Washington: Soldier of the King.*

Goodhart, Sir Philip. (2005) *The Royal Americans.*

Goodhart, Sir Philip. (2006) *A Stab in the Front: The Suez Conflict – 1956.*

Graham, Professor Dominick. (2000) *The Escapes and Evasions of an Obstinate Bastard.*

Green-Wilkinson, John. (1998) *Bishop Oliver: Letters and Reminiscences: Soldier 1939-1946, Priest 1947-1970.*

Greenhill, Denis. (1992 & 1993) *More by Accident.*

Grewal, Dr Anthony, abridged by John Luck. (2006) *History of the Windsor Medical Society.*

Guy, Roland. (1999) *Reflections.*

Halifax, Dorothy. (1980) *A Story for Dorothy's Grandson.*

Halifax, Edward. *Christmas at Hickleton* (from 'Fulness of Days').

Herbert, John. (1994) *London Corinthian Sailing Club Centenary.*

Hildyard, Myles. *The Hildyards.*

Hildyard, Myles. *The Thorotons.*

Hill, Roy Gray. (1997) *And So It Happened.*

Holderness, Richard. (1998) *I Like My Choice.*

Holland-Hibbert, Thurstan. *Dad's Memories.*

Holman, Betty. (1998) *Memoirs of a Diplomat's Wife.*

Hudson, Charles Edward. (1994) *Poems of Charles Edward Hudson.*

Hudson, Miles. (2001) *Mercedes.*

Hudson, Myles. (1992) *Two Lives 1882-1992. The Memoirs of Charles Edward Hudson VC, CB, DSO, MC, and Miles Matthew Lee Hudson.*

Ikin, Reginald. *Thought for the Day.*

Jameson, Geoffrey. (1996) *To War with Friends: The War Diaries, September 1941-43.*

Johnson, Rosemary. (2008 & 2015) *Ripples of War.*

Kerr, Michael. *As Far as I Remember.*

King, Betty. (1994) *Rabbits or Romans.*

King, Betty. (1998) *Gadding with Gran.*

King, Betty, *Mortals and Maltsters.*

Lancaster, Estelle. (2001 & 2004) *Please Remember.*

Lancaster, Nancy. (2003) *A Lightning Sketch.*

Lancaster, Nancy. (2003) *Childhood Reminiscences of Mirador and Nancy Astor.*

Leatham, P. E. (2009) *The Short Story of a Long Life.*

Lindsay, T. M. (1992) *The Story of the Nottinghamshire Sherwood Rangers Yeomanry in the Second World War.*

Lumsden, Jane Forbes. (1994) *Regency Recollections: As told by Mrs Clements Lumsden to her daughter Katherine Maria.*

MacAlpine, Daphne. *Hunting in Ireland.*

May, Diana. (1998) *Miscellennium.*

Moore, Peter. (2001 & 202) *No Need to Worry: Memoirs of an Army Conscript, 1941-1946.*

Moore, Peter. *Adolescence.*

Moore, Peter. (2004) *Ah! Happy Years!*

Moore, Peter. (2011) *French Journal: 14 January to 21 March 1988.*

Nash, D. E. *The Fox's Prophecy.*

Ness, Brigid. *Nelly in the Forest.*

Ness, Patrick. (1986) *Also Ran.* (And eight further books.)

Onslow, Dorothy. (1984) *Early Victorian Wisdom.*

Onslow, Dorothy. (1984) *Stories from a Victorian Nursery.*

Onslow, Dorothy. *Trex and Mousey*.

Onslow, The Earl of. (1999) *Men and Sand*. (Facsimile reprint.)

Page, Jack. (2000) *A Page at a Time*.

Paradine-Palmer, Greta. (2002) *Jhools in the Dust*.

Pemberton, Hester, *Chemins de Prières*.

Phillips, Carol, *The Sofa*.

Phillips, Sir Horace. (1995) *Ihsan Dogramaci – A Remarkable Turk*.

Pinhorn, Malcolm, *Courts of Equity*.

Poole, Peggy. (2011) *Mirror Child*.

Poole, Peggy. (2011) *One Chaplain's War*.

Prudham, Rosemary, *Diary of Irene Fern Smith*.

Puxley, Aline. (2008) *John Philip Lavallin Puxley: 28th June 1915-28th June 2006*.

Quoist, Michael. (2003) *Pathways of Prayer*.

Reddish, Arthur. (1997) *The Sherwood Rangers: Final Advance*.

Rhodes James, Richard. (1993) *The Years Between: A Tale of the Nineteen Thirties*.

Roberts, Hugh. (1995) *Tenterden: The First Thousand Years*.

Robertson, Bobby. (1996) *The Stowaways and Other Stories from St Helena*.

Robinson, Ian. (2013) *An Engineer's Journey*.

Robinson, Peter. (2012) *Eshton Hall*.

Rolph, H. C. (1990) *Letters to Both Women*.

Rowan Robinson, Jeremy. (2012) *Who Weeps for Strangers*.

Rowlandson, Richard. (2001) *Two Bites of the Cherry*.

Russell, Louis R. (2008) *The Russells in Horticulture, 1800-2000*.

Schaller, Jane G. and Türmen, Tomris. (2003) *Children in his Heart, Youth on his Mind: tributes to Ihsan Dogramaci in honour of his 65 years of service to Child Health and Education*.

Seymour, Thomas. (2010) *Heraldry, Genealogy and the 8th Lord Howard de Walden*.

Shields, Gillies. (2000) *Donington Oak Poems*.

Simmonds, C. (2012) *Hermione: After 'To War with Whitaker'*.

Smyth, A. J. M. (2001) *Abrupt Sierras*.

Smyth, A. J. M. *Magic Casements*.

Stennett, Peggy. (1996) *Pram, Plough and Putter*.

Swire, Sir Adrian. (2010) *John Kidston Swire*.

von Preussen, Brigid. (1993) *Diaries 1949*.

von Preussen, Brigid (1994) *Those Boys*.

Vorley, J. S. (2003) *The Road from Mandalay*.

Webb-Carter, Celia. (2011) *Neville Francis Fitzgerald Chamberlain*.

Whetton, John. (2013) *Rodman Wanamaker: Edward VII's American Friend*.

Whitelaw, Celia (ed.). (2003) *Riddell Estate Roxburghshire, Volumes 1 and 2*.

Whitelaw, William. (1998) *The Whitelaw Memoirs*. (Reprint from the original).

Wilcox, A.F. *Sally and Belinda*.

Williams, Max. *Wild About the Law and No Time for Modesty*.

Willshire, Henry. *Nobody's Wall*.

Winn, Alice. (2003) *Sketch in the Canvas*.

Winn, Alice. (2004) *A La Recherche du Temps Perdu*.

Winn, Alice. *War Diary*.

Winn, Alice. *Random Jottings from a Disordered Mind*.

Winn, Elisabeth. (2005) *Nancy Lancaster and Her Gardens*.

Wood, Leonora, *Leo's Limericks*.

Woolley, John. (1994) *Deliver Me from Safety*.

China produced at Q.E.F.D.

When Richard ceased to be in the Government and was given a peerage we decided we would like to try and develop the work done by the disabled at Dorincourt Industries, which was part of Queen Elizabeth's Foundation for the Disabled, to which we had both been connected for almost all our married lives. The workshop was producing fairly basic things like tiles and we thought that with the help of the artist Graham Rust, and all that John Cowdray was willing to do for us through Royal Doulton, we would be able to train badly disabled people to produce small quantities of high-class decorated china, much of it to order and often through friends. Below is a list of many of the plates and other china which we produced and marketed, using the name 'Wilton 65'. Sadly, it all came to an end when the main building was gutted by fire one night in 1989, when almost all the china and much of our equipment and designs were destroyed.

It was hard to give up this work, but in life things must move on, and the Foundation now cares for more seriously disabled people and they have developed different activities. But I am very glad that we did this when we did. It was enjoyable and we both felt it very well worthwhile, both for the disabled people, but also for the people for whom we were able to produce small quantities of something no big firm would undertake, such as crested dinner services and big wedding presents.

Emma Bridgewater asked us if we would be interested in decorating earthenware with her designs. She came down and was very enthusiastic, at a time when she was just starting up. We would have loved to do it, but the Foundation felt that it would over-pressurise the workers, so we had to refuse. Would that we had been able to accept her suggestion, as she really has gone from strength to strength.

I have listed below many of the special orders we produced:

Purdeys. Fine bone-china. Large plates accompanied by five small octagonal plates with designs of game birds, and mugs rimmed with gold with crossed guns on the reverse.

Fountains Abbey, commemorative plate designed by Sir Martyn Beckett for the National Trust.

Two sets of octagonal Country House plates designed by Graham Rust: Arundel, Auchmacoy, Balmoral Castle, Blenheim Palace, Bowood, Chatsworth, Clandon, Claverton Manor (the American Museum in Britain), Cranborne, Firle, Harewood, Hatfield, Hever Castle, Ragley, Sudeley Castle, Syon Park.

Set of plates of important chateaux in the Medoc, also designed by Graham Rust: Beychevelle, Cos d'Estournel, Lafite-Rothschild, Latour, Margaux, Mouton-Rothschild.

Two designs of fine bone-china sets of plates for King Hussein's Silver Jubilee, 1977.

Plates of Aqaba for Prince Hassan, with 22ct gold rims.

Selection of plates commissioned by King Hussein and the Royal Jordanian Government.

'The Two Longfellows': Fred Archer centenary & Lester Piggott retirement plates.

Limited edition of plates with signatures of the Cabinet formed by Margaret Thatcher in 1981.

Plates of Lord and Lady Attlee to celebrate the 40th anniversary of the foundation of the Welfare State.

Plates of Chequers for her PPS, Peter Morrison, to present to Margaret Thatcher.

Made for the Food Halls at Harrods: art nouveau tiles, plates and coasters from their designs by Neatby, together with patum pots for sale there.

Plates made for the MFH Association with a portrait of the 8th Duke of Beaufort, a running fox above and a 22ct gold rim.

Royal Opera House, to commemorate the 250th anniversary in 1982. Fine bone-china plates.

Plates of Queen Mary for holders and medallists of the Order of the British Empire.

Plate with Gainsborough's house in sepia by Graham Rust.

Commemorative mugs when Prince William was born, each carrying his name and the names of individual children born the same year.

Plates for the Concert Hall in St John's Smith Square.

Plates designed by Graham Rust of Mawley Hall.

Fine bone-china mugs made to order for Eximious, with people's names on each.

Commemorative plates to mark the 40th anniversary of the Allied landings in Normandy. The plate carried a reproduction of the original map of the Allied landings and the subsequent advance in the summer of 1944.

Large fine bone-china plates for the Player's Theatre, commemorating Marie Lloyd.

Plates for the East Grinstead Operatic Society's Diamond Jubilee (1982).

Plates for the Queen's Silver Jubilee with her coat of arms.

Sets of octagonal plates for François Spoerry, the architect of Port Grimaud.

Porcelain plates after the manner of Creil plates from an old engraving of Southill Park.

Coupe plates for the opening in 1979 of the Polka Children's Theatre by the Queen Mother.

Large fine bone-china plates for sale in the Westminster Abbey bookshop.

Fine bone-china plates with a guardsman on a horse for the Blues & Royals, with the regimental badge in 22ct gold. Also for the Scots Guards and the Royal Green Jackets, together with decorated mugs.

Fine bone-china plates of Lord Montagu and his family in a motor car outside Palace House at Beaulieu.

Limited edition of fine bone-china plates with a view of Knaresborough for the funds of St John's Church.

Hohenzollern plates with coats of arms for the museum at Doorn in Holland.

Large fine bone-china plates of Karl Marx with his facsimile signature on the centenary of his death in 1983.

Presentation plate to Queen Elizabeth of Roy Plomley and choristers taking part in a musical evening at St James's Palace in 1982.

Limited, numbered edition of large fine bone-china plates to commemorate the voyage of the replica of the *Golden Hinde*.

Fine bone-china limited edition of fluted plates with an old engraving of Bridlington Priory Church, with gargoyles on the rim by Francis Johnson. Hand coloured.

Large fine bone-china plates designed for the 60th anniversary of the 1922 Committee. Hand coloured.

Limited-edition plates in fine bone china of an old engraving of Hughenden to commemorate the centenary of the death of Benjamin Disraeli, for the National Trust.

Limited, numbered edition of fine bone-china plates of the Dome of the Rock. Hand coloured. For fund-raising for the Order of St John of Jerusalem.

Small octagonal plates for the centenary of the Ophthalmic Hospital of St John of Jerusalem.

A limited edition of 200 mugs for the Young England Kindergarten on the occasion of the marriage of The Prince of Wales and Lady Diana Spencer.

A beaker with the design of the Duke of Edinburgh's Award scheme.

China mugs for the 40th anniversary of the Salvation Army Nurses Fellowship.

Ashtrays with coats of arms for the refurbished and named suites in the Ritz Hotel.

Ashtrays for the House of Keys, Isle of Man.

Coasters, dishes and earthenware mugs for the Cheshire Homes.

Coupe plates for the 75th anniversary of the Caravan Club.

Large stoneware octagonal plates with design commissioned and drawn by Gerard van der Kemp (curator of the Royal Palace at Versailles) for the Monet Museum at Giverny and, also by him, coupe plates of the design in green.

Identical-shaped plates of Putney Parish Church, hand coloured, for fund-raising.

Fine bone-china coupe plates with a figure of Britannia in 22ct gold for the Bank of England, boxed for presentation to overseas clients.

China coupe plates with platinum rim, partly hand coloured, to celebrate the opening of the Thames Barrier in 1982.

Large porcelain plates with a reproduction of the opening of the South Durham Railway in 1857.

Large stoneware octagonal plates 'In Memory of the flying Duchess', Woburn Abbey, 1981.

Small plates heavily decorated in blue and silver for the silver jubilee of the Army Air Corps.

Small china plates for the Wireless Section of the Royal Corps of Signals.

Coupe plates for the diamond jubilee of the Royal British Legion in 1981 and the same for the Scottish British Legion.

Small octagonal plates for the Society of Archers, decorated in blue for the Scorton Silver Arrow.

Hand-coloured coasters designed by Graham Rust of the Orangerie in the French Garden at Moët & Chandon. Packed in scarlet presentation boxes.

Small octagonal ashtrays for the Wellington Country Park at Stratfield Saye.

Numbered edition of china plates for the millennium of the Tynwald, designed by Alan Kitson Towler and commissioned by the Manx Millennium Committee.

Fine bone-china plates for the centenary of the Royal College of Midwives in 1981, designed by Alan Kitson Towler.

China coasters for the 40th anniversary of the WRVS, designed by Caroline Fellowes.

Graham Rust did two standard designs, both in colour, which could be decorated for private orders with monograms, crests, racing colours, names of yachts and more, and another suitable for one or more initials.

We also decorated many ordinary tiles, mugs and plates which are not listed here.

Things We Have Imported from America

These are a combination of things which my parents told us about when they had been to America in the 1930s with the Marlboroughs and Cecil Beaton, and the things that Richard and I saw for ourselves when we went to America in the 1950s. With one or two exceptions, every single one has since been copied in Britain.

Few Americans had servants.

Even fewer had nannies and they disapproved of those who had living-in ones. (This was still true in the late 1940s.)

Few gents were in the Army or Navy.

People seldom dressed for dinner.

No one was offered the loo after lunch or dinner, as they used to be here. You had to ask for the 'bathroom'. This is one thing we haven't copied. Kick used to ask Richard for the bathroom, which meant please stop the car so she could go behind a hedge to pee.

Women didn't leave the men at the end of dinner (one of the very few good things we copied!).

Instead of Bromo loo paper (considered essential for all gents – in the war George VI wrote to my father-in-law and asked if he could send some from Washington as it had become unobtainable in England). But it didn't exist in the USA, instead they used rolls of soft paper such as we now all use (perhaps the other good thing we copied).

They seldom had home-made jam but always bought it in shops, which now we largely tend to do.

They had few people to stay and, except for the very rich, had no spare rooms. (They put people up in clubs. Something we haven't copied.)

People were judged by the amount of money they had. The very rich all stuck together, unlike in England where who you were mattered much more than your money. And the Americans talked about the money people had, which was strictly not done in England until after the war. Now we do the same.

Taxi-drivers kept the radio playing, wore scruffy clothes and had no glass partition. We have still kept a partition in black cabs, though not in others.

If you went for a walk in the country, people thought something was wrong and stopped to offer you a lift (this happened to me three times in California).

They used tissues instead of handkerchiefs, which more and more people now do in England, and handkerchiefs are hard to buy.

Even quite poor families had two cars.

People travelled with very little luggage.

They started jeans, then called Blue Jeans – now worn here by almost everyone. If women in England wore trousers it would have been corduroy ones, which we all did in the war.

Very few children went to boarding schools unless they had some kind of problem or were very very rich. Boarding is now getting less in England.

What we called a wireless the Americans called a radio.

Few people had educated handwriting, and the same is happening in England now.

Most people sent typed and not handwritten letters. This was thought to be very rude in England unless it was an official letter, and even then they were always topped and tailed by hand.

Children were spoilt and allowed to help themselves to food from the fridge at will and allowed not to get up when people came to see them. This again is something we are copying here.

Index

The abbreviations D and R have been used for
Diana and Richard Holderness

R to Rome in 1940, 54; and husband for Anne, 63, 97; proposes to Lady Dorothy, 64; D's relationship with, 68, 89-90; importance of religion to, 68, 90, 100, 130; advises D to sell houses, 78; offers to buy houses for R and D, 82, 85, 89; eccentricities of, 89-90; generosity of, 89; death of, 114; disapproves of unmarried women, 122; and Baba Metcalfe, 165; statue of, in India, 196

Halifax, 2nd Viscount, 50, 53
Hambleden, Lord, 100
Hamilton, Corinna, of Dalzell, 224
Hand, Nancy, 213
Harrison, Corporal, 33-4
Hartington, William, Marquis of, 58
Harvey, Major General Sir Charles ('C.O.'), 70
Hassan, Prince (formerly Crown Prince of Jordan), 186, 187
Hayter, John, 226, 240
Head, Antony, Viscount, 20, 62, 180, 217
Heath, Sir Edward, 114, 120-1, 136, 163, 210, 216, 217-18, 223
Heathcoat-Amory, Derick (later Viscount Amory), 91
Helpmann, Robert, 44
Henry, Prince (later Duke of Gloucester), 16, 34
Hepple, Richard, 54
Hernes Keep, 234, 237
Highclere Castle, 24, 26
Hildyard, Myles: 226, 239-40; in the war, 39, 40, 112-13, 151; D's long friendship with, 61, 113, 235

Hitchcock, Alfred, 94
Hillman Minx cars, 17
Hills, John (housemaster), 53
Hills, John (soldier), 153, 156
Hohenzollern, Schloss, 138
Holland-Hibbert, Diana, 228
Holland-Hibbert, Julian (later Lord Knutsford), 211
Hong Kong, 168
Hoole, Alan, 229-30, 231-2
Hoole, Delia, 229-30
Hope, Arthur (later Lord Rankeillour), 32, 197
Hopkinson, Reverend Philip, 148
Hornsea, 77, 107
Howard, Lady Anne (later Lady Herries), 100, 101
Howard, George, 119
Howard, James, 68, 69, 157
Howard, Virginia ('Bidger'; later Ker), 68, 238
Howorth, Frances, 223, 224, 236, 242
Howorth, Georgina, 223, 236
Howorth, Michael, 223, 236, 242
Hughes, Canon F. L., 67
Hussein, King of Jordan, 173, 182-4, 187

Idris, King of Libya, 133-4, 154
India: 35, 51-2, 162; R and D visit, 176-9, 195-7
Indonesia, 169-71
Intrepid, HMS, 165-6
Irwin, James, Lord, 235-6
Islamabad, 165, 195
Isle of Wight, 14, 28-9

Masters (butler and soldier-servant), 32

Mauritius, 207

Maydon, Lynch, 127

Menzies, Sir Stewart, 48

Metcalfe, Lady Alexandra ('Baba';
   formerly Curzon), 120, 165,179

MI6, 47-8, 62

Miers, Christopher, 122

Milton Manor, 27-8, 29, 35-7, 46

Mirfield, 93

Miss Sprules' Secretarial Academy, 44

Mogg, Nigel, 122

Mohato, King of Lesotho (formerly
   Prince), 190

Monckton, Sir Walter (later Viscount),
   39, 103

Montgomery, General Bernard (later
   Viscount), 58

Montgomery, David, Viscount, 224-5

Montserrat, 181-2

Morocco, 148-9

Morrison, Peter, 127

Morton, Jane, 200

Moshoeshoe, King of Lesotho, 188-9

Mounsey, Eleanor, 219

Moyne, Lord (Bryan Guinness), 74

Moyne, Lord (Walter Guinness), 18

Muna, Princess, of Jordan, 173

Mussolini, Benito, 55, 132

Nairobi, 158, 160, 205-6

Napoleon, 228, 230-1, 239

Ness, Brigid. *See* Guinness, Lady Brigid

Ness, Patrick, 198, 224, 226

Nevis (island), 182

Newall, Mary, 39

New York, 57, 94

Ngurdoto and Ngorongoro craters,
   158-9

Nicolson, Sir Harold, 223

Nicolson, Nigel, 222-3

Nicolson, Vita, Lady, 223

Nile, River, 161-2

Niven, David, 61

Norfolk, Bernard, Duke of, 100, 101

Norfolk, Lavinia, Duchess of, 101, 102

Normandy, 155-6

North, David, 243

Northumberland, Hugh and Elizabeth,
   Duke and Duchess of, 134

Norton, Sarah (later Astor, then
   Baring), 125

Norway, 164

Nutting, Sir Anthony, 103

Omaha beach, 155-6

Onslow, Arthur and Pam, Earl and
   Countess of, 116

Onslow, 4th Earl of, 50, 209

Onslow, Victor ('Huia'), 209

Ord River Dam, 168

Orchid Room (nightclub), 59

Ormerod, Frances, 242

Orpheus (submarine), HMS, 170

Pakistan, 164-6, 175, 194-5

Parker, Cecilia, 148

Parker Bowles, Anne, 180

Parker Bowles, Derek, 104, 119, 180

Paris, 28, 106, 199-200, 230

Parish, Michael, 112

Parkinson, Sir Kenneth, 118